SPY FOR NO COUNTRY

THE STORY OF TED HALL, THE TEENAGE ATOMIC SPY WHO MAY HAVE SAVED THE WORLD

Dave Lindorff

Prometheus Books

Essex, Connecticut

🅿🅑 Prometheus Books

An imprint of Globe Pequot, the trade division of The Rowman & Littlefield Publishing Group, Inc.
4501 Forbes Blvd., Ste. 200
Lanham, MD 20706
www.rowman.com

Distributed by NATIONAL BOOK NETWORK

British Library Cataloguing in Publication Information Available

Library of Congress Cataloging-in-Publication Data

Names: Lindorff, Dave (David P.), author.
Title: Spy for no country : the story of Ted Hall, the teenage atomic spy who may have saved the world / Dave Lindorff.
Other titles: Story of Ted Hall, the teenage atomic spy who may have saved the world
Description: Lanham, MD : Prometheus, [2024] | Includes bibliographical references and index. | Summary: "Spy for No Country tells the gripping story of a brilliant scientist whose information about the plutonium bomb, including detailed drawings and measurements, proved to be integral to the Soviet development of nuclear capabilities"— Provided by publisher.
Identifiers: LCCN 2023015429 (print) | LCCN 2023015430 (ebook) | ISBN 9781633888951 (cloth) | ISBN 9781633888968 (epub)
Subjects: LCSH: Hall, Theodore A. (Theodore Alvin), 1925- | Hall, Theodore A. (Theodore Alvin), 1925—Friends and associates. | Espionage, Soviet—United States—History—20th century. | Manhattan Project (U.S.)—History. | Spies—United States—Biography. | Nuclear Weapons—History—20th century. | World War, 1939-1945—Secret Service—Soviet Union. | Nuclear weapons—History—20th century. | Venona Project (U.S.)
Classification: LCC D810.S8 H3475 2024 (print) | LCC D810.S8 (ebook) | DDC 327.1/2/092—dc23/eng/20230411
LC record available at https://lccn.loc.gov/2023015429
LC ebook record available at https://lccn.loc.gov/2023015430

♾™ The paper used in this publication meets the minimum requirements of American National Standard for Information Sciences—Permanence of Paper for Printed Library Materials, ANSI/NISO Z39.48-1992.

To all those who put their lives on the line over the decades to
end war and the nuclear threat hanging over humankind

CONTENTS

REMEMBERING "TEDDY" HALL

After a three-day shoot in Cambridge interviewing Joan Hall, wife of former teenage atomic spy Ted Hall, and their two surviving daughters, Ruth and Sara, in 2019, the film crew working on *A Compassionate Spy* gathered around a table at dusk outside the historic eighteenth-century Blue Ball Inn and Tavern in neighboring Grantchester Meadow. Tavernkeeper Toby Joseph, apologizing that the kitchen was closed, offered to bring us a couple of pitchers of ale and some nachos.

As we sat there, mugs in hand, discussing the weekend's work and what would come next when we got back to the United States, Toby asked, "So what are you Yanks doing here in Cambridge?"

Director Steve James said, "We're working on a film."

"A film, eh?" said Toby, his interest piqued. "What kind of film—drama or documentary?"

"A documentary," Steve told him.

"A documentary? What's it on?" Toby inquired.

"You tell him, Dave," Steve said, nodding in my direction. "It's your film."

Caught by surprise, because I hadn't really thought about what to call our film, I said, "It's about a teenage spy who saved the world."

Toby immediately responded, "Teenage spy . . . saved the world . . . are you talking about fuckin' Teddy Hall?"

We all laughed, astonished that he'd guessed right.

"Yeah, fuckin' Ted Hall," I said.

"You're doing a documentary about fuckin' Teddy Hall? Good for you! He bloody deserves a documentary. He did save the fuckin' world!" said Toby, explaining that he'd grown up as a neighbor of the Halls, was friends with the Hall daughters, and was there in 1995 when "Teddy" was publicly identified as a spy in the Manhattan Project.

PREFACE

A Note to Readers

A man's every action is inevitably conditioned by what surrounds him.

—Leo Tolstoy

Reading a work of history, just like writing one, is not a passive activity. It requires reader and author alike, both of whom live in the present, to attempt to enter the mindset of people living in an altogether different time and, usually, place. Sometimes our modern assumptions can lead us to see as villainous acts or beliefs that are actually the opposite in the context and the conditions of an earlier time.

Consider the Revolutionary War era in the United States. For those of us who grew up in the United States, the mythology regarding that period portrays an earnest and honest bunch of Patriots standing up heroically in the name of freedom and liberty to the brutal tyrant King George III and his equally brutal Redcoat army of occupation. In fact, as Shannon Duffy, senior lecturer in early American history at Texas State University, writes in a short article published by the Center for Digital History at the Library of Mount Vernon, the Revolutionary War of 1776–1783 was "in many ways also a civil war."[1]

As she points out, the population of the thirteen colonies was bitterly divided into Patriots and Loyalists. Commitment to ideas like liberty and freedom, attributed in our official history exclusively to the Patriots, was actually often also held by many of those who were Loyalists—and some-times was not held by those known as Patriots. Among the Loyalists, too, were a fair number of pacifists, mostly Quakers, who opposed the violence and compulsory service in the Continental Army.

Advocates of independence in the Revolution were not all noble pro-claimers of human rights and freedom like the radical pamphleteer Thomas Paine. Many, in fact, were notoriously enslavers, including such notable revolutionary leaders as George Washington and that eloquent principal author of the Declaration of Independence, Thomas Jefferson. Meanwhile, many opponents of slavery, and thousands of enslaved people themselves, favored and even fought and died as Loyalists for continued colonial rule by Britain, which offered and granted freedom to those who came over to its side. One of these was Loyalist John Murray, 4th Earl of Dunmore, a Scottish peer who in 1771 became the last royal governor of Virginia. In 1775, he issued Dunmore's Proclamation, offering freedom to any enslaved person who left his enslaver to fight for the Crown against Patriot rebels in his state. Viewed as a loathsome Loyalist in U.S. history, Dunmore's action contributed to the escape of an estimated one hundred thousand enslaved people during the Revolution.[2]

Even decades after U.S. victory in the Revolution, voting was limited in all states exclusively to property-owning adult white men. As Ed Crews, a contributor to the *Colonial Williamsburg Journal*, has written:

> At its birth, the United States was not a democratic nation—far from it. The very word "democracy" had pejorative overtones, summoning up images of disorder, government by the unfit, even mob rule. In practice, moreover, relatively few of the nation's inhabitants were able to participate in elec-tions: among the excluded were most African Americans, Native Americans, women, men who had not attained their majority, and white males who did not own land.[3]

To move beyond the mythology and understand the complex history of that era, one must step back mentally into that era, when slavery existed in all thirteen colonies (and, later, states) and when only a minority of the popula-tion of white males owned sufficient property to be allowed to vote (facts that many Americans even today are unaware of).

Similarly, in reading a history like this one about Ted Hall and Saville Sax, two young U.S. volunteer Soviet spies in the Manhattan Project that created the atomic bomb, and others like Communists Julius and Ethel Rosenberg or the German physicist Klaus Fuchs, one needs to go back to the world and the United States during the first part of the twentieth century, when the Soviet Union, beginning with the German invasion of that country on August 25, 1941, even before Pearl Harbor, was the main nation battling Adolf Hitler's Nazi war machine.

One needs also to understand that all the way back to 1917 and the Russian Revolution that overthrew the tsar and the fledgling Duma, establishing a workers' state, from the moment of the Bolshevik triumph, the United States had been—and in large part continued to be through World War II and beyond—hostile to the Soviet Union. In fact, even before the end of World War II, the United States was plotting to use its new atomic bombs to intimidate and even perhaps destroy the USSR after the war.

It is with this reality in mind that one must consider the audacious actions of two young U.S. college students who endeavored to break through what they saw as an unconscionable and dangerous wall of secrecy intended to keep the Soviet Union in the dark about the U.S. atomic bomb project, even as the Red Army, by the time the two became spies in late October 1944, had beaten the Nazi Wehrmacht and was driving Hitler's battered troops back to Germany. Hall and Sax shared a common goal: to prevent what they viewed as a nightmare postwar era in which the United States had an unchallengeable monopoly on the atomic bomb.

Readers are, of course, invited to reach their own conclusions about the decisions and actions of these two young Americans, Ted Hall and Saville Sax, in becoming volunteer Soviet atomic spies during 1944–1945. That said, in doing so I hope they will make the effort to consider the pair, as I have tried to do, from the perspective of the extraordinary times in which they were living.

Additional note to readers: This book adopts the commonly used convention of using all capital letters for spy code names of spies and places, except for several excerpts from journalist Alexander Vassiliev that appear throughout the book.

FOREWORD

We don't know when Theodore Hall first met Klaus Fuchs at Los Alamos in 1944, as World War II was raging intensely in the Pacific and Europe and the scientific staff at Los Alamos was ballooning from a few hundred to thousands of people. Ted, an eighteen-year-old Harvard physics major from New York City, recruited in November 1943 by the Manhattan Project, had arrived in New Mexico in late January 1944. Klaus, a thirty-three-year-old German refugee physicist attached to a British team of scientists, first arrived in Los Alamos that August.

Ted, the youngest physicist in the supersecret Manhattan Project at Los Alamos, learned only upon his arrival that he would be part of a crash program to build an atomic bomb before Nazi Germany could do it. Klaus had already been working on that project for several years in the United Kingdom.

Hall was one of four Harvard undergraduate physics students recommended by Professor John Van Vleck for what the Manhattan Project recruiter who interviewed them disclosed only was a top-secret wartime project somewhere out west.

Hall and Fuchs were similar in that both were recognized—even in the rarified circle of senior physicists on the Manhattan Project, some with Nobel Prizes, many destined to earn them—as extraordinarily brilliant, despite their relative youth.

Fuchs, a physics student and Communist activist being hunted by the Nazi Gestapo, had fled Kiel, Germany, for England in September 1933. His father, Emil, was a well-known Lutheran minister and a Quaker. Klaus Fuchs and his siblings were active members of the German Communist Party. In England, Klaus was soon recognized as a brilliant graduate student, first with Neville Mott in Bristol and later with Max Born in Edinburgh, both top scientists who by 1940 had begun working secretly on the British atom bomb project that was known only as "Tube Alloys." Even before Operation Barbarossa, the Nazi invasion of the Soviet Union, in June 1941, Fuchs had already established himself as a reliable Soviet spy operating in England and was passing copies of his own work on to Simon Kremer at the Soviet Consulate in London via German Communist friends, the Kuczynski family.

Interned by the British as an enemy alien in 1940, Fuchs ended up with Hans Kahle and other refugee German Communists at a camp in Canada before being returned to England and his twin careers as nuclear scientist and Soviet spy. He signed the Official Secrets Act in June 1942 and a month later became a naturalized British citizen, swearing allegiance to his new homeland.

Hall's Russian Jewish father, who had fled Tsarist Russia for America because of anti-Semitism, and mother, a child of Russian Jewish immigrants who probably did the same, were Roosevelt Democrats during his youth. During the war, like many Russian émigrés, they were rooting for their old homeland as it battled an onslaught by the Nazi Wehrmacht.

By 1943, the Soviet Union had become a critical ally of the United States and Britain in the war against Hitler's Germany. As the Red Army, despite huge losses, rallied and began pushing the Wehrmacht back out of Russia and Ukraine, its troops were widely viewed by Americans as embattled heroes. The United States at that time was supplying Joseph Stalin's military with vast quantities of planes, tanks, weapons, and ammunition.

At Los Alamos, Ted was assigned to work on testing and refining the complicated implosion system needed to detonate a bomb made with plutonium. During the months that he worked on his task, it became increasingly clear that Germany was losing the war, with the German army getting hammered on its eastern front by the Red Army and, after the June 6, 1944 Normandy landing, also facing U.S., British, and Canadian forces in France and the Low Countries, as well as in Italy. As this shift happened, Ted, like many more-senior scientists, began to wonder why the bomb was needed and why its development was being kept secret from the Soviet Union, a U.S. ally.

While some top scientists were vainly petitioning President Franklin D. Roosevelt to bring the Soviets in on the project or at least to inform them about it, Ted decided to act. Completely unaware that Soviet spies (like Fuchs) were already inside the Manhattan Project, in mid-October he used the excuse of visiting his family in New York for his nineteenth birthday and set off, with the help of Harvard friend and roommate Saville Sax, who met him in New York, to locate a Soviet spy and volunteer to provide information about the secret Manhattan Project plutonium bomb he was helping to make.*

Incredibly, Hall and Sax, through luck and persistence, succeeded in connecting with a Soviet spy on that October trip to New York, and Hall told him about the secret operation at Los Alamos, offering to help the Soviets to develop their own bomb. While certainly dangerous, providing such information may not have seemed all that treacherous to Hall at the time: The Soviets were U.S. allies, after all, and although Hall didn't know it, the secret Quebec Agreement reached between FDR and Winston Churchill in 1943 permitted sharing atomic secrets between the United States and another wartime ally, Britain.

While both worked on the plutonium bomb, Hall and Fuchs were in different divisions, experimental and theoretical, respectively. But because the Soviet spy network kept its spies from knowing about each other (even maintaining separate couriers for each spy), even if they met in passing or conversed on issues, they never knew they were fellow Soviet spies, even in the months after the war and into 1946, when Los Alamos scientists began exploring the possibility of a superbomb based on hydrogen fusion rather than the fission of heavy elements. At that point, Fuchs returned to England to run the theoretical division of the British nuclear research facility at Harwell, in the countryside southwest of London. Hall, meanwhile, moved to Chicago, where he enrolled as a graduate student at the University of Chicago, pursuing a program of biophysics and sharing space for a time in the office of Edward Teller, who would later be widely known as the "Father of the H-Bomb."

Hall, who had lost his security clearance as of his departure from Los Alamos, maintained some contact with New York–based Soviet spy Lona

---

* When I published *Klaus Fuchs: Atom Spy* (1987), which included that physicist spy's confession of espionage, the name Ted Hall was unknown beyond his scientific work at Los Alamos and to a few key people inside U.S. intelligence. Only with the public release in 1995 of some of the Venona transcripts of wartime U.S. decryptions of Soviet intelligence cables was there public knowledge that Hall and Sax had spied for the Soviets at Los Alamos during the war.

Cohen, who had replaced Sax as his courier in mid-1945, but that connection likely ended in 1948, when Hall seems to have rejected a KGB request that he resume spying for the USSR. Picked up by agents with the Federal Bureau of Investigation (FBI) in March 1951 and interrogated intensely at the bureau's Chicago office, Hall and Sax both denied all accusations of spying and were not questioned again by the bureau.

Although they were working independently as providers of secret information to Soviet bomb makers, Fuchs and Hall separately confirmed one another's information about the plutonium bomb in reports that reached Igor Kurchatov, director of the Soviet bomb project, at a crucial time for the financially strapped and struggling Soviet bomb effort. Fuchs had a much broader grasp of the bomb project and its theories of fission and fusion, explosion and implosion. Hall had more detailed and intimate knowledge of the lens system for imploding plutonium in a sphere. Fuchs conducted his espionage for almost a decade and was a true believer in Communism as the best path to the destruction of Nazi Germany, to world peace and a better world. Hall was a short-term teenage spy who wished to help a wartime ally in 1944–1945 and prevent a postwar U.S. atomic monopoly.

When the war was over, Fuchs continued his espionage, passing secrets to Moscow through Alexander Feklisov ("Eugene"), an agent of the People's Commissariat for Internal Affairs (NKVD) previously active in New York and later the Committee for State Security (KGB) station chief in Washington, DC. Hall, after graduating with his doctorate, took a job in 1952 in biophysics at the Sloan Kettering Institute in New York City and bought a house in Greenwich, Connecticut. A decade later, in 1962, he moved with his family—wife Joan Krakover, who he had married in 1947, and their three young daughters—to the United Kingdom, taking up a research position in electron microscopy at Cambridge University's Cavendish Laboratory.

Curiously, Ted Hall was never arrested or charged with spying, while Klaus Fuchs continued his spying undetected through the 1940s. He was arrested in Britain in 1950 after he confessed.

By the mid-1950s, Edward Hall, Ted's older brother, who in 1950–1951 was an Air Force major designing engines for nuclear-capable missiles in a top-secret lab, had become the chief inventor and director of ballistic missile development from the Thor and Atlas to the solid-fuel Minuteman and Poseidon missiles. Ted's espionage never impeded Edward's career with the U.S. Air Force, where he continued to be promoted, reaching the rank of colonel by 1957—a second enigma few atomic historians realized, or, if they did, were unable to explain. In this book, investigative reporter

Dave Lindorff, who obtained Edward Hall's FBI file for the first time, convincingly explains this mystery, as well as why the FBI and the Justice Department were blocked from arresting and prosecuting Hall and Sax for espionage (much as they clearly wanted to).

Klaus Fuchs died in Dresden in 1988, like fellow Manhattan Project veteran and fellow spy Ted Hall in 1999, of a cancer likely caused by Manhattan Project work. A memorial service celebrated Fuchs's life as a German Communist and scientist. The Soviets did not send any official delegate but permitted the attendance of a thirty-five-year-old KGB agent in Dresden named Vladimir Putin. After Ted's death, Cambridge physics colleague and friend Mick Brown suggested at a memorial that besides saving lives through his electron microscopy research, Hall "may have saved the world" by helping prevent just one country from possessing atomic bombs after the war's end.

Lindorff has done a marvelous job researching and telling the largely overlooked story of Ted Hall's life and career as a scientist and a onetime spy and its significance, using documents not available to earlier historians of the era. Hall's surviving widow, Joan, has contributed her own knowledge, archives, and love of Ted to the story.

Klaus Fuchs was the only nuclear scientist to work with the American, British, Soviet, East German, and Chinese bomb projects. His contributions after 1940 in Birmingham and Harwell in the United Kingdom and Los Alamos in the United States were truly significant. He remained convinced to the end of his life that sharing nuclear secrets was the best tool for achieving arms control and the best route to global peace through mutual deterrence. Ted Hall was a teenage genius from Harvard caught up in the scientific excitement of the Manhattan Project during World War II, who came to believe that a U.S. monopoly on the bomb would be a threat to the world. He concluded that two rival nations with the bomb could lead to its being banned, or at least could prevent its being used again. Typically relegated to only a few lines or a footnote in atomic histories, his full story is now getting its due as a significant chapter in the complex history of nuclear weapons, espionage, cryptography, and the politics of the Cold War.

Robert C. Williams
Vail Professor of History Emeritus
Davidson College
Topsham, Maine

PROLOGUE

A Soviet Atomic Spy Is Publicly Outed after Fifty Years

I . . . have the feeling that England is a far better place to live, and I am seriously considering moving—to Cambridge perhaps. . . . To live here peacefully, tranquilly, is a poor policy. The tranquil life can be led better elsewhere (I hope), and the only workable basis on which one can enter into society at large here is that of trying to change it.

—Ted Hall, letter from Los Alamos to his
brother Edward, dated August 8, 1945, the day
before the Nagasaki plutonium bomb[1]

In the fall of 1995, Theodore Hall, a seventy-year-old physicist and bio-physicist, was at home in the comfortable Newnham rowhouse he and Joan, his wife of forty-eight years, had continued to share since his retirement from Cambridge University's biology department. It had been a rough few years, during which Ted had been fighting a losing battle against a terminal case of kidney cancer and worsening Parkinson's disease. He and Joan were also trying to come to terms with the tragic death of their middle daughter, Debbie, killed in March 1992 when a truck hit her as she was riding her bike to a law class in London. Only thirty-seven, she left two young daughters motherless and two sisters and parents bereft.

In the midst of all this, Ted, looking through the day's mail, found a letter from physicist and author Arnold Kramish, a colleague from his time at Los

Alamos in the mid-1940s, when Ted had been the youngest physicist working on the Manhattan Project that developed the world's first atomic bomb. Another young Manhattan Project physicist undergrad, two years older than Ted, Kramish had gone on after Los Alamos to work at the Atomic Energy Commission (AEC), which took over from the Manhattan Project when that entity was disbanded after the war. In his out-of-the-blue letter, Kramish asked if Ted could confirm whether he was the "Teodor Kholl" referred to in a just-released decrypted and translated 1944 Soviet spy cable from New York to Moscow concerning the enlisting of a young new volunteer spy based at Los Alamos.

Recalling that letter and its shocking resurrection and revelation of Ted's spying days in an interview with me, Joan said Kramish claimed to her husband that he was working on a memoir of his Los Alamos years and wanted to include Ted in it. It was the first time Ted heard the explosive news that his name—or a close approximation of it—as well as the name of his Harvard roommate, friend, and spy courier Saville Sax (also misidentified by Soviet agents as "Savil Saks"), had been mentioned in the decrypted and declassified Soviet cable.

For the previous three decades, the Halls had been living quietly in Cambridge, believing interest in Ted's sharing of information about the design details of the Manhattan Project's first bomb—the plutonium devices used in the Trinity Test at Alamogordo, New Mexico, on July 16, 1945, and on Nagasaki, Japan, on August 9, 1945—about which the FBI had first been secretly informed in April 1950, had been long since consigned to the archives by the Bureau and the U.S. Justice Department. Because they'd heard nothing from the FBI or from Britain's intelligence service MI5 since the mid-1960s, they'd optimistically assumed the secret of his spying would likely die with him. Instead, they suddenly realized—to their chagrin and horror—that they had to start worrying anew about whether Ted, and possibly Joan too, would spend their remaining lives being questioned by reporters and historians, perhaps being hounded by the FBI and even indicted for spying, or, almost as bad, harangued by anti-Communist critics of his actions in sharing U.S. bomb secrets.

Joan recalls that Ted ignored Kramish's request for a phone interview or visit. It was probably a wise decision, given that Kramish, while at the AEC, had worked as a liaison with the CIA on Soviet bomb progress estimates and had earlier assisted the FBI and the Justice Department in the interrogation of Soviet spy David Greenglass. The brother of Julius Rosenberg's wife, Ethel, Greenglass in 1944 had come to Los Alamos as a technician. His arrest as a spy in June 1950 and his subsequent confession and provision of information about other spies—including his own sister and brother-in-law—led to the unraveling of much of the Soviet Union's largest U.S. wartime spying network. Hall was likely not privy to any of these details at the time of Kramish's letter, but in any event, Ted chose not to respond to his request for details. The memoir Kramish alluded to writing never materialized, suggesting it may have been just a clumsy ploy to elicit Hall's cooperation. But Kramish's letter and his later uninvited appearance at their door did serve to alert Ted to the tsunami of notoriety and attention headed his way following the seismic release of decrypted Soviet spy cables. It also prompted him to hire and seek advice from one of Britain's most prominent activist defense solicitors, Benedict Birnberg—apparently the first time he had ever consulted an attorney about his legal jeopardy in half a century.

That wave of notoriety didn't take long to surge up and break against the Hall doorstep. Several weeks after Kramish's inquiry, a phone call came from Ralph Kinney Bennett, a senior staff writer and later assistant managing editor of *Reader's Digest* magazine, a right-wing U.S. publication with a strong anti-Communist editorial stance. Bennett also later showed up uninvited at the Hall home in Newnham, accompanied by Herbert Romerstein, a historian of the Soviet Union and a former Communist turned anti-Communist who later coauthored *The Venona Secrets: Exposing Soviet Espionage and America's Traitors* with Eric Breindel. The title alone gives away the authors' political perspective, since "treason" and being a "traitor" are defined in the law as acting *in wartime* to aid the *enemy* of one's country. However, through all but a short period in the very beginning of the European theater of World War II—before the United States had even entered the war—the Soviet Union was not only an *ally* of the United States and Britain but was the recipient of huge amounts of U.S. military aid, including ammunition, tanks, fighter planes, and the like, much of it transported via a specially built highway through the Canadian Yukon and into Alaska. From there, planes and ships transported the materiel across the Bering Strait to Siberia and the western terminus of the Trans-Siberian Railway. That railroad carried it all to the eastern front, where the Soviet Union's Red Army was battling the Nazi Wehrmacht.

Romerstein and Breindel write in *The Venona Secrets* that Hall, in a brief meeting in Cambridge, told them he had seen only the one partial Venona cable decrypt that provided a mangled but still obvious rendering of his and his spy courier Saville Sax's names. But, they add, after they showed him the other Venona files referring to him, "he did make comments acknowledging the truth of some of the information and expressed concern [that] even at that late date he might be prosecuted." While "not confirming that he was engaged in World War II espionage," they claim he "promised to write a statement" for them by December, which they say he never followed through on.[2]

Joan Hall says her husband never made such an offer, as he had no trust in the two men—apparently with good reason. Romerstein and Breindel's disdain for Hall is made evident in a comment in their book about the authors' visit to his home in Cambridge: "When author Romerstein spoke to Hall in 1995, he appeared to be the same brilliant airhead he had been as a teenage spy years earlier."[3] Not the slightest evidence was offered for the random, gratuitously disparaging non sequitur.

Romerstein and Breindel were followed by a visit from a husband-wife journalist team from Cox Newspapers, both foreign correspondents posted in Moscow. Upon learning about Hall's spying, the two raced over from Russia to try to talk with him. Joseph Albright (former husband of Madeleine Albright, who at the time of their visit was serving as President Bill Clinton's ambassador to the United Nations), was a career journalist and a grandson of Joseph Medill Patterson, who founded and long owned the New York *Daily News*. Marcia Kunstel, also a career journalist, had previously worked for C-SPAN. Joan recalls that unlike the inquiring visitors who had visited (or tried to visit) them earlier, she and Ted found Albright and Kunstel to be "interesting and sympathetic." After several meetings and one almost missed opportunity for a meeting, the Halls agreed in January 1996 to tell their story to the two reporters, who said they intended to write a book. The Halls agreed to the idea with the stipulation that the authors would not publish anything for a year. In a 2021 interview for the film *A Compassionate Spy*, Kunstel said of that agreement, "I think Ted believed he would be dead by the time our book would be published."

In fact, Ted battled his kidney cancer and Parkinson's disease for almost two more years, dying on November 1, 1999, a few weeks after his seventy-fourth birthday.

Ted and Joan both were able to read not just their manuscript, but also the published book, *Bombshell: The Secret Story of America's Unknown Atomic Spy Conspiracy*, which the couple pronounced themselves "mostly happy" with—especially the part on the testing, development, and working of the complex implosion system for detonating the plutonium bomb and the description of the design of the bomb that he provided to the Soviets—a technically detailed section that Joan claims Ted was largely responsible for writing.

During their last years together, Ted and Joan also endured many lurid stories about his spying. *People* magazine, read widely in the United States and Britain, ran a piece with the headline "A Shy Scientist Is Exposed as a Traitor"—heavy word inflation for the actual charge of espionage, conspiracy, or theft of government secrets actually lodged against the Rosenbergs and other spies like Klaus Fuchs (although "treason" was used in many of the tabloid headlines). One British tabloid asked rhetorically, "Should traitors escape the death penalty just because they lived a long time?" Others ran with everything from the *Daily Mail*'s "Hall of Infamy" and "Years of Treachery" to the London *Times*'s "Cambridge Scientist 'Leaked' Atom Bomb Secrets to Moscow."

Eventually, when no arrest or official investigative questioning by law enforcement or prosecutors followed the public disclosure of Ted Hall's spying, and with coconspirator Saville Sax—who had died of a heart attack more than fifteen years earlier, well before his name appeared in the Venona decrypts—long gone, media interest in Hall's atomic bomb spying died down. Not, however, before the 2002 airing of a PBS special on its popular program *Nova*. Titled "Secrets, Lies and Atomic Spies," the documentary labeled him, rather ludicrously, as "a teenaged master spy." That program included an interview with Manhattan Project physicist Sam Cohen, a former close friend of Ted's at Los Alamos who, half a century later, turned on his dead friend viciously. Asked by the interviewer what should have happened to Hall, Cohen (who, after leaving the Manhattan Project and earning a doctorate at Berkeley, worked at the RAND Corporation and invented and advocated for the controversial neutron bomb), spit out his answer angrily:

> Shot! He was a military man, he's a soldier in the United States Army, he was not subject to civil law, he was subject to military law. Military law called for a traitor being executed and that son-of-a-bitch should have been retrieved once we found out what he'd done, called back into the Army, court-martialed and executed![4]

Cohen's sharp view reflected a common attitude among a sector of the U.S. population, though the documentary didn't bother to note, in airing that clip, that by the 1990s, U.S. court decisions had established that military personnel, once returned to civilian life, could not be put back in uniform and tried in a military tribunal. Instead, they must be tried as civilians, even for crimes committed earlier while in uniform. Nor did the film note that since Hall and Sax had engaged in their espionage at a time when the Soviet Union was a U.S. ally, and even after the war ended was not at war with the United States, treason was not an appropriate charge for what they did.

Even the Rosenbergs, indicted in 1950, were not charged with treason. The heaviest charge leveled against them was conspiring to pass atomic secrets, or espionage.

What has remained for several decades regarding the case of Ted Hall and Saville Sax was an unsolved mystery: Several thousand pages of Venona Project decrypted intercepts of Soviet wartime spy cables were released publicly in a series or tranches during 1995–1996 by the National Security Agency (NSA). But the actual partial decryption of the file that concretely revealed the identities of Hall and Sax had been made by the Signals Intelligence Service (precursor to the NSA) in late 1949 and provided to the FBI in early 1950. FBI agents in the Chicago bureau office even interrogated both young men for hours a year later in early 1951. But then, keeping all information about the two identified spies secret, even for a time from the CIA, the bureau ceased following them; the Justice Department never prosecuted either man. Remarkably, their names were never leaked to journalists despite J. Edgar Hoover's well-deserved reputation as a skilled and prolific leaker to the media. These two young men, amazingly, were never hauled before either the House Un-American Activities Committee or Senator Joseph McCarthy's Government Operations Committee's permanent subcommittee on investigations, both of which knew nothing about them all through the Red Scare era.

Why? The answer only came to light during my research for this book, and unfortunately came too late to make it into the film I coproduced, *A Compassionate Spy*, which was completed and shown by Participant Films to critical acclaim on the film festival circuit in the late summer and fall of 2022, with a world premiere on September 2 at the Venice Film Festival in Italy and a U.S. premiere a day later at the Telluride Film Festival in Colorado.[5]

1

THE NURTURING OF
A YOUNG GENIUS

*Neither a lofty degree of intelligence nor imagination nor both
together go to the making of genius. Love, love, love, that is the
soul of genius.*

—Wolfgang Amadeus Mozart

Theodore Alvin Holtzberg was born on October 20, 1925, in Far Rocka-
way, Queens, New York, the youngest child of a Russian Jewish father,
Barnett "Barney" Holtzberg, who had immigrated to the United States dur-
ing the last years of Russian tsar Nicholas II, and an American-born mother,
Rose Moskowitz, the daughter of Eastern European Jewish immigrants.
Barney and Rose married in 1908.

In addition to Ted, there were two daughters, Frances (b. 1909) and
Selma, who were born first, followed by Edward Nathaniel (b. 1914). Ted
was a doted-on late addition to the Holtzberg family—the more so because
he was unexpected, as Rose had earlier been informed by her doctor that she
could no longer get pregnant following the difficult pregnancy and delivery
of his older brother.

Ted grew up healthy and quickly showed himself to be extraordinarily
intelligent.

Help came early in nurturing that innate genius. Edward, who was
quite intellectually gifted himself, especially in math and science—realized by the age of fifteen, when his younger brother was just four, that

the family had an exceptional child on their hands. He brashly informed his non-college-educated parents that he would be taking charge of Ted's education from that point on. Ted's parents agreed to the unorthodox arrangement so assertively proposed by their older son, and so it was that while other kids Ted's age were playing with blocks or maybe learning letters and numbers if they were bright, Ted was being taught to read books and to do arithmetic. Under his older brother's dedicated tutelage, he was already a math prodigy accomplished at doing algebra by the time he turned seven.

In 1936, at age eleven, he sat for a set of citywide exams and scored high enough to win one of the eighty highly competitive spots available each year at the Townsend Harris High School, a free public three-year secondary school "hothouse" for gifted boys located at the time on several floors of City College of New York's (CCNY) School of Business and Civic Administration (later to be named Baruch College) on 23rd Street near Gramercy Park in lower Manhattan. Founded as a one-year training school for CCNY in 1849, after 1904 it became a three-year accelerated high school before closing for budget reasons in 1942. Among its distinguished alumni, Townsend claimed such notable figures as polio vaccine creator Jonas Salk, Nobel physicist Julian Schwinger, Nobel economist Kenneth Arrow, Supreme Court Justice Felix Frankfurter, physicist Gilbert Perlow, astronomer and physicist Robert Jastrow, and Nobel mathematician Herbert Hauptman.*

Ted's intellectual gifts did not pigeonhole him as a nerd. Fit and athletic, he played stickball in the streets with the neighborhood kids, was popular with fellow students, and also developed an early interest in progressive politics. In stickball, he made use of his math skills to explain to his friends on the team (dubbed "The Underdogs") how to predict on the hilly streets of their Washington Heights neighborhood where a ball would go after hitting a curb or a building wall—with the angle of bounce reflecting the angle of approach. Such inside knowledge, courtesy of trigonometry and physics, surely helped the team give the lie to their perhaps deceptively chosen team moniker.

Joan writes in a memoir about her late husband regarding his being pushed early into high school and later college:

* The school was reopened in 1980, this time in Flushing, Queens, New York, as a coeducational institution associated with Queens College. Among its prominent alumni the still-functioning school lists "Theodore Hall, atomic spy."

Though it certainly hampered Ted's social development to be at school with kids up to four years older than himself, I think it would have harmed him more to be held back. . . .

Despite his exceptional mind, he had a very happy, normal childhood and youth. In spite of his dislocation in school, Ted had a very active social life with boys of his own age in the neighborhood. I gather he was popular, a natural leader, athletic and well-coordinated.

. . . In school, he sailed effortlessly through the curriculum, and was often asked by the teacher to give coaching in mathematics to other (older) pupils who found it difficult. To me it is significant but not surprising that he managed to do this without antagonizing them—even as a child, apparently, he had a sort of natural modesty and grace that disarmed people (actually I never knew or heard of anyone who didn't like Ted). He told me his mother objected to this informal tutoring, not because it took him away from other studies, but because it might give the other child a competitive advantage over him! She was proud and jealous of his pre-eminent standing in the class. Ted thought this was silly and just laughed it off.[1]

In terms of his political development, meanwhile, the experience of seeing his father lose his furrier business to bankruptcy during the Great Depression, compelling the family to move from their spacious apartment in Far Rockaway to a small flat in Washington Heights in uptown Manhattan, certainly made an impression. He also had the firsthand experience of seeing inequality all around him—particularly at that time and in that part of the city. The experience produced, as it did in many young people of that time (at least among those with any sense of empathy), a political perspective that was left leaning. This was evidenced by the popularity in New York City in that period of socialist and communist political parties. Indeed, New York City—where almost half of the U.S. Communist Party's claimed seventy-five thousand members lived in 1938—was where the party had its national headquarters, located in a building it owned at 35 E. 12th Street, just two blocks downtown from Union Square. In 1938, a CP candidate for the city's board of aldermen received one hundred thousand votes, and during World War II, when the Soviet Red Army was fighting Nazi Germany alongside the United States and the rest of the Allies, two Communists, Peter V. Cacchione of Brooklyn and Benjamin Davis of Harlem, were elected to the New York City Council.

Young Ted was no doubt also influenced by the leftist pamphlets and books, including Karl Marx and Friedrich Engels's *Communist Manifesto*, that his elder brother Ed, an engineering student at the City University of

New York (CUNY), who found himself briefly interested in Marxism and CCNY's Communist Party chapter himself, used to bring home from class. CUNY, along with Columbia University and other tertiary educational institutions in the city in the late 1930s and early 1940s, were hotbeds of Communist support, with hundreds of students joining the Young Communist League and thousands joining the American Student Union (ASU), a CP front organization.[2]

As Jews (albeit not observant ones), the Holtzberg brothers were acutely aware of and were following carefully the rise of Nazism with its virulent anti-Semitism—something that was also present and on the rise in the United States.

It was around that time too that Ed, who had personally experienced the prevailing U.S. anti-Semitism that made landing a good job difficult for Jews—even in New York City, with its large Jewish population—decided to change both his and his young brother's surname from Holtzberg to the more Anglo-Saxon Hall. It was an action that would catch the eye of FBI sleuths when they began investigating the two as possible spies.*

In truth, far from espionage, back in 1939, thirteen-year-old Ted's primary concern was about whether he wanted to be a journalist, a comedian, or a physicist. The two-year-long internal contest among those career tracks wasn't a fair one, though. His brother and tutor was an engineer and fond of math, and two years earlier, when his mother had asked Ted what gift he'd like for his approaching twelfth birthday, he asked for a copy of *The Mysterious Universe*, a primer on physics sufficiently up to date to include chapters on cosmic rays, Albert Einstein's theories of relativity, and even an introduction to the new field of quantum mechanics—a concept most U.S. schools ignored in science classes and textbooks well into the 1960s, when the atom was still being misrepresented to most junior high school students as being more like a tiny "solar system" of planet-like electrons "orbiting" a star-like nucleus of protons and neutrons portrayed as solid balls. Somebody must have told him about or shown him that inspiring tome, and the most likely person to have done that was his older brother.

---

* Although the idea of a name change was Ed's, and though Ted was just eleven when the legal change was made in the courtroom of a New York State judge, it was noted down in Ted's and Ed's FBI files years later as if it might suggest sinister preparation for later becoming spies. That was during an investigation conducted during 1950–1952 by agents of the New York FBI office as part of an exhaustive nationwide bureau investigation into Ted (and Ed) Hall's early years, part of building a potential case against Ted and Saville Sax as Soviet atomic spies and about finding if Ted's brother might have had any connection with him in that activity.

Before wrapping that present, his mother rather prophetically inscribed the volume: "To My Son Theodore On his 12th Birthday. As you say, perhaps with this book, 'You have started your career.' Many happy returns of the day son. And good luck. Mother."[3]

It wasn't long after that birthday that Ted took his New York Board of Regents exams, a set of tests the Empire State still uses to help determine which of its public university campuses should accept the students in each year's high school graduating class. Again, Ted scored exceptionally high. Two years later, Ed encouraged him to take the entrance exam at Columbia University. Though just fourteen at the time, Ted reportedly notched one of the highest scores on record at the urban Ivy League university. Indeed, he might well have enrolled there the coming fall, and he and his family were seriously considering it. Joan Hall writes,

> For a short time it looked as if Ted would go to Columbia—he received an invitation to a freshman smoker, and got worried because he didn't smoke. But then came an interview, which he attended with his mother. The admissions officer wisely told her that despite his ability, Ted was too young for college, and believe it or not he suggested that her son should "travel" for a year! Apart from his tender age, and the fact that the family had no money, this was 1939, when Japan was already at war in China and Europe was about to erupt into World War II. One has to wonder what world the man was living in.[4]

Since travel was not an option the family even considered, Ted could have continued at the highly regarded City College of New York, the main undergraduate college within the City University of New York system, which was known as the "working-class Ivy League" school. But his parents, who lived in Queens at the time, opted instead to keep him closer to home, enrolling their precocious youngest child in the borough where they had moved as their fortunes improved. So he began his college studies in Flushing, at Queens College, another undergraduate campus in the CUNY system. He began his freshman program there in the fall of 1940, a few months before his fifteenth birthday, starting with a course in calculus to support his career goal of becoming a theoretical physicist. Had his parents allowed him to attend the main CCNY campus, Ted might well have come to know—or at least know *of*—a somewhat older young activist of the American Student Union there, a working-class engineering student named Julius Rosenberg.

As a high school student—and a young one, at that—at Townsend Harris, Ted had already joined the ASU, a group covertly organized as a front organization by the Young Communist League of the U.S. Communist Party. Rosenberg was one of the founders of the CCNY ASU chapter. That would be enough of a "link" to excite FBI Director J. Edgar Hoover more than a decade later, when he got wind of Ted's espionage for the Soviet Union inside the Manhattan Project.

In reality, it's unlikely Ted, as a very young high school student, would have known the older college leftist Rosenberg, or that Rosenberg would have noticed Ted. Rosenberg was not the type to deliver fiery speeches. Still, his older son, Michael Meeropol, notes that there was an alcove in the CCNY dining hall where Communists like his father held forth in discussions on various political issues. Meeropol suggested to me that it's "certainly possible to imagine" that if the precocious and politically intrigued Ted had listened in at any of those occasions in the alcove when Communist students were speaking, the person he was listening to might well have been Meeropol's father, Julius.

But in any case, by the time he was a fourteen-year-old freshman at Queens College, Ted was well on his way to getting an education in both physics and leftist politics. Just four years later, he would, rather incredibly, be a physicist at Los Alamos working alongside the most brilliant scientific minds in physics and math in the world, all of them trying to create, as quickly as possible, an atomic bomb.

2

EDWARD HALL JOINS THE ARMY AIR CORPS AND SHIPS OFF TO ENGLAND

Be so good they can't ignore you.

—Steve Martin

When Ed Hall advised his younger brother, Ted, during his second year at Queens College in 1942 to apply as a transfer student to Harvard University, he had to communicate that advice by mail from a Royal Air Force base in Rushden, UK. That was where the U.S. Army Air Corps had a group of mechanics tasked with repairing damaged bombers returning from battle.

Ed, who had graduated from CCNY's School of Engineering in 1936 with a BS in engineering and an MS in chemical engineering, later wrote a never-published book-length memoir of his World War II and Cold War days titled *A Nation at Risk*. In that work, provided to me by Ed's daughter Sheila, who had acted as his editor, Ed wrote first about his struggles in a Depression-plagued job market to find engineering work. Finding only short-term contract jobs and taking positions between those professional gigs working at everything from auto mechanic and radio repairman to an electrician and plumber, he longed for something more steady and demanding. He writes, "I reviewed my sad career and decided a major change was necessary."

And so, with war heating up in Europe in 1939, he enlisted. He chose the Army Air Corps, explaining, "I felt that the growing Air Corps would eventually need engineers so I packed my ancient car and headed west to Chanute Field, Illinois, home of the Air Corps mechanics school, getting sworn in there as a private."[1]

His assumption about the army's need for engineers proved decidedly optimistic. Instead of being snatched up and applying his engineering degrees and on-the-job work skills, he found his education to be an obstacle to his advancement. Asked by a sergeant who was interviewing new recruits and assigning them to appropriate tasks on the base what his reason for enlisting was, he replied, "Becoming an Air Corps engineer." He says the sergeant filled out a paper, put it in an envelope, and told him to go see another sergeant. That second sergeant, after appearing have trouble reading the note, asked Ed if he was a draftsman, and when he said he had done some drafting work, the "relieved-looking" sergeant sent him on to see yet another sergeant, this one named Browning.

Of Sgt. Browning, Ed writes,

> He showed me the control mechanisms of a Hamilton hydromatic propeller and a constant speed unit. He wanted sectioned plates made of these as instruction aids. I said I'd be glad to do this if I could have a set of Air Corps drafting standards. He produced these, conducted me into an adjoining room fitted with drafting equipment, and left.
>
> He returned after two days and found the plates nearly complete. This surprised him and he asked about my background. I informed him of my college degrees and my checkered engineering career. He seemed well satisfied, and asked how I was referred to him. I described my initial interview, the letter, and the second sergeant's reaction to the note, including his direction to Browning's office. Browning then requested that the original note be sent to him. It directed that I be given the job of painting GI cans [lavatories].[2]

Things didn't improve much for Ed during his early years in the army. He spent some time working at March Field near Riverside, California, as a mechanic, repairing and maintaining planes like the B-18, A-17, and P-36, before being shipped on to Elmendorf Field near Anchorage, Alaska. His efforts to get his commanding officer to recommend him to officer training school going nowhere, he had a friend in the radio room at the base transmit a letter from himself directly to the school. He was accepted and soon found himself back in Chanute, Illinois.

He was there when Pearl Harbor was attacked by Japan on December 7, 1941. By then a freshly minted Army Air Corps lieutenant, Ed found his transport group, after a series of delays—including a "useful" period spent attending the Pratt & Whitney engine school in East Hartford, Connecticut—being shipped to Labrador, Newfoundland, and later to Greenland. In early 1942, he was sent on to Britain, where engineers capable of repairing damaged planes were, as he had presciently anticipated, in serious demand—though, as he would quickly learn, not particularly appreciated by the senior officers overseeing them, who had no engineering training.

During his time in England, Ed distinguished himself by designing a quick fix for returning badly flak-battered and cannon-damaged bombers to the air with a "spar cord that didn't require removal of the damaged fuselage"[3]—an innovation for which he received his first of several Legion of Merit awards. He also gained notoriety for regularly insulting superior officers who ignorantly interfered with his work by trying to impose their own authority without, in his view, the expertise to justify it.

Even in the military, Ed didn't suffer fools, even significantly higher-ranking ones. For example, he recounts one incident where a badly damaged B-17 had managed to crash-land in England after limping back across the English Channel from a bombing run. It was sitting in a hangar being repaired.

Ed writes,

The repair was being performed on the lower spar cord of the inward panel about twenty feet from the fuselage. This was a region of very heavy load. The spar cords of the B17 are closed squares in cross section, extruded and varying wall thickness with length. The repair consisted of a thin stainless steel saddle with four holes in each of the two splice plates of specified thickness attached to two sound spar-cord ends with a carefully designed pattern of drive fit bolts.

I called up to the man on a ladder doing the work and asked where I could find the crew chief. I found him and asked who had designed the repair being installed. He replied, "Boeing." Astonished, I asked to see the paper submitted by Boeing. It read, "Boeing Burtonwood" [a nearby town in Britain]. I then ordered his men off the job. They refused, and since I felt that the first flight of that B17 would be its last, I took out my .45 service pistol and told them I'd give them five minutes. They left. About five minutes later I was called to the phone and heard, "This is Col. Short at Burtonwood." I replied, "This is Lt. Hall at Basingbourne."

"Did you order my men off the B17 they were repairing?"

"Yes," said I.

"By what authority did you do that?"

I read him the letter signed by Gen. Clark at headquarters, placing me in charge of repair of all battle-damaged airplanes in the United Kingdom. He chose to ignore my statement and ordered me to put his men back to work. I said that I could do no such thing as it would assure the loss of an airplane and crew. He continued to insist and I replied, "I cannot possibly do such a thing, you son of a gun," and hung up.

Two weeks later, I was called into Bush Park to the desk of a major. He said that I was in very serious trouble. Court Martial charges had been filed against me and I was ordered to fill out a charge sheet and return it within two days. I left his desk, sat down and read the sheet. It was signed by Col. Short and accused me of gross technical incompetence. I left Bushy Park and proceeded to the Boeing office in London. There, I conferred with two Boeing Engineers, Mssrs. Butler and Martin. They inspected the charge sheet and I filled in the details of the encounter at Basingbourne. Yes, they said they would be glad to give me a paper attesting to my engineering ability. This was prepared immediately, and included the statements that my mobile repair group was far better equipped to repair B17s than any other organization in Britain; that the work on B17s at Burtonwood was generally poor and frequently unacceptable; and that removal of my organization would be disastrous.

I returned to my major's desk and he asked whether I had any comments. I handed him the paper prepared by the Boeing engineers. As he read it his face reddened. He asked whether I had any more copies of the document, to which I replied that I had. He requested that I give them to him. I informed him that that was impossible, since I had sent them to friends in various parts of the United States with instructions to hand them to their newspapers if they did not hear from me in two weeks. He asked me to stay put and hurried off to a high-ranking officer's office at a corner of the building. In five minutes he returned with a general officer who shook my hand and said, "Go back to work and keep them flying."[4]

Another illustration of Ed Hall's dismissive attitude toward military rules and the authority of rank occurred a bit later. It was at the Warton Air Depot, where there was a serious lack of supplies and equipment because of the losses among U.S. supply ships crossing the Atlantic. He recalls that "the British construction detachment was commanded by a wing commander whom I felt must have been involved in the Crimean War. To exacerbate this minor lack of engineering skill, the US Air Corps people assigned to help were equally competent." He continues,

The supply bins at Warton were unpredictable. Occasionally I was hard pressed to locate a needed material or device and had to exercise ingenuity on the telephone to seek a replacement. On one such occasion, I had located an essential tool at a British shipyard nearby (we often helped each other informally since we were sure that formal requests would have to go through Washington and Whitehall). I drove to the shipyard, a distance of four miles, in my coveralls and was picked up by a military policeman on my way back for leaving the base while not in a class A uniform. This dastardly act delayed my promotion to captain.

On another occasion, heavy structural steel sections were needed to build a special press and none could be found. My friend Lt. Maurice Comman-day and I had a great idea. On the road, a few miles from Wharton, was a steel tank trap. During the evening we removed a section from the trap and modified it to fit a press I had designed to aid in the development of a new technique to simplify repairs to B17 spar cords. We installed it. It worked, and permitted B-17 spar cords to be repaired more simply, better and faster.[5]

Ed Hall was, if nothing else, self-confident to a fault. He demonstrated this confidence when his wife, Edith Shawcross, was in a life-threatening medical crisis. It happened in early 1944, shortly after he had been reposted to a location near Bournemouth, some distance from his home and his preg-nant wife of less than a year. As he relates the story, a few days after arriving at his new post, he received an alarming call saying his wife had gone into labor unexpectedly and was delivering their baby, but that there was a seri-ous problem. Recalling that "for some reason I cannot recall," when he put on his Class A uniform for the headlong drive to Oxford, he unthinkingly strapped on his holster and .45-caliber pistol. He recalls,

I went immediately to Edith's Boar's Hill home where I was directed to the Radcliffe infirmary and found the obstetrician treating Edith. By this time, Edith had been in labor for about 50 hours. I discussed the case with the doctor, who was very worried. He informed me that the baby's heart had weakened, and that my wife was rapidly failing. He seemed thoroughly con-fused and could not answer my question as to what he would do now. It was evident that time was now critical. I pulled my .45 out of its holster, pressed it to his chest, and ordered him to remove the fetus immediately. He actually seemed relieved and proceeded at once to remove the baby with high forceps. I suppose this makes my son David a son of a gun! This baby suffered in early life from the prolonged birth and almost certain anoxia he suffered, causing us much anxiety. He now holds a PhD in physics from Cal Tech.[6]

Such self-confidence and daring end-runs around standard procedure and dismantling of defense systems in the name of efficiency, as well as

run-ins with superior officers, were characteristic of Ed—once actually landing him in the brig—but he inevitably came out on top each time, albeit with
a list of bitter enemies in the Army Air Corps and later in the U.S. Air Force
as well as in the arms industry establishment.

Ed and his much younger brother were as different in personality as
they were in stature, Ted a lanky 5-foot-11, with a quiet voice and almost
shy demeanor hiding a sharp wit, and Ed, at 5-foot-8, brusque and self-
confident, though also with a sense of humor. Even as youngsters, both
brothers showed themselves to be capable of remarkable decisiveness when
they knew something needed to be done and that they had to act.

3

EINSTEIN WARNS FDR ABOUT A POSSIBLE GERMAN A-BOMB

$E = MC^2$

—Albert Einstein

About the same time Ed Hall was enlisting in the army, Albert Einstein, the scientist who created the nuclear age with his discovery that matter and energy were different states of the same thing, was also thinking about the looming conflict in Europe—and worrying about the wartime implications of his discovery. He sent President Franklin D. Roosevelt a historic letter. In it, the world's preeminent physicist alerted the president about research conducted by Enrico Fermi and Leo Szilard, two other foreign but U.S.-based physicists who, along with a physicist in France, had discovered it was possible to create a fission reaction that, given a sufficiently large amount of refined uranium, could produce "vast amounts of power." This release of energy, he noted, could "lead to the construction of bombs that, if delivered to a port, might very well destroy a whole port together with some of the surrounding territory."[1]

The letter was actually the idea of Szilard, a Hungarian physicist who was a student of Einstein's. In 1932, Szilard had read H. G. Wells's prophetic 1914 novel *The World Set Free*, which predicted that air-dropped "atomic bombs" would change the nature of warfare forever. A year later, he conceived the concept of nuclear fission, which he realized could power nuclear reactors and also produce horrific atomic bombs. Indeed, Szilard filed a patent application for such a bomb made from uranium, not with an eye to profiting from the weapon, but in hopes of keeping anyone else from making it. As a new world war became a reality and (as Szilard knew) there were eminent physicists in Nazi Germany who were, like him, clearly aware of the possibility of creating an atomic bomb, he encouraged Einstein, because of his fame and his celebrated research position at Princeton's Institute for Advanced Study, to send a warning to FDR about the risk of a Nazi atom bomb. Einstein, to his later profound regret, agreed to do so.

The resulting letter, drafted by Szilard but signed on August 2, 1939, by Einstein, was hand-delivered to FDR by a friend of Einstein's who was a Wall Street investment banker. It included a warning that there was disturbing evidence that German scientists might have already set about planning to develop such a superweapon:

> I understand that Germany has actually stopped the sale of uranium from the Czechoslovakian mines which she has taken over. That she should have taken such early action might perhaps be understood on the ground that the son of the German Under-Secretary of State, [Ernst] von Weizsäcker, is attached to the Kaiser-Wilhelm-Institut in Berlin where some of the American work on uranium is now being repeated.[2]

Around the time Einstein's letter was making its way to the Oval Office, Ed was advising his seriously bored younger brother that he should transfer out of Queens College, which he derisively called a "glorified high school," and apply to Harvard to pursue his interest in physics.

After receiving Einstein's troubling warning letter, on October 21 FDR established the Advisory Committee on Uranium, headed by scientist Lyman J. Briggs, director of the U.S. National Bureau of Standards, and including a mix of scientists and military leaders. In early 1940, the committee recommended that the federal government fund research into uranium isotope separation (U-235, constituting only a minute fraction of naturally occurring uranium, is the only fissionable form of the element) and further work on fission chain reactions using a reactor at Columbia University that was available to Fermi and Szilard.

By June 1940, FDR had replaced the uranium committee with a new organization, the National Defense Research Committee (NDRC), composed only of scientists and headed by Vannevar Bush, president of the Carnegie Foundation. For security reasons, foreign-born scientists—including even Fermi and Szilard—were kept off the new committee, and any further research on uranium was barred from publication (a decision that, in retrospect, may have done more harm than good in terms of keeping the nascent U.S. bomb project secret, since the sudden blackout clearly showed that ongoing research into uranium fission had become a secret).

The plan was to fund research into four possible methods for refining pure U-235 until the best path to producing significant quantities of bomb-grade material was developed. A year later, on June 28, 1941, the president issued an executive order establishing the Office of Scientific Research and Development (OSRD), tasking it with coordinating all military research and development. Bush remained in charge, reporting directly to the president, and was provided with an unlimited budget. Because of the importance attached to the atomic bomb research, the NDRC's earlier ban on foreign-born scientist participation was dropped, and Fermi was put on the OSRD's board.

Interestingly, while the NDRC and OSRD initially left research into uranium largely in the independent hands of various federally funded researchers like Fermi and Szilard, the committee took a different approach with another major challenge—an urgent need to expand on the successful, carefully guarded secret invention of radar by British scientists who were using the novel idea of generating microwaves and picking up the reflected radiation with large antennas stretched along the eastern coast of the British Isles as a way to spot incoming German bombers and V-1 drones. With this earlier scientific challenge, the goal was to figure out how to significantly upgrade the power of Britain's invention, a top-secret ten-centimeter cavity magnetron, to produce much shorter-length microwave signals of sufficient power to enable radar to be placed on weapons systems as small as torpedo-carrying dive-bombers. So equipped, the planes could use the revolutionary new device to locate and attack German U-boats as they raised their metal periscopes or antennas above the sea's surface. Small radar systems could even eventually be used to aim air-mounted guns on bombers.

Established in October 1940, the Radiation Lab, known familiarly as the Rad Lab, became the model for the of the ultimately much larger Manhattan Project, established two years later, on December 28, 1942.* Based at MIT,

---

* One reason I initially became interested in the story of Ted Hall was that it resembled somewhat the experience of my own father, David Lindorff, the first of his immigrant German family to go to and eventually graduate college (MIT), where he earned a BS in electrical engineering. Dad was eighteen when he was hired in 1941, at the end of his freshman year, by the Rad Lab. As he recounted the story, he was leaving the school after his second semester of study because of the sudden death of his own father from colon cancer. Dad had to find full-time employment to support his widowed mother and his seven-year-old brother. Having just filed leave of absence papers with the college, he decided to use as

the Rad Lab, under tight security, recruited all the genius scientists and engineers it could find, giving them as much freedom as possible to share information among each other, as well as freedom from military interference, in hopes that they could solve an urgently important and daunting scientific problem. The Manhattan Project subsequently adopted the same approach, though there was more military oversight than at the Radiation Lab, which didn't have a general overseeing it.

Like the Manhattan Project—which is often credited, controversially, with having ended the war with Japan—the Radiation Lab is often credited with having contributed significantly to an earlier-than-anticipated defeat of Germany and Japan by enabling Allied planes and ships to locate and target enemy planes and submarines from the air, easing the transport of men and military materiel from Canada and the United States to Britain and later to the western front in Europe.

By early 1941, well before the Manhattan Project was established, U.S. government-funded research into an atomic bomb had already begun to produce results. It was discovered, for example, that a fairly small amount of pure U-235 (early estimates were as little as ten kilograms rather than the actual forty-seven kilograms needed) could produce a massive nuclear blast. It was also discovered in 1942 that another newly discovered element, plutonium—a by-product of the nuclear fission created in uranium-fueled reactors but rarely found in nature, and then in only minute amounts—could

---

a shortcut a tunnel that led from the basement of Building 10—the iconic Great Dome classroom and administration building at the main entrance to the campus—to the Red Line subway. He found the door to the tunnel locked, with two signs taped on it. One read, "Top Secret. No Admittance"; the other read, " Looking to Hire: Lab technician."

In the market for a job, Dad knocked on the door, and an older man opened it a crack, asking him what he wanted. When my father said he was interested in the tech job, the man, who turned out to be the famed Nobel physicist Isidore Rabi, responded, "What can you do?" My father replied proudly that he'd just completed MIT's first-year engineering program with straight A's. Rabi responded, "You and a hundred other students. But what can you do?" My father told him that he had built his own ham radio set in high school, to which Rabi responded, "Oh, so you can solder?" My father said, "Sure," and he was hired on the spot. Dad thus became the youngest engineer at the Radiation Lab, much as Ted two years later became the youngest physicist at Los Alamos. Like Ted, too, within a year, with the war raging, Dad was drafted, in his case by the U.S. Navy. Loathing the uniforms assigned navy recruits, with their funny-looking bell-bottom trousers and back flaps, he decided on a whim, while heading to his induction, to instead enlist in the Marines at a recruiting office he was walking past. The Marine uniforms in the posters, he explained later, looked much sharper. The eager Marine recruiter falsely assured him he would make certain my father would be allowed to continue his "important national security work" with the Radiation Lab. When Dad instead found himself in basic training being prepared for transfer to combat in the Pacific theater, he contacted senior people at the Rad Lab. To the intense irritation of the base commander, the lab pulled strings with the Marines and had his orders changed to the Vero Beach Naval Air Station in Florida. There he spent the war flying shotgun on dive-bombers attempting to test and harden the delicate glass tube–based radar devices, which the huge G-forces the planes created pulling out of their dives tended to destroy as soon as they were used.

also work as an atomic bomb. There were initial predictions (optimistic, it turns out) that an atomic bomb could be produced within two years' time using one of these elements. But those predictions did not anticipate the obstacles to moving from theory to the engineering realities of constructing an atomic bomb, which proved to be daunting for both types of bomb, but for completely different reasons.

The basic design of a uranium bomb had been obvious to Einstein and Szilard as soon as they thought about it: basically a "plugged cannon" inside of which one subcritical hunk of fissionable uranium would be fired into a stationary subcritical hunk of the same metal at the other end of the "barrel" to create a fission reaction. But this seemingly simple weapon required an isotope, U-235, that represents only 0.73 percent of the uranium atoms in a given mass of refined uranium metal. Most of the rest of the shiny silver metal consists of the much more stable isotope U-238, which has three more neutrons in its nucleus and, while radioactive, does not create a chain reaction of ever more neutrons and splitting atoms, releasing in the process enormous amounts of energy and producing the desired fission explosion. Figuring out how to separate out just the lighter fissionable isotope of uranium was a challenge (since the isotopes are chemically identical and so cannot be separated by chemical reactions), requiring massive construction of high-speed centrifuges working with hot vaporized uranium gas along with significant amounts of electrical power as well as other elaborate, costly, and energy-hungry equipment.

Meanwhile, the problem with plutonium was almost exactly the opposite. Plutonium in the pure form of its most common isotope, P-239, might possibly be able to work in a simple cannon-type bomb, but it turned out the new element, relatively easy to isolate and extract chemically from the waste stream of a nuclear reactor, also always included a small amount of the isotope P-240, with one more neutron than P-239, which made it one thousand times more fissile than the more common isotope. This "contamination" made it so that subcritical plutonium pieces, if blasted together in a "cannon" system like U-235, even at the maximum obtainable speed of 1,000 mph, would start fissioning as they approached each other. This would heat both pieces into liquid before they even made contact and cause a small premature explosion that would destroy the whole bomb, with a resulting blast being no bigger than a large chemical bomb. It would require two years and a major engineering feat to make plutonium work as an atomic bomb, as was finally accomplished with the "Gadget," the first atomic bomb constructed and tested in the Manhattan Project's Trinity Test on July 16, 1945. (This was the task that Ted Hall, in June 1944, was heading up a team working to accomplish.)

By the time the plutonium bomb was successfully detonated, Germany had already surrendered and Japan's surrender was imminent.

4

TED HALL

From Student Physicist to Manhattan Project Recruit

You have to learn the rules of the game. And then you have to play it better than anyone else.

—Albert Einstein

While the U.S. atomic bomb project was moving along in what was (at least during the years the Manhattan Project was underway) believed to be total secrecy, even within the federal government, Ted Hall had been growing up quickly. Following his brother's advice—or perhaps one could say insistence—during the spring of 1942, Ted applied to Harvard as a transfer student from Queens College. The application deadline for transfer students had already passed, but his stunning New York Board of Regents exam scores and glowing recommendation letters from his teachers at Queens College won him admission anyway. And so, in the fall of 1942, Ted began classes at Harvard as a junior physics major while he was still just sixteen.

By the luck of the draw, Harvard assigned this young transfer student to Leverett House, which had become by reputation (reinforced by self-selection among upperclassmen, who got to request and sometimes obtain specific room assignments) a residence hall of choice for student leftists. This led to its becoming known around the college as "Moscow-on-the-Charles." Ted found himself randomly assigned to a dorm room with two upperclassmen who, like a number of students at the school in those days, identified themselves as Marxists. Jake Bean (who never graduated from Harvard but ended up as curator of drawings at the Metropolitan Museum of Art in New York) was chairman of the school's John Reed Society, a legacy relic of the old Communist-front John Reed Club, which was at the time a small assemblage of some dozen students, with no Party connection needed and no ideological requirement. Hall's other roommate was Barney Emmart, another John Reed Society stalwart who, after a stint in the Army Air Corps as a meteorologist, became a journalist like his father and later a media critic and professor.[1]

The John Reed Club, which at one point boasted thirty chapters in as many cities around the United States, was named after the Harvard alum who became famous as an advocacy journalist for his "embedded" and sympathetic coverage of the Mexican Revolution during 1914 and the Bolshevik Revolution in St. Petersburg in 1917. The club, originally established in 1929 by the U.S. Communist Party, was operated as a "mass organization" or "front" until 1936, when the Party, following instructions from Moscow, abandoned it as part of a change in strategy to align the U.S. Communist Party with Roosevelt's New Deal under an antifascist united front strategy. By 1943, "any vestiges of the John Reed Clubs had vanished as an organization within the Communist Party USA."[2]

But at Reed's alma mater, the organization continued—though no longer as a front organization—with its name changed to society from club. This society, with no Party backing, struggled through the war years, at one point before Hall and Sax arrived splitting in two over the issue of admitting non-Marxists as members. Several years later, after the war was over, Hall described the Reed Society to his then-girlfriend Joan Krakover as "more of a joke" by 1943 when he was frequenting its meetings—a way to seem edgy, perhaps, and to get together with smart young leftist-leaning students who wanted to kibbitz around while also discussing politics and Marxist philosophy.

One of those smart young leftists in the society was Harvard mathematics major Horace Chandler Davis. A year younger than Hall, Davis had joined the Communist Party in 1943 at the age of seventeen. Another resident of Leverett House, Davis became friends with Hall, Sax, and another young physics major, a month older than Hall, named Roy Glauber. In a conversation with me in early 2022, Davis—ninety-six years old and still living with his wife, noted historian Natalie Zemon Davis, in Toronto (where they were both emeritus professors at the University of Toronto)—recalled his three young schoolmates, Hall, Sax, and Glauber, as being "all leftists of a sort like most of those at Leverett House." He added, however, that "as a member of the Party, I was always looking for potential recruits, but I never thought of any of the three of them as candidates for recruitment. I don't think I ever had the feeling, 'Hey I should try and sign these guys up.'"

As a serious and committed Communist, Davis (who died on September 24, 2022, his mind still so sharp he insisted on speaking remotely from his hospice bed at a meeting he had organized to support Azat Miftakhov, an outspoken Russian mathematics graduate student imprisoned on a trumped-up charge) was likely a good judge of people's political sentiments even at a young age. Hailing from a radical family of upper-class Boston "Brahmins," he never hid his political beliefs, boldly identifying himself as a socialist and Communist, except during his years in the U.S. Navy, when, "in accordance with Party policy to support Roosevelt," he quit the Party, rejoining only after his discharge.

Returning to Harvard after the war, Davis went on to graduate in 1950 with a doctorate in math. He landed a job as an instructor on the math faculty of the University of Michigan, only to be fired in 1954 because of his prior Party history. That was when he became "something of a legend and hero" among leftist opponents of that witch hunt era in academia, according to HUAC/McCarthy-era historian Ellen Schrecker, who highlighted his experience at the opening of her groundbreaking book on that era in academia, *No Ivory Tower*.[3]

Like many dedicated Party members, Davis quit the Communist Party for good in 1953 as Stalin's epic crimes and atrocities were confirmed by the new reformist Soviet premier Nikita Khrushchev. Nonetheless, his youthful Party history followed him during that paranoid decade. When he and two other professors at the school were called before the notorious House Un-American Activities Committee later that year, Davis refused to cooperate with the demand that he name fellow Communist Party members or former members allegedly lurking unrecognized in academia. Cited for contempt of Congress, he was sentenced to six months in FCI Danbury, a federal prison in Connecticut, and was controversially dismissed by the university. Locked up and serving his sentence once his appeals had been exhausted, he wrote a research paper behind bars that, when it was later published in the American Mathematical Society's journal, included a note saying, "Research supported in part by the Federal Prison System. Opinions expressed in this paper are the author's and are not necessarily those of the Bureau of Prisons."[4]

There is no evidence that Ted Hall was a Communist as a Harvard student, much less a Party true believer, as some historians of the era have baselessly claimed, usually on the thin "reed" of his early teenage membership in the American Student Union and his later college participation in the Harvard John Reed Society. Clearly a socialist and interested in Marxist economic theory, Ted was also admiring of the Soviet Red Army's heroic resistance to the German invasion of the country—but so were many, if not most, Americans at that time.

Like many a young student, Hall found diversions aplenty to his studies, like the Reed Society, as well as interesting courses outside his major in physics. Also competing for his attention was the Harvard campus's heavy emphasis on the war effort, with large numbers of students in the Reserve Officer Training Program (ROTC) and with the navy operating an officer training program on the campus. All this served to make it difficult for a young student with wide-ranging interests, including in the war, to focus on the challenging science program he had selected for his first semester, which included optics, electricity, magnetism, and mechanics, along with German language and a philosophy course titled "Fundamental Issues at Stake in the War."

He wrote to his brother in April 1943 describing his program:

Dear Ed,
    As an educational institution the spirit is all wrong. THERE IS NO LAUGHING IN THE CLASSES. What it boils down to is that there is no appreciation of the lusty beauty of effective learning—learning that is to be applied to world-building. That is perhaps the basis of education. In this sense the process of education depends as much, maybe more, on the student as on the prof, where one authority is thumping his irrefutable facts into the heads of good students who will learn it all.[5]

Frustrated, Ted began participating in a lot of extracurricular options, ranging from guerrilla warfare training and lessons on how to parachute behind enemy lines (on offer because of student expectations of being drafted, interest in the war, and all the Navy personnel attending classes at the university) to tennis and sculling on the nearby Charles River. All that and meetings of the John Reed Society too.

Ted's work suffered—ironically, in view of his future activities—as he began questioning the relevance of his physics major and related classes to the real world. Part of the problem was that Ted, long accustomed to being considered the smartest person in any classroom, was for the first time finding himself to be not the only brilliant student in class. Instead, because he entered Harvard as a junior, he was for the first time in his life struggling to catch up with what was happening in courses where the other students had the benefit of earlier Harvard-level preparatory coursework. In another letter he sent to his brother in early 1943, after he'd regained his academic footing and some of his old confidence, he wrote,

> Personally, I have been suffering psychological violence. I almost quit college last December—I had absolutely no interest in work in any field. I decided to leave but Mom and Dad got me back against my will. That was lucky—now for the first time I am going steadily and securely in several fields under my own power—and I know I shall continue that way.[6]

Had he not gotten his act together, or even had he taken longer to pull himself out of his emotional funk and instead allowed his malaise and distraction to continue into the fall term of 1943, it would have surely meant he would not have been recommended to a recruiter dispatched by Robert Oppenheimer, science director of the Manhattan Project. Instead, he gave up hanging out with a guitar and became fascinated with quantum mechanics. At the same time, though, he managed to prepare and present a Marxist analysis to the John Reed Society in which he sought to demonstrate that any economic system could be explained by a series of mathematical equations.

By the mandatory summer term of 1943, his grades had recovered to the point that he was awarded a $200 scholarship (almost $3,500 in today's dollars), an honor not often bestowed on transfer students. As an indication of the high regard in which he was held by the physics department faculty, he was asked to fill in as an instructor in an elementary physics class offered to U.S. Army soldiers being boarded at Leverett House.

There was, however, a second blow that struck him late that summer. His mother, Rose, with whom he was always very close and who was the one person who could tell him what to do (as she did when she insisted that he return to Harvard after the winter holiday), died of cancer at age fifty-seven, after two weeks in a coma.

Speaking about that loss with *Bombshell*'s authors, Hall told them, "Superficially this had very little effect on me, but looking back, I think it made me a little more lost."[7]

Joan, in her memoir of Ted, writes,

> Talking to me four years later [at around the time they met, fell in love, and got married in 1947], he did not recall being terribly upset about his loss, though

he loved his mother very much. He described his father's reaction with admiration: "I could say he accepted my mother's death with equanimity."

Ted must have aimed for something like that. He went back to Harvard and carried on. In October 1943, just after his eighteenth birthday [and a month before he was invited to an interview for the job at Los Alamos], he wrote his brother Ed a long letter, evidently in response to Ed's exhortations to stop being lazy and behave like a "grade A individual" [replying]: "I could spend a whole summer strumming a guitar and not feel the summer was wasted at all. Sure it's fine to hit on all cylinders and . . . I like being grade A. But I also like being grades B, C, D and E. I think most of my time will be in A blocks. It happens. I hope it will. I have no inclination to avoid the other levels though."

Joan adds, "Here is a rare, characteristically modest expression of Ted's attitude to his own remarkable gifts. His aim, he wrote, was, 'to be able to enjoy capability without depending on the feeling of superiority.' This was the young man I married three and a half years later."[8] Ted eventually fully overcame his crisis of confidence and the loss of his mother, and he began to excel.

That fall, Hall and Glauber, by then good friends and both eighteen-year-old whiz-kid juniors majoring in physics, decided to room together in Lowell House, a building adjacent to Leverett. They were later joined by Saville Sax, a disheveled, wiry, and witty bohemian student who showed up one day after being belatedly assigned (or perhaps successfully having requested assignment) by the overcrowded school to their dorm room.

5

ENTER SAVILLE SAX

*Differences are not intended to separate, to alienate. We are
different precisely in order to realize our need of one another.*

—Desmond Tutu

Saville Sax (Savy to friends and family), though new to Roy Glauber, was
hardly unknown to Ted Hall when the two roommates found him in
their dorm room, where he had been added as a third roommate. A regular
at Harvard's John Reed Society meetings, Sax had similar leftist politics, age
(Sax, born on July 26, 1924, was a bit more than a year older than Hall),
and background (both being born to Russian Jewish immigrant parents
and raised in New York City) as Ted, creating an instant and strong bond
between them.

Sax's children, Boria and Sarah, and Joan Hall (who knew Saville as a
fellow student at the University of Chicago and for most of the late 1940s
and early 1950s as a friend of hers and Ted's) all note that he had an unusual
and traumatic childhood. Born into a family who spoke mostly Yiddish at
home, he wasn't taught to speak English until he went to school at age six.
He was virtually an immigrant himself when he began school—and one
with a deformed hand, the result of an entanglement in the umbilical cord
that prevented it from developing properly in the womb. A smart child, he
seemed to make his way through school easily enough, performing sufficiently well in grade school to gain admittance into DeWitt Clinton, a special

high school in the Bronx for gifted students, and later to Harvard. Age six or seven, as it turns out, is a good time to pick up a new language through immersion, as I know from experience.* But it can also be a challenge being different, and Saville was certainly that.

Boria writes that Savy's parents, Boruch and Bluma, both hailed from nameless villages in the region around Vinitsa in what today is Ukraine. They emigrated, he says, at a time when many Jews were attracted to the new Communist movement. When they left for America in 1914 to escape the frequent violent and deadly pogroms launched by anti-Semitic Ukrainians, his parents, especially his mother, brought that movement with them and settled alongside other leftist Jews from the same area, establishing their own "ghetto" in New York, where Yiddish remained the lingua franca and Communism, in its various versions and sects, rather than Judaism, was the common belief system. As he writes, "They all moved into the same apartment building, got together every day, and regarded the rest of the city, indeed American society, as heartless and corrupt."[1]

The 1917 Bolshevik Revolution, besides being a source of pride and identity for this little ghetto-within-a-ghetto in New York, also proved to be a financial boon to the enterprising Boruch. The new Russian government was desperate for hard currency, and there was, fortunately, a lot of expropriated property in the new Soviet Union, including valuable items "liberated" from the homes of the wealthy families who had backed or been part of the old tsarist regime.

Boria writes,

My grandfather saw his chance and began importing these for the American market. He quickly prospered, without the need to make any real accommodation to his new society. I suspect him of having converted to Communism mostly because it was good for business. He lived what is commonly referred to as "the American Dream." But that ideal had merged in his imagination with the Communist utopia.[2]

---

* In 1991–1992, I received a Fulbright Professor fellowship to teach journalism at China's Fudan University in Shanghai. I went there with my wife, Joyce, and our seven-year-old daughter, Ariel. While I spoke Chinese, which was my college major, my daughter knew not a word of the language. We managed to get the elementary school in our neighborhood to let her enroll in the first grade with forty other students, mostly a year younger than her, and a seasoned teacher of fifty who spoke no English but was very dedicated to her students. To my amazement, my daughter picked up the language both in class and on the playground and was fully fluent in less than three months, with no English accent! By December she was even dreaming in Chinese and speaking the language in her sleep.

Boria says his grandmother Bluma, who died in 1986, remained the "simple peasant woman" she had always been, but with a difference: She was an ardent Communist "peasant" and a passionate supporter of the Soviet Union.

A major tragedy in Savy's life came when he was twelve. As Boria tells it,

> A few weeks after a vehement argument with his father, Savy . . . was entrusted with administering heart medication to his father at specified times. But one day . . . [he] fell asleep and failed to perform that task. When, shortly afterwards, a heart attack killed Bernard, Bluma placed the blame on her son. Savy, carrying an enormous burden of guilt about his father, even named me after Bernard (using his nickname) as an attempt at expiation. Savy's guilty conscience gave Bluma enormous emotional power over him.[3]

Joan, who met and befriended Sax at the University of Chicago in 1947, recalls him as an interesting if unkempt young man, with wild hair and wilder ideas, "some of which Ted went along with." She thought Hall, who she was introduced to by his college friend, was also drawn to Sax because they could "talk knowledgeably together about Marxist and socialist ideas."[4]

Where Hall was precise if nonconformist in his dress and conversation and a scientist in his thinking, Sax was more scattershot in his thinking and oblivious to his appearance—smart, to be sure, but lacking focus. What the two shared was a kind of unconscious sexual attractiveness to women and a sense of humor. (Maybe the two things go together.) In his effort to explain the friendship between Ted and Savy, Boria put it this way in an interview included in *A Compassionate Spy*: "My father admired Ted, and in a way wanted *to be* Ted."[5]

Sarah Sax, Saville's artist daughter, says she thinks Ted liked her father's "creativity, his impulsivity and his sometimes crazy ideas, which he often rejected but sometimes went along with."

Future Physics Nobel laureate Roy Glauber, in an interview with the authors of the book *Bombshell*, recalled returning to his dorm room one day to find Sax, a student he didn't know, crouching near the fireplace and nursing a flaming bunch of crumpled paper. "I asked him what he was doing and he said, in a kind of husky voice, 'I'm roasting eggs,'" Glauber said. "Somehow the dining halls weren't open and he had a couple of eggs that he'd put into the fire, and of course they burst, and scattered egg about. And I thought this was one of the strangest people I had ever met."[6]

Saville Sax, who adopted the dorm room's sofa as his bed, was indeed unusual. Like Hall and Glauber, Sax had graduated from a select secondary public institution in the New York City school system, DeWitt Clinton High School, which emphasized literature and the arts, not science and math, and produced such prominent graduates as James Baldwin (a close high school friend of Sax's), William Kunstler, Burt Lancaster, and Richard Rogers. Sax himself was of a bohemian bent, unconcerned about his grooming or his grades. It seems likely that Sax's irreverent dismissal of social norms and his general disestablishmentarianism—as well as his sharp intelligence, wit, and dark sense of humor and imagination—appealed to the more taciturn, scientific-minded, but also nonconformist Hall.

Both these Harvard students shared leftist politics, though Sax's were more fully formed, thanks no doubt to his mother's strongly held Communist beliefs and longtime Party membership. An FBI report from the Boston Bureau office in 1950 notes that Sax was "one of the key leaders" of the Cambridge chapter of American Youth for Democracy (which it labeled a Communist front organization originally called the Young Communist League) and was also in the Boston chapter of the Wendell Phillips Club, another Communist Party front group.[7] His FBI file labels Sax as a Communist, though there is no evidence offered of his being a Party member at the time he worked as a spy courier when Ted was working at Los Alamos.

One thing the two teens had in common was that they were the American-born sons of Russian Jewish immigrant parents—or, in Ted's case, of a Russian Jewish immigrant father, as his mother, Rose Moskowitz, was the U.S.-born child of Russian Jewish immigrant parents and not herself an immigrant.

Ted's parents were struggling economically because of the Great Depression's devastating impact on his father's furrier business. In contrast, Sax's father's upholstery business, which enabled people to repair their furnishings instead of having to buy replacements, continued to thrive, as did his profitable sideline enterprise importing expropriated Russian valuables like samovars and jewelry. Helping provide the USSR with hard currency needed for buying war supplies and weapons also helped provide the Sax family with a secure income through the Depression years. Indeed, Boruch Sax saved enough money to buy a large tract of land outside Wallkill, New York, on which he built cabins to make a summer retreat for Communist Russian Jews—property that is still in the possession of Sax's children Boria and Sarah, though most of the buildings have rotted away. Sarah says her father always loved to spend time there. Sax's mother worked for the Soviet War Relief Agency during the war, helping to raise funds and other aid for the Soviet Union during the war.

Whereas Hall was naturally athletic—he was an ace at ping-pong and stickball and loved tennis and sculling on the Charles River—Sax's deformed hand kept him from engaging in most sports and, to his dismay, prevented him from enlisting in the military during the war, as many students at Harvard were doing. Both friends were highly intelligent, but while Ted, except for an early period of ennui shortly after his arrival at Harvard, thrived in college, Sax had a difficult time applying himself and suffered from chronic depression—a condition he at one point claimed only his friend Ted was able to pull him out of. He twice flunked out of Harvard and never graduated.

Sax's sudden appearance as a third roommate in Hall and Glauber's dorm room during their junior year at Harvard seems an improbable start to what would become a crucial pairing of two bold but novice and untrained future spies whose actions would help set in motion the Cold War, a decade of duck-and-cover atomic attack drills, and a nearly eight-decade era in which no nuclear weapons were used in war. But that's what happened. Sax would be Ted's coconspirator and courier; Glauber, despite sharing his roommates' sympathy for America's wartime ally, the Soviet Union, steered well clear of spying for that nation. Still, both he and Sax, in their own ways, would play crucial roles in the course of Ted's life, both in terms of Ted's future evolution from bomb maker to bomb secret sharer as a Soviet atomic spy as well as in his (and Sax's) improbable escape from U.S. prosecution as spies.

Indeed, it was Sax who would first suggest out loud, when he heard that Ted had been interviewed for the job on the Manhattan Project, the rash idea that Ted should become a spy if hired onto a secret weapons project. Recalling this, Hall still always insisted that when he was being interviewed for the job and before he knew what the project was, he found himself thinking, without any outside prompting, about the need for the United States to share with the Soviets whatever secret weapons the country (and he himself) might be working to create.

6

HIRED ONTO THE
MANHATTAN PROJECT
AT LOS ALAMOS

*If this turns out to be a weapon that is really awful, what you
should do is tell the Russians.*

—Saville Sax

Amid fears that Germany, despite increasing Allied bombing, might still
be able to produce an atomic bomb first, the Manhattan Project in 1943
was in need of more hands on deck at Los Alamos to help with the work of
creating the two types of atomic bombs. The pickings were getting slim.
According to Joseph Albright and Marcia Kunstel, by late 1943, Vannevar
Bush had already scooped up two-thirds of all the physicists in the country
for various other crash military projects related to the war effort, leaving
many universities and colleges scrambling to find qualified professors to
teach their advanced physics courses.

The idea of hiring grad students and even brilliant undergrads like physics major Ted Hall or the mathematics undergrad Peter Lax, who was seventeen when he began working on the Manhattan Project at the suggestion
of John von Neumann, might seem odd today. But in fact, while there were
plenty of Nobelists and prominent senior scientists and engineers working
at Los Alamos, there were many brilliant physicists and other scientists
and engineers in their twenties and thirties, too; Samuel T. Cohen was
hired at the age of twenty-three, Hans Bethe at thirty, and Klaus Fuchs at
thirty-three. Robert Oppenheimer was only thirty-nine when he was named

scientific director of the project and had already been doing leading-edge work on nuclear fission before his appointment.

In any event, because of the shortage of senior talent, and feeling the pressure from General Leslie Groves and from Washington war, foreign policy, and national security strategists for a faster development of a working atomic bomb if the weapon was to be operational before the war ended, Oppenheimer authorized Bush, still President Roosevelt's chief of research and development, to contact Professor John Van Vleck at Harvard asking for recommendations of exceptional physics majors to recruit. At the time, Van Vleck, a venerated astrophysicist, had both Hall and Roy Glauber in his quantum mechanics course and was impressed with both young men. He and Physics Department chair Edwin Kemble recommended Hall and Glauber along with two slightly older Harvard seniors, twenty-one-year-old Kenneth Case and twenty-year-old Austrian national Frederic de Hoffmann as ideal candidates.[1]

Bush dispatched Merriam Hardwick Trytten, his chief of personnel, to Harvard to interview the four potential recruits. A professor of physics at the University of Pittsburgh prior to the war, Trytten had not been involved in recruiting for the Manhattan Project up to that point. Rather, he had been tasked with recruiting physicists and engineers for three *other* top-secret projects for the War Department. The first of these was the radar miniaturization program of the Radiation Lab at MIT. The second was development of a proximity fuse at a project based at Johns Hopkins University, aimed at enabling bombs and cannon shells to explode a short distance away from a target or the ground instead of only on direct contact. (It was passing of details about the proximity fuse to the Soviet Union that was one of the major charges on which Julius and Ethel Rosenberg were convicted.)

The third project, based at the California Institute of Technology in Pasadena, was to develop solid-fuel rockets.*

Trytten held his top-secret interviews with the four young graduates in a musty empty faculty office at Harvard over the course of one day in early October, when Ted was still just seventeen, two weeks ahead of his eighteenth birthday. According to Albright and Kunstel, both Glauber and Hall recounted being informed at the time only that there was an important war project they were needed for, but they were not provided any details;

---

* Interestingly, Cal Tech is where Ted's brother Ed would earn his master's degree in aeronautical engineering after the war. By the mid-1950s, he had become director of the Pentagon's solid-fuel rocket development program and later headed up the U.S. Air Force's ballistic missile program. He was recognized as the air force's top rocket engineer during that period.

all they were told by Trytten was that it was urgent and top secret. Glauber also noted that he had to fill out a form listing "every organization he had ever joined and every place he'd ever lived."[2]

In their book *The Venona Secrets*, Herbert Romerstein and Eric Breindel write that "Ted asked if he, too, could be recommended for the project. Glauber, to his later regret, recommended him."[3] This assertion, made with no citation, is simply wrong, and ludicrously so. Bush and Trytten had asked Van Vleck and Kemble for recommendations and scheduled all the interviews for the same day, so Trytten couldn't have taken recommendations from Glauber, who he only first met at the interview. Furthermore, he certainly wouldn't have asked an eighteen-year-old student for suggestions about whom to recruit. The idea that Hall sought out the position rather than being recommended as a candidate is likewise nonsense and in any event would have been brought up by FBI investigators when Glauber was questioned by Boston bureau agents about Hall in 1966; the FBI report on that two-hour questioning session shows it was not. Romerstein and Breindel also mistakenly write that "one other" undergraduate Glauber "friend" was hired along with him and Ted to go to work at Los Alamos.[4] In fact, *two undergraduate seniors*, T. K. Case and Frederic de Hoffmann, were interviewed and hired along with Glauber and Hall. That information was published by Albright and Kunstel in their 1997 book and should have been known to Romerstein and Breindel by the time they wrote their book two or three years later.

After their interviews, the four job candidates gathered at Lowell House and began joking around and excitedly speculating about the mystery project for which they were being considered, all of them curious about what it might be. They were all promising young scientists studying under some of the leading theoretical physicists in the world, but the idea of an atomic weapon apparently never seems to have occurred to them at the time. They recognized that the project they were being considered for must involve a scientific breakthrough of some kind—but what? The idea of some kind of superweapon seems like it should have been obvious, given all the secrecy, but a fission bomb—which not only didn't exist but wasn't even speculated about in textbooks—reportedly didn't occur to them.

Ted recalled that evening to Albright and Kunstel, telling them that he had returned to Lowell House after his job interview for the secret war project at Los Alamos and discussed the possible offer with Glauber, Case, and de Hoffmann. Sax was in the room listening.

As the *Bombshell* authors wrote,

When Savy realized that Ted might be sent off to do secret military research he murmured something in Ted's direction. As best those words of Saville Sax can be reconstructed they went like this: "If this turns out to be a weapon that is really awful, what you should do is tell the Russians . . ."

Ted Hall wasn't outraged at the suggestion of passing secrets to the Soviet Union; actually, his mind was already turning that same possibility. What really startled Ted that day was that the idea had occurred to Savy. Ted took him aside. "Never never talk to anyone else about this," Ted said. "Not even as a joke."[5]

It was a caution he would find himself uttering to another close person a few years later, after the war had ended, when for the first time he admitted his spying to his girlfriend and future wife, Joan Krakover, as their relationship grew more serious.

What shocked Hall about Sax's comment was that the idea of a super-weapon had occurred to his more humanities- and arts-oriented classmate and friend, and not to any of the four young physicists, himself included. Perhaps Savy had read H. G. Wells's prophetic 1914 science-fiction novel *The World Set Free*, which imagined wars being fought using "atomic bombs" of massive power, unleashing mushroom clouds and scattering deadly radioactive fallout.

During their last two months in residence at Harvard, during which Ted, Glauber, and the other two student physicists learned that they had all been hired and would be traveling together to a remote place called Los Alamos located on the Pajarito Plateau, a seventy-two-hundred-foot-high mesa in the Jemez Mountains of New Mexico some twenty-five miles northwest of Santa Fe, Ted had finished the coursework required for graduation. This meant that although he would be in a fenced-in and carefully secured compound in one of the most remote locations in the continental United States, he could graduate at the end of the spring 1944 term, even if he would not likely be returning to Cambridge for the commencement ceremony.

Near the end of January 1944, Hall, Glauber, Case, and de Hoffmann headed off to the location known variously, for secrecy's sake, as "Project Y," the "Zia Project," or "Area L." The four traveled together by rail from New York City via Chicago, arriving in Santa Fe on January 27, 1944. They were met at the station by a man dressed like a cowboy, who they didn't recognize, even when he introduced himself as "Mr. Neumann." It was only later, according to Albright and Kunstel, that an awestruck Glauber figured out that their "driver" to the site of the Manhattan Project was the brilliant Princeton University mathematician John von Neumann, transferred to Los

Alamos from the equally top-secret MIT-based Radiation Lab in Cambridge to help the weapons laboratory solve the problem of designing an atomic bomb.

It was a day later, on January 28, the date they officially began working on the Manhattan Project, that they first learned what the project was all about: the goal was to develop a nuclear weapon before the Germans managed to do it.

The project was laid out to them by Cornell University physicist Robert Bacher, at that time head of the project's Experimental Physics Division (P-Division for short). They would each be working on one of the two concurrent programs to develop an atomic bomb. One bomb design being explored would be based upon U-235, a fissionable isotope of uranium, an element with atomic number 92 (for the ninety-two protons in its nucleus). The other path to a bomb, being pursued simultaneously in case there were problems coming up with the necessary amount of U-235, was a device based upon the newly discovered element plutonium. This was an artificially produced element with atomic number 94, found only in trace amounts in nature as a product of radioactive decay but produced deliberately in greater amounts as a by-product of the fission process of uranium undergoing fission in nuclear reactors. Discovered in August 1942, this new addition to the atomic chart of elements, which, like U-235, was capable of producing a fission chain reaction and thus was at least theoretically suitable for producing an atomic bomb, was so secret it was referred to even within the Manhattan Project by the code name "49" instead of by its scientific name or correct atomic number.

Bacher explained to the four Harvard recruits the unique environment at Los Alamos. Located on the grounds of a former private boys' prep school taken over by the U.S. government through eminent domain, the project was entirely fenced-in, with access—if one ignored the various holes in the fencing that people could sneak through—permitted only through a gate guarded around the clock by armed soldiers. These military police monitored all those leaving and arriving at the compound, checking government-issued badges and also outgoing bags, pockets, and envelopes. Security was as tight as possible, including deliberate misinformation spread in Santa Fe and other nearby communities that the mysterious work up on "the Hill" was about developing "electric propulsion systems." But within the confines of the project, the resident scientists could freely discuss anything. Oppenheimer, the project's scientific director, believed that to create the bomb quickly, it would be necessary for the six hundred assembled scientists, tech staff, and other workers to have complete freedom to share and challenge each other's ideas. But that openness ended at the fence and the gate. Nothing about the project was to be communicated by those working on the project to the outside world, even to relatives.

This secrecy, backed by tight security, including even the reading of all incoming and outgoing personal correspondence, was about to be shattered, although it would be well after the war ended and the Manhattan Project had been shut down and replaced by the Atomic Energy Commission that U.S. intelligence and counterintelligence agencies realized it.

7

THE SOVIET BOMB PROJECT

Build the uranium bomb without delay.

—Georgy Fliorov, young physicist and Soviet fighter pilot

The Soviet Union first began investigating the possibility of creating an atomic bomb based upon the principle of a neutron fission chain reaction in 1939. That was when Igor Kurchatov, a brilliant thirty-six-year-old physicist, alerted Soviet leaders to the potential for a fission bomb based upon uranium. Work on that project began soon after that warning, but with only limited funding and few scientists involved, the effort essentially came to a halt in 1941 with Hitler's launch of Operation Barbarossa, the massive full-scale surprise Nazi invasion of the Soviet Union.

Work on a Soviet atomic bomb picked up again in 1942 when another young Russian physicist, twenty-nine-year-old Georgy Nikolayevich Fliorov, sent an alarming message directly to Soviet leader Joseph Stalin, chairman of the Council of People's Commissars and commander of the Red Army. At the time he sent his letter, Fliorov was an engineer and pilot in the Soviet Air Force, but he was also well known as a scientist: Two years earlier he had distinguished himself by discovering spontaneous nuclear fission. That background surely lent a sense of urgency to his letter, which warned the Soviet leader that it was critical for the USSR, even while fighting an existential war against Nazi Germany, to "build the uranium bomb without delay." Explaining his concern, Fliorov said that he had noticed a "conspicuous lack" for more than a year of any research articles being published on nuclear fission in scientific journals in the United States, the United Kingdom, and Germany, which he correctly deduced meant that all those countries were already investigating the idea of an atomic bomb—secret work that was being held back from publication.

Soviet military forces at that time were hard-pressed by the rapid onslaught of the better-armed and more mechanized German Wehrmacht, so Stalin was perhaps understandably reluctant to devote too much scarce funding to what was clearly a quite speculative project, particularly as he had no knowledge at all about the concept of nuclear fission. But the Soviet leader took Fliorov's alert seriously enough that he approved a concerted research effort into creating an atom bomb. Kurchatov was put in charge of that program at the age of thirty-nine (coincidentally, the same age his U.S. counterpart, Robert Oppenheimer, was when he took over the reins of the Manhattan Project's secret laboratory as scientific director at Los Alamos later that same year).

At least equally important, and less costly, was the establishment by Lavrentiy Pavlovich Beria, head of Soviet intelligence and secret police and Stalin's right-hand man, of a dedicated atomic spying program in the United Kingdom and the United States. The program was focused on developing sources inside those countries' programs to learn what they were up to and gather all the information they could about what was being developed in secret from not just Germany, but also the United States and United Kingdom. The operation inside the United States was coordinated by the NKVD, precursor of the KGB. The NKVD's U.S. headquarters, located in the Soviet Consulate in New York City, was referred to by the code name *Rezidentura.* Also involved in atomic espionage work in the United States, as well as in Canada and the United Kingdom, was the People's Commissariat for State Security (NKGB), the Soviet military intelligence organization.

A key figure in the Soviet spying campaign in the United States was a colorful character named Sergei Kurnakov. A former tsarist cavalry officer and former member of Tsar Nicholas's Palace Guard, he had fought with the counterrevolutionary White Army against the Bolsheviks in the Soviet civil war during the early 1920s. But after immigrating to the United States following the Bolshevik government's victory in that war, he became a secret ardent supporter of the new Communist regime he had once fought against. This personal history no doubt helped divert attention from him as he became an important Soviet agent in America. Kurnakov used his work as a journalist and novelist in the United States as cover for his work in the

NKVD, which included being a courier of documents for various Soviet spies and, more importantly, as a valued talent spotter with a knack for vetting potential spy recruits. Although he had been accused of being a spy himself in a 1944 article in *Time* magazine after teaching a Russian class in 1943 at Cornell University, and although his son Nick, a soldier in the U.S. Army in Europe, defected to the Soviet Red Army and was quickly made an officer, Kurnakov was not conclusively identified as a Soviet spy until the publication in 1995 of the Venona decrypts of Soviet wartime spy cables. It was a disclosure that came forty-six years after his death.[1]

Kurnakov's work as a Soviet spy and an expert at vetting recruits and volunteers was destined to play a crucial role in the story of Ted Hall and Saville Sax.

The first reports to Moscow and Soviet atomic scientists concerning serious work underway on an atomic bomb in the United States and Britain came from a significant spying operation in the United Kingdom.

First came word from a British spy, likely John Cairncross, one of a group of five former Cambridge university students who reported on the nascent British Tube Alloys Project (the code name for Britain's atomic bomb development program). He gave word of a disturbing and ultimately overly optimistic British estimate that a uranium bomb could be made within two years. Then along came a young German physicist, Klaus Fuchs, who would ultimately prove to be a much more important atomic spy for the Soviets.

A Communist activist who had fled to England just ahead of arrest by the Nazi Gestapo, Fuchs, despite being marked early on as a potential risk by MI5 because of a warning from (of all places!) the German Gestapo that he was a "Marxist," succeeded in gaining refugee status in the United Kingdom. Although he made no serious effort to hide his German Communist Party membership when he arrived in Britain in the winter of 1933–1934, he nonetheless managed to gain admission to Bristol University to pursue graduate work in physics, earning his doctorate there in 1936 at the age of thirty-four.

Fuchs's Communist background and continued association with German Communist Party refugees living and working in Britain did lead MI5 to open a file on him, and this eventually led, after Stalin and Hitler signed a non-aggression pact in 1939, to his being classified as an enemy alien. Although the Soviet Union and Britain were not at war, in the view of MI5 and the British Home Office, Fuchs and other German Communists in the United Kingdom, who had been viewed before that pact as at least antifascist, became suspect because of the USSR's neutrality in the war between

Britain and Germany. They were interned for several years as security risks. Confined in a stark, crowded, dirty, and cold Canadian prison camp during the late 1930s, Fuchs and his fellow German Communists found themselves thrown together with suspected German Nazi refugees—an undoubtedly awkward situation.

By 1941, Britain, which had been excluded from the Manhattan Project, leaving it to work on an atomic bomb on its own, was forced to identify and gather together all the first-class nuclear physicists it could find. This led to Fuchs's release and return to the United Kingdom at the direction of the British Home Office. Hired that May by another German refugee physicist, Rudolf Peierls, who had been similarly rehabilitated, Fuchs soon found himself working on atomic bomb research at the University of Birmingham. That was his circuitous entry into what became the Tube Alloys Project.

MI5 had been right to suspect Fuchs's allegiance to the USSR, though: He had in fact already signed up as a Soviet spy even before he was brought onto the Tube Alloys Project. Indeed, when Russia was attacked by Hitler on June 22, 1941, Fuchs, as a dedicated Communist internationalist and no longer considered an enemy of Britain, had made the decision to volunteer to provide the Soviet Union with information about the British atomic bomb project. It was important information he had, too, as British scientists, ahead of their U.S. counterparts, had already come up with the conceptual design for what would have been a successful uranium-based atomic bomb had British scientists had available to them a sufficient quantity of pure U-235. Fuchs's spying for the Soviets in Britain continued until 1943, when he, along with other British atomic bomb researchers, were transferred to the United States to join the Manhattan Project.

After the war, in early 1946, what was known as the British Mission to the Manhattan Project, including Fuchs, returned to the United Kingdom, only to be cut off early that year by President Harry Truman from further information on or access to the U.S. nuclear weapons project, which by that point was under the direction of the Atomic Energy Commission. This presidential freeze out was formalized under the terms of the Atomic Energy Act passed by Congress in 1946.[2]

The British responded by establishing their own project, called the Atomic Energy Research Establishment (AERE), headquartered in the farming community of Harwell, just fifteen miles from Oxford University.[3] The project was divided into a number of divisions, as had been done in the United States at Los Alamos. Fuchs, rather incredibly given the file MI5 had maintained on his Communist past since before he fled from Germany to England in the late 1930s, was made head of the theoretical division and physics department of the AERE in mid-1946, and with a top security clearance, he basically oversaw the development of both Britain's fission bomb and fusion bomb projects.[4] That position lasted through late 1949, when the Venona Project's decryption of several spy cables identified him, when taken together, as the only possible suspect. At that point he was questioned by William "Jim" Skardon, a special branch officer skilled at interrogation.[5] Skardon skillfully maneuvered Fuchs into confessing, which he did in an effort to spare his Communist sister Kristel Fuchs Heineman, who was living in the United States at that time, from being pursued by the FBI.[6]

Interestingly, Fuchs was not charged with treason in Britain, not because British prosecutors didn't have the evidence about the bomb project secrets he had passed to the Soviets—he ultimately confessed about that—but because his information had been provided to a country that was, at the time of his spying and later through his time of arrest, a British ally against Nazi Germany and not an enemy at war with Britain. He was instead led by his interrogator to plead guilty to theft of state secrets, a serious but lesser charge that didn't carry a potential death penalty, for which he received a fourteen-year jail sentence. He ended up serving only nine of those years before being released and allowed to return to his home in what had become the German Democratic Republic.

There were other spies within the British project as well as Britain's security agencies MI5 and MI6—a group of upper-class young British men from Cambridge who shared Communist sympathies, known as the Cambridge Five—but none of them provided the kind of detailed information Fuchs did about the uranium and plutonium atomic bomb designs and later about the hydrogen thermonuclear fusion bomb.

The information provided to Soviet bomb makers by the Soviet spies Fuchs and Hall, as well as others in Britain and the United States, was crucial to the Soviet Union's rapid development of an atomic bomb of their own. That could never have happened, however, had the Soviet Union not had a significant number of brilliant theoretical and experimental physicists and engineers of its own to take advantage of that information.

As the Soviet atomic bomb project scaled up dramatically toward the end of the war in Europe and in the years after the war, these scientists and engineers succeeded in developing, despite the massive destruction of much of the USSR's industrial base during years of all-out war with Germany, a nuclear industry on a scale that eventually resembled what the United States created during and after the war.

During the war, the number of Soviet scientists working on developing an atom bomb numbered in the dozens, compared to the hundreds involved in the Manhattan Project at Los Alamos (not counting the project's staff of workers, who numbered in the thousands, many at Oak Ridge, Tennessee, and Hanford, Washington, early on). By war's end, the Manhattan Project's workforce numbered more than one hundred thousand.[7] But after the war against Germany ended, the Soviet bomb project expanded exponentially too, spurred by the reality of the two bombs the United States dropped on Japan, which led Stalin to fund a "cost-is-no-object" crash program to produce the USSR's own atomic bomb. (Comparing the ultimate scale of the U.S. and Soviet bomb projects in terms of number of workers is difficult because much of the Soviet project's vast facilities were constructed using prison labor.)

In truth, however, despite all the talk of spies like Fuchs, Hall, and the "Rosenberg ring" giving away "atomic secrets" to the Soviets, developing a nuclear bomb was not really a matter of stealing scientific secrets possessed by a more advanced project in another country. The basic *scientific* principles of a fission bomb were just as well known to Soviet scientists as to their U.S. and British (and even German and Japanese) counterparts. The problem was a matter of having the resources to devote to the project, and being able to solve the very major *engineering* problems involved in creating a reliable implosion system for a plutonium bomb and to refine large quantities of relatively pure U-235 for a uranium bomb. It was this information that Fuchs and Hall had to offer, and what they both separately provided allowed the Soviet project, once the funding spigot was opened, to move forward quickly to a successful initial test in the Semipalatinsk desert on August 29, 1949, just over four years after the United States used its bombs on Japan.

8

TED HALL AT LOS ALAMOS

There is no such thing as chance; and what seem to us merest accident spring from the deepest source of destiny.

—Friedrich Schiller

Within a few days of their arrival up on what was known among the Manhattan Project residents there as "The Hill" at Los Alamos, the four newly hired Harvard student physicists got their assignments. Ted Hall, along with Frederic de Hoffmann, was put in the Theoretical Division, known as the T-Division, joining senior scientists who were engaged in complicated mathematical and experimental efforts to calculate the actual critical mass of uranium. This was an urgent task, because isolating the trace amounts of U-235 from the vastly more common U-238 isotope in refined uranium was proving very difficult, and the lower the critical mass found to be required for a chain reaction explosion to occur, the sooner the Manhattan Project could produce a uranium bomb that would reliably work. Roy Glauber, meanwhile, was assigned to the experimental team, the P-Division, headed at that time by Cornell physicist Robert Bacher. The P-Division at that point was busy developing and producing super-fast neutron counters that could be used to measure, for example, tests of an implosion system being designed to successfully detonate a plutonium bomb. The devices had to take an accurate measure of the initial neutron burst in test explosions of an imploding mock "pit" composed of a different non-fissile radioactive element to find a configuration that would reliably produce a completely symmetrical spray of neutrons—a daunting challenge.

Ted was happy with his T-Division job assignment, as it was at that time the most urgent task underway at Los Alamos. That was because even as late as February 1944, General Leslie Groves, chief of the Manhattan Project, was reporting to President Roosevelt the discouraging news that the uranium bomb might well require as much as 175 pounds of U-235 to go critical and explode as a bomb. (It turned out to be 104 pounds if not compressed by conventional explosives, as was done in the case of the 85 pounds eventually used successfully in the bomb used on Hiroshima. And there just was not the prospect of that quantity of that rare isotope becoming available in the near term—and certainly not enough to find out its critical mass by experimenting with a smaller amount by trial and error!)

Establishing U-235's critical mass was clearly a critical issue in more ways than one. But within a few days after they began their assigned tasks at Los Alamos, Glauber expressed unhappiness with his assignment to the P-Division, leading Hall to generously offer to swap assignments with him. The switch was approved by higher-ups on the project without any problem. "That was all right with me," Hall told Joseph Albright and Marcia Kunstel in an interview. "I wasn't particular, and so I swapped. And that is how I got into Bruno Rossi's lab."[1]

Once in Rossi's P-Division lab, Hall was teamed up with senior physicist Philip Grant Koontz, who had worked in Chicago with Enrico Fermi on the original experimental uranium pile that demonstrated a fission chain reaction. Working with a few valuable and hard-to-come-by samples of foil composed of pure U-235, which they blasted with high-energy neutrons, Hall and Koontz managed to experimentally establish the probability that a given U-235 atom would split and release a cascade of more neutrons if approached by a fast neutron—the key to producing a fission chain reaction. Their test result made establishing an accurate critical mass measure for a uranium bomb into a relatively straightforward math problem for the T-Division to work out. Rossi gave Hall equal credit with Koontz and himself, deciding to list their names alphabetically in a paper later circulated within the security perimeter of Los Alamos. *Bombshell*'s authors compare that authorship listing honor to that of "a copyboy getting a byline story on the front page of the *New York Times*."[2]

A Jewish Italian physicist who had left Italy in 1938 with his wife after Benito Mussolini approved anti-Semitic laws that deprived Jews of their citizenship and him of his university job, Rossi was invited to Denmark by Niels

Bohr. The Danish Nobel physics laureate later helped arrange a position for him at the University of Manchester, in the United Kingdom. With war clouds gathering in Europe, Rossi later moved to the United States on the recommendation of Hans Bethe, landing a position as associate professor of physics at Cornell University. Because of his pioneering work on cosmic rays, which led him to develop measuring devices for capturing rapid ionization changes on a subatomic scale caused by fast-moving particles, he was invited onto the Manhattan Project, where he was put in charge of a group working to develop an implosion system for detonating a plutonium bomb.

While that innocent job switch between schoolmates Hall and Glauber was proposed as a generous act by Hall on behalf of a friend, it would prove to be critically important to Hall's later volunteer espionage work. Had he remained in the T-Division working on uranium, he would not have had that much to offer the Soviets as a volunteer spy. Even if he were taken on as a spy, he would have been far less impactful on the course of Soviet bomb development. The USSR had many highly competent mathematicians and physicists who were as capable as those at Los Alamos of figuring out uranium's critical mass. Their problem was that the Soviet Union at that time had no uranium mines or even any known uranium ore deposits. And even if it could obtain the ore, the embattled country lacked the resources to refine out the required quantity of the isotope U-235 needed for a bomb. If the United States was having a hard time doing it with unlimited resources, the Soviets would have found it impossible to do under conditions of a full-scale war on their territory. At the same time, the Soviets didn't have a clue how to make a successful bomb with the newly discovered and hard-to-work-with element plutonium. As fate would have it, accomplishing that would, over the course of 1944, become Ted's challenge in the P-Division and his real area of expertise. Offering himself nine months later as an atomic spy to the NKVD, Hall must have seemed to the Soviet spy he first located like director George Lucas must have felt when Harrison Ford showed up to work on a set for use in the Han Solo role auditions in his first *Star Wars* movie.

In June 1944, a few months into his work in the P-Division of the Los Alamos Weapons Lab and based upon academic credit he was awarded by the Harvard physics department for the secret work he had been doing, Ted Hall was graduated with honors in absentia. With that prestigious BS degree in hand, the young Harvard graduate, who at eighteen was the age of a typical entering college freshman, was promoted by Rossi to a supervisory position as team leader on a project directed by physicist Luis Alvarez. There he found himself working alongside senior scientists Hans Staub and

David Nicodemus, designing and building glass sensors that, linked by wire to oscilloscopes, would allow them to instantly measure, in the nanoseconds before the sensors were destroyed, the all-around release of gamma rays by the blast of an imploded sphere containing at its center a small amount of lanthanum-140, a highly radioactive element that produces a large amount of gamma rays. Each sphere was made of a heavy metal—iron or copper initially, and later cadmium, which metallurgists advised the experimental team would compress more similarly to plutonium. Since four sensors had to surround the implosion sphere to measure the symmetry of each gamma burst and were destroyed along with the sphere by the blast, Ted was kept busy making new ones as the ones he'd made were blown up by one test after another.

The radioactive materials used in these radioactive lanthanum—or Ra-La—tests, as they were called at Los Alamos, had to be very carefully handled. Even though the lanthanum was encased inside the exploding pellet and tampers and the whole explosion was contained inside a heavy blast container, putting a highly radioactive lanthanum slug in place required using a ten-foot fishing pole to keep the test personnel conducting the experiment relatively safe from radiation exposure. After the explosion, most of the exploded radioactive material would have been changed into the nonradioactive element cesium, but significant amounts of the highly dangerous biologically active nucleotides cesium-140, barium-140, and especially strontium-90, were also produced. All three are highly radioactive and attracted biologically to certain parts of the human body, meaning that such chemicals, if inhaled or ingested, become concentrated in certain organs, where the radiation they emit for a considerable time can cause cancers in surrounding tissues.

During each test explosion—and there were many—the scientists and tech people would retreat to a wooden shed, and later, as they began using larger amounts of lanthanum and bigger explosive charges, into a sealed M4 Sherman army tank equipped with its own air supply. Despite such precautions, significant radiation exposure occurred during these tests, including contact with the radioactive atoms of the three toxic nucleotides Cs-140, Ba-140, and Sr-90. (Back then, there was not much attention paid to the danger caused by ingestion or inhalation of such minute radioactive alpha-particle emitters, where exposure can be measured in days, weeks, or even years, as opposed to the more powerful gamma radiation and neutron particle radiation that can be easily measured with a Geiger counter as it is released, or exposure over time measured by a dosimeter badge, and where risk is often calculated in seconds or minutes. Wearing a radiation exposure badge is useless in determining the exposure level to alpha-emitting particles, which, once in a body, cannot even be detected by a Geiger counter or badge.)

Exposure to these nucleotides may well have caused the aggressive terminal kidney cancer and perhaps Parkinson's disease that would later kill Ted in 1999. Indeed, it is likely no coincidence that both Hall and Fuchs, along with a number of other scientists at Los Alamos and other Manhattan Project sites, died prematurely of cancer resulting from their wartime atomic bomb work. Fuchs died at age seventy-six of rectal cancer, and Hall's Ra-La experiment colleague Hans Staub died at seventy-eight. (His other fellow Ra-La tester, David Nicodemus, died the same year as Hall, in 1999, at age eighty-three, but of heart failure.) Even Robert Oppenheimer himself died of cancer of the throat at the relatively young age of sixty-two, though this was attributed to his forty years of cigarette smoking.[3] In the end, though, despite the risks they took, the scientific team working on the plutonium bomb succeeded in coming up with an implosion design involving thirty-two perfectly fitting lenses and tampers assembled such that they could reliably be slammed together by chemical charges on the outside, compressing a sub-critical plutonium and gallium "pit" in the middle into a much denser, smaller one and producing the desired massive chain reaction.

The reason for this complex system and all the testing was that the plutonium used for a fission bomb presented its own challenge—one almost opposite from the one posed by uranium. Generated through a kind of nuclear alchemy as part of the waste stream from operation of the Oak Ridge reactors, in the case of plutonium it was the most common isotope, P-239, that could produce a fission chain reaction perfect for a fission bomb. But that plutonium was found to also unavoidably contain some small amount of contamination by the isotope P-240 (a variant of plutonium one thousand times more fissile than P-239). The scientists discovered that even that small amount of difficult-to-remove plutonium 240, if included in the relatively common U-239 isotope of plutonium used with the "cannon-type" system being designed for a U-235 bomb, would begin fissioning as the halves approached each other instead of exploding in a massive blast. Such premature fissioning would cause the whole plutonium "pit" to melt into a liquid even at the highest speed possible, using a chemical blast in the cannon of about 1,000 mph. This blast would blow the melted plutonium—and the rest of the bomb—apart, in what was called a "fizzle," with the reaction initiating before the full chain-reaction nuclear explosion could take place. The resulting "dud" bomb blast might blow up a building or maybe a few city blocks, but not a city.

It was physicist Robert Serber—the scientist who put together a booklet summarizing the work on the bomb and an oral introduction to the project to bring up to speed each new recruited scientist arriving at Los Alamos, as he did with Hall, Glauber, Case, and de Hoffman—who solved the plutonium bomb's premature detonation problem. He came up with the Rube Goldberg–like idea of taking a smaller, safely sub-critical mass of plutonium, then somehow smashing it from all sides into a much denser hunk of the metal, causing it to fission instantly despite its sub-critical mass. How to cause that implosion—which had to produce a perfectly symmetrical burst of neutrons in all directions for the process to work—was the engineering challenge. Eventually Ted and his team of Ra-La experimenters succeeded in accomplishing that feat. For the actual bomb, a tiny core inside the center of the plutonium sphere called a neutron actuator or initiator, composed of beryllium-9 and polonium-210, was added. Bolted into a one-inch-diameter hollow spot at the core of the plutonium sphere, it kick-started the neutron chain reaction when crushed inside the surrounding plutonium, releasing a spray of neutrons that caused the plutonium to instantly go critical.

David Hawkins, an assistant administrator of the Manhattan Project at Los Alamos and later one of the project's official historians, wrote in his history of the project that "Ra-La became the most important single experiment affecting the final bomb design."[4] That "final design," provided by Hall to NKVD courier Lona Cohen in the short period between the dropping of the bomb on Nagasaki and Japan's surrender on August 15, was also almost certainly the most important information Ted was able to convey in detail to Soviet scientists working to create an atomic bomb to match what the Americans had created.

Ted's Ra-La group began their testing and tinkering on July 25, 1944, and by the end of February 1945, the design that was to be used for the implosion core of the bomb dubbed the "Gadget," exploded successfully in the July 16 Trinity Test, was set. Bruno Rossi, who was in charge of that project, reported having heard a relieved Oppenheimer say, after at a top-level meeting of top scientists and General Groves where the decision was confirmed, "Now we have our bomb."[5]

It was later estimated that some 30 percent of the 6.2 kilograms of plutonium in that first test at Alamogordo underwent explosive fission, producing a blast of about 22 kilotons. The "Fat Man" bomb detonated over Nagasaki was estimated at 21 kilotons.

One can readily imagine how exciting it must have been for Hall and Roy Glauber, both just eighteen and not yet even graduates with their physics degrees in hand, to be suddenly working daily with some of the greatest physicists in the world on something Oppenheimer, referencing a then-popular science fiction hero, had called "a somewhat Buck Rogers project." Working with luminary physicists like the Nobel laureate Bohr and renowned colleagues like Hans Bethe, Joseph Rotblat, Leo Szilard, and Enrico Fermi—scientists whose discoveries they had been studying about in their Harvard physics classes—sharing lunch in the same mess hall, discussing the solutions to various problems that were facing the project, and also debating the future of the bomb they were making and the awesome moral and political issues it raised must have electrifying. During a taped interview made a year before his death in 1999, Ted admitted that it was "exciting—even exhilarating."[6] He looked almost embarrassed as he heard himself saying that on camera, but there's no denying that he and the other scientists working there realized they were involved in something both demonic and at the same time situated at the fascinating event horizon between science and science fiction.

For Ted, it was also—both morally and politically—a deeply vexing time. Even before he learned that he'd be working on a nuclear bomb, just knowing he was going to be working on some kind of secret weapon, he admitted, got him thinking that it would be proper and important for America's wartime ally, the Soviet Union, to be included in what was being created. It was a view shared by his friend, roommate, and eventual courier and coconspirator Saville Sax and by many scientists working for the project. And by mid-1945, when it was evident that the bomb was ready to use, the moral imperative to do something to prevent its use after the war ended, should the United States remain the only nation possessing it, became to Hall and Sax vastly greater.

9

1944 AND THE WAR'S
END IS IN SIGHT

*You realize, of course, that the whole purpose of the Project is
to subdue the Russians.*

—General Leslie Groves

As Ted Hall's first year at Los Alamos progressed and the technical problems of creating an atomic bomb—two different atomic bombs, really—were gradually being solved, one by one, the question of building an atomic bomb, for the scientists of the Manhattan Project, had become one not of if, but of when.

It was also evident that the same was true of Germany's and Japan's defeat and surrender. This was causing anxiety among and tension between some project scientists and many of the military and foreign policy leaders in Washington, many of whom wanted to avail the United States of an opportunity to demonstrate its new atomic bomb's awesome destructive power under wartime conditions, if only to establish America's unassailable power in the minds of the world's leaders—especially Stalin. They wanted to make clear to potential postwar rivals that the United States would be dominant in future world affairs. The idea of the war's ending before they could have a chance blow up something with the atomic bomb—a dramatic blast that would destroy a whole city and hundreds of thousands of people—was too awful for them to permit. Especially after the surrender of Germany, the pressure from Washington and many of the military brass advising President

Harry Truman, relayed through General Leslie Groves to the scientists at Los Alamos, to get the bomb tested and one or both versions of it fully assembled and shipped off for use on Japan in a hurry was palpable.

Meanwhile, among some of the scientists on the project, even as early as the fall of 1944, a growing awareness that the war was heading toward a conclusion, probably within a year, was creating a sense of unease and dread. For many, overshadowing the excitement of harnessing the raw power of the atom was an increasing concern about how the new weapon, once created, would be used, and whether atomic bombs should ever be used or even made at all. Also troubling some was why the USSR, America's most important ally in the war in Europe, was being kept completely in the dark—or at least thought to be—about the bomb project.

A major reason young untested physicists like Hall, Roy Glauber, Frederic de Hoffmann, and Kenneth Case had been hastily recruited in late 1943 was that Robert Oppenheimer himself felt the urgent need for more hands on deck to get past the remaining scientific and engineering roadblocks, create the two atomic bombs, and have them ready for use before peace broke out, rendering them unnecessary without having had a real-world wartime test. As Joseph O. Hirschfelder, a chemist at Los Alamos, recalled, at one meeting to discuss the future of the bomb, Oppenheimer "argued with his usual eloquence that, although they were all destined to live in perpetual fear, the bomb might also end all war. . . . Such a hope, echoing [Neils] Bohr's words, was persuasive to many of the assembled scientists."[1]

But not to all. By middle to late 1944, some leading scientists, most notably Bohr and Joseph Rotblat, had made their feelings clear to Washington. Bohr did this by writing in July directly to President Roosevelt, urging him to bring the Soviets in on the project or at least inform them about it. He argued that this would prevent a dangerous competition in secret after the war. The proposal was summarily rejected by the ailing FDR, but it led him to have the FBI closely monitor the eminent Danish scientist to prevent his leaving the country.[2]

Meanwhile, Rotblat, a Polish physicist less prominent than Bohr who had fled to the United Kingdom before the war began, resigned in November 1944 from the Manhattan Project. He took this dramatic step because of a conviction that with Germany on the ropes, the bomb wouldn't be needed and would instead end up being used later against the USSR. He didn't want anything more to do with it. In response to this principled move, the FBI launched an investigation into whether Rotblat was a spy. He was questioned, his books and research were confiscated (and never returned), and he was prevented for some time from leaving the United States, though he had already become a British citizen. While he was cleared of suspicion of espionage, he later expressed the belief that *actual* spies in the Manhattan Project were missed for years because FBI officials and Los Alamos security personnel were so preoccupied with trying to prove that he was one. Joseph Albright and Marcia Kunstel report that Rotblat, who had come to Los Alamos from the UK's Tube Alloys Program as part of the British Mission to the Manhattan Project, told them, "I was accused of all sorts of things. This was a terrible shock to me. [James] Chadwick [head of the British Mission] of course never believed it, because he knew me sufficiently. But still, this all is written down."[3]

Rotblat was eventually permitted to return to Britain, where he became an early and outspoken activist calling for a ban on nuclear weapons. A signer of the 1955 Russell-Einstein Manifesto calling for peaceful resolution of international disputes, he was later a founder of the antinuclear Pugwash Conference on Science and World Affairs, established in 1957, serving as that organization's secretary general until 1973.[4]

At Los Alamos, the thirty-five-year-old Rotblat's concern about completing the bomb had been sparked by a dinner he attended in March 1944, when the team of British Tube Alloys Project atomic bomb scientists, who had recently arrived at Los Alamos to work directly with their American counterparts there, were guests at the cabin of James Chadwick, head of the British Mission to the Manhattan Project. The guest list that night included General Groves as well as a number of senior Los Alamos scientists. Recalling that gathering years later during an interview with the *Bombshell* authors, Rotblat remembered being shocked to hear Groves state bluntly that the atomic bomb was never really intended for the war against Germany, much less Japan. Rotblat said he specifically recalled Groves saying, "You realize, of course, that the whole purpose of the Project is to subdue the Russians."[5]

Stunning words, indeed, expressed as they were even as Soviet soldiers on Europe's eastern front were at that time still dying under German fire as the Red Army was relentlessly driving the battered but still deadly Wehrmacht back toward Germany's eastern border.

As word of Groves's startling admission inevitably spread around the close-knit Los Alamos scientific community—a unique environment where secrets were kept tightly held behind a fenced-in and guarded camp, but where communication among the scientists and staff inside that fence was openly encouraged—many scientists shared young Ted Hall's growing concern about the weapon they were working on. By fall, with Germany's heartland cities, industrial centers, and infrastructure being battered almost daily by waves of heavy British and especially U.S. bombers, it also was becoming increasingly clear to Hall that the implosion design he was fine-tuning was going to work, producing a horrific explosion that would change the world forever—and not in a good way.

As authors Kai Bird and Martin Sherwin put it in their book *American Prometheus*,

> By September 1944, Ted Hall was working on the calibration tests needed for the implosion-design bomb. Oppenheimer heard that Hall was one of the best young technicians on the mesa, when it came to creating a test implosion. An extremely bright man, Hall that autumn was sitting on the edge of an intellectual precipice. He was a socialist in outlook, an admirer of the Soviet Union, but not yet a formal communist, and neither was he disgruntled or unhappy with his work or his station in life. No one recruited him. But all that year he had listened to "older" scientists—in their late 20s and 30s—talk about their fears of a postwar arms race. On one occasion, sitting at the same Fuller Lodge dinner table with Niels Bohr, he heard Bohr's concerns for an "open world." Prompted by his conclusion that a postwar US nuclear monopoly could lead to another war, in October 1944 Hall decided to act.[6]

By October, Ted had come up with a seemingly cockamamie and personally highly risky plan to prevent what he foresaw as the catastrophe of a U.S. monopoly on the bomb: He would share what he knew about the plutonium bomb—which was a considerable amount—with the Soviet Union. In other words, he would become a Soviet asset or, to put it bluntly, a spy.

The thought process Ted went through in concluding that he had to take the dangerous step of spying for the Soviets was recounted decades later in a short essay he wrote over the course of a year beginning in 1995, when his name was first made public in the NSA's initial release of English transcripts of coded Soviet wartime spy cables known as the Venona decrypts. In that essay, which was provided to me by Ted's wife, Joan, and was initially published in *Bombshell*,[7] Ted wrote,

> I have occasionally been asked to explain what motivated me in 1944. Thinking back to the rather arrogant 19-year-old I then was, I can recall quite well what was in my mind at the time.
> My decision about contacting the Soviets was a gradual one, and it was entirely my own. It was entirely voluntary, not influenced by any other individual or by any organization such as the Communist Party or the Young Communist League. I was never "recruited" by anyone, nor was I prompted

by any personal problems. I had grown up in a very loving family and had a successful and happy life.

During World War II, I shared the general sympathy for our allies, the Soviet Union. After they were attacked, everybody knew that they were bearing the main load in the fight against Nazi Germany. Their propaganda was characterized by a craving for peace deeper than was apparent in the Western countries. I think that this came about partly because the Soviet Union suffered devastation far greater than anything experienced in the West.

My political views had been shaped by the economic depression of the 1930s. With the New Deal Roosevelt had tried to restore prosperity, but that was only partially successful and it was not until the war that the depression really ended. What would happen when the war was over?

At nineteen, I shared a common belief that the horrors of war would bring our various leaders to their senses and usher in a period of peace and harmony. But I had been thinking and reading about politics since an early age, and had seen that in a capitalist society economic depression could lead to fascism, aggression and war—as actually happened in Italy and Germany. So as I worked at Los Alamos and understood the destructive power of the atomic bomb, I asked myself what might happen if World War II was followed by a depression in the United states while we had an atomic monopoly?

In fact, I was very optimistic. I didn't believe that there would necessarily be a depression or that a depression would necessarily lead to war. But it seemed to me that an American monopoly was dangerous and should be prevented. I was not the only scientist to take that view: For example Einstein and Bohr both felt keenly that the best political policy was to reach an understanding—the opposite of the Cold War. I remember reading that Bohr tried to persuade Roosevelt to send him to Stalin to work out a peace-directed alliance and policy.

I did not have an uncritical view of the Soviet Union. I believed that the Soviet Union was a mixture of good and bad things, and hoped it would evolve favorably. But in any case there was no question of the Soviet Union ever having an atomic monopoly.

Of course, the situation was far more complicated than I understood at the time, and if confronted with the same problem today I would respond quite differently.[8]

Ted's concerns about a fascist America were not absurd—certainly no less absurd than concerns about a growing fascist movement in the United States today. Bear in mind that by the time Ted Hall was contemplating the next step to deter a U.S. atomic bomb monopoly after the war, he had already, as a politically savvy and knowledgeable young man traveling in leftist intellectual circles in college, learned about a major fascist plot hatched in

1933, the first year of Roosevelt's presidency, involving major business and financial leaders, members of Congress, and prominent right-wing Christian leaders to overthrow the U.S. government. The plot, called ULTRA, was backed by the Christian Front, the Silver Legion fascist militia, the America First movement, and other fascist organizations.[9] It was exposed by U.S. Marine hero Major General Smedley Butler, who blew the whistle to Congress, and was reported on in the U.S. media at the time. Though shocking, the story has been largely buried today in what passes for history in U.S. public secondary education.

In 1941, when Ted was a politically involved teenager, there was a prosecution and trial of elements of that U.S. fascist movement, which had, among other things, blown up several explosives plants around the country at a time when Britain was already at war with Nazi Germany and the United States was itself preparing for possible war with Germany and Japan. The case fizzled out with a hung jury unable to convict those who were arrested, but the sedition charges and evidence presented were lurid. While open support for Hitler and Nazism wasn't possible once the United States was at war with the Axis powers, quiet support for fascism and racist white nationalists continued underground* and welled up again after the war, providing fertile ground for the McCarthyism and witch hunts to come.[10]

Joan Hall said during a taped conversation with her oldest daughter, Ruth, in October 2022 that while Ted had come to believe that it was wrong for the Soviet Union to be excluded from the U.S./British atomic bomb project during the war, at a time the country was an ally in the fight against Hitler, and as he was working on the bomb's development, he increasingly felt that it would be dangerous for the United States to have a monopoly on atomic weapons after the war, he was not particularly anxious to take that dangerous task on himself. "He would have done anything in the world not to have had to do it [give the bomb secrets to the Soviet Union]," she said, "but he was also brave enough not to pull away from doing it himself when he thought it had to be done." She also noted that Ted confided to her that his friend and later spy courier Sax had been critical of him, even as they were trying to make connection with the Soviet NKVD spy organization in

---

* My father told me that while his grandmother, who emigrated with her husband from Germany in the late nineteenth century, was a lifelong Socialist and proudly voted in every presidential election for Eugene Debs and later for Norman Thomas on the Socialist ticket, her sister, Feenie Kerpol, a pianist of some note in the New York City classical music scene, was an ardent Nazi backer who hosted fascist meetings at her Manhattan apartment, at least until the United States entered World War II. (Somehow, despite their starkly conflicting politics, the two women managed to jointly run a successful private piano school in Manhattan.)

New York, "because he [Ted] was so loath to take such a step" as spying for the Soviets. "Savy, I recall him saying, was very keen on reporting on the whole thing to the Soviets," she said.[11]

In any event, once Ted made his fateful trip to New York and his rendezvous with Sax, he quickly overcame or set aside all second thoughts and committed himself to his plan to share what he knew about the atomic bomb with America's wartime ally, the Soviet Union. The plan was that the two friends would come up with some way to contact a Soviet official and provide the details of the plutonium bomb and any other useful information Ted had about the atomic bomb project to the Soviet Union so that nation could make its own atomic bomb and prevent the United States from obtaining the nuclear monopoly its leaders so badly wanted.

10

FINDING A SOVIET SPY
TO SIGN UP WITH

When one's mind is made up, this diminishes the fear; knowing what must be done does away with fear.

—Rosa Parks

So how did two novice teenagers who didn't know any Soviet officials, or anyone who might know one, locate a reliable Soviet contact—perhaps a consular officer or even an intelligence agent—and then get that person to listen to them? And after getting past that major challenge, how did they manage to convince wary Soviet intelligence agents to *believe* that a recently graduated college student, still just a teenager, could actually be working in a significant capacity on a top-secret superweapon—an atomic bomb!—and wanted to just hand over the plans for that bomb to them?

Spies don't advertise themselves as spies. In fact, they go to extraordinary lengths to avoid arousing suspicion or disclosing information about themselves. That makes the whole idea of finding a spy or spy organization to connect with hard to imagine, especially absent any intermediary. Then, too, hard as the task would be, how were they to accomplish it during the strict two-week home leave Ted Hall was able to obtain from authorities in Los Alamos right as the plutonium bomb project was finally coming together?

The whole plan, viewed from the outside, appears outlandish, naive, and foolish. But it was all they had.

The first challenge was for Ted to get away from Los Alamos and to New York City without arousing suspicion. That problem was solved because of the fortuitous timing of Ted's nineteenth birthday in mid-October. Saying he wanted to go visit his family in New York, who he had not seen since he left for Los Alamos ten months earlier, Ted managed to get a leave for two weeks. His timing was good for another reason too: There was a sense at the Manhattan Project that the biggest hurdles to constructing both types of atomic bomb had finally been overcome, and more specifically that the operation Ted had been put in charge of—fine-tuning the plutonium implosion design—was finally accomplished except for a few final tests of the implosion design and the assembly of the test bomb, the "Gadget." As a result, project leaders were willing to let him have a two-week furlough.

Departing Los Alamos on October 15—it's unclear whether by plane or train, though a plane seems likely given the limited time he had for the task at hand—Ted arranged to meet up in Manhattan with his friend and Harvard classmate Saville Sax, whose family had a home on West 75th Street near the Museum of Natural History, just off Central Park. The pair would then figure out a plan to somehow make a connection with the Soviets.

Consider the challenge this plan presented. Clearly the U.S. government was suspicious of the Soviets and was attempting to identify and monitor suspected agents in the United States, even though Washington was providing billions of dollars' (in current terms) worth of arms to Moscow and considering the USSR to be a critically important wartime ally. This state of affairs meant that Soviet officials who were spies would naturally be worried about being set up and falling into a trap if they met with someone promising top-secret military information. This was especially true for a superweapon development project they knew was underway but about which they knew almost nothing, as they still, even as late as October, had nobody on the inside (at least in the United States) and not even a clear idea of where it was happening. And, as Sax pointed out to Ted, the FBI was certain to be constantly monitoring the comings and goings at the Soviet Consulate in New York, which was located at 7 East 61st Street, right off the intersection with toney Fifth Avenue where it runs along the eastern side of Central Park. This meant visiting the consulate would pose an enormous risk for someone like Ted, whose photo image as a scientist at Los Alamos would likely be available to them were he to just walk in the consulate's front door.

So, in a series of brainstorming sessions at Sax's home on West 75th St.; wandering the halls of dinosaur skeletons, meteors, stuffed and preserved animals, and glassed-in dioramas of early humans and Native Americans in the Museum of Natural History across the park on Central Park West; or in a rented rowboat in Central Park, they discussed what to do. They settled on a division of labor: Sax would approach the Soviet Consulate, calling in advance to say he wanted to inquire into whether any of his Russian Jewish family had survived the German invasion and occupation of the Ukraine Soviet. Upon gaining admission and a chance to speak with a consular official, he'd tell them his real reason for visiting. If that approach failed, he would try the Soviet art and culture building, and then, if necessary, try to see Earl Browder, head of the U.S. Communist Party, which had its head-quarters in lower Manhattan.

Meanwhile, Ted opted to try his luck at the Soviet import/export trading company Amtorg, which was playing a critical role in lining up buyers of Soviet products and artifacts to raise funds for the war effort and in buying needed supplies and arms to ship to the USSR. Maybe, he hoped, someone there would be able to steer him toward an interested Soviet official.

Sax decided on his own to first try finding someone at Artkino, a Soviet-run cultural office that distributed Soviet films. The opposite of a dapper dresser, Sax likely wouldn't have made a great first impression, but he nonetheless managed to meet Artkino's president and manager, Nicola Napoli. The director probably had his doubts about this disheveled young man with his extraordinary tale about having a friend who was working on a superweapon and who wanted to tell the Soviets about it. But instead of tossing Sax out of his office, Napoli figured out a safe way to fob him off that wouldn't put Napoli himself in jeopardy of an espionage arrest, leaving it to someone else to consider whether the young man's wild story was real. He suggested that Sax locate and visit a former tsarist cavalry officer named Sergei Kurnakov, a Russian expatriate novelist/journalist living in Manhattan. A colorful character who had fought on the side of the counterrevolutionary White Army during the postrevolutionary Russian civil war of 1917–1922, Kurnakov was said to know most of the Russian community in the New York area and might be able to help Hall and Sax locate someone who could connect them with a Soviet spy.

Unimpressed and disappointed with the contact he had been given, Sax moved on to the New York headquarters of the U.S. Communist Party, where he sought the ear of Party general secretary Earl Browder. Perhaps he felt that his mother's membership in the Party would make Browder more willing to listen to him, but in fact, he fared worse with the CP than he had at Artkino. He couldn't even get past Browder's office secretary.

Meanwhile, as Sax was pressing ahead with his efforts to find a Soviet official, Ted was heading on foot to the lower part of New York's Garment District, which at that time was a one-square-mile region of loft buildings, many with freight elevators opening directly onto the street, bounded roughly by Fifth and Ninth avenues to the east and west and by 42nd and 26th streets to the north and south. His destination was Amtorg (short for Amerikanskaya Torgovlya). His hope was that the "businessmen" at Amtorg might be more inclined than Soviet government officials to listen to him and might be convinced to pass on his information to someone at the Soviet Consulate.

Amtorg was running a $1.5 billion operation selling Soviet products and confiscated artifacts in the United States and buying weapons and other needed equipment for the war effort. But as Robert Chadwell Williams, a noted Russia historian and expert on Soviet atomic espionage, explained to me in an interview, Amtorg was also "a nest of Soviet spies," thanks to the handy cover of "trader" or "businessman" that it offered. Its staff likely also included an FBI informant or two, since the FBI was well aware of its convenience as a cover for Soviet agents. (In fact, the building had been covertly burgled in the 1930s by the FBI, which bagged an old Soviet code book, later supplied to code breakers at the SIS's Venona Project. That find would, a decade later, help the SIS begin the painstaking decryption of the Soviet Union's wartime spy code.)[1]

Ted walked into that center of intrigue, known to Soviet intelligence as "The Factory," on a cool day in mid-October. He took the freight elevator up to the floor marked "Amtorg" and found himself in a typical unpainted loft space where a man who turned out to be an American was busy stacking large crates and cartons.

One can easily imagine that conversation. Turning from his work to see a strange teenager exit the lift, the startled worker, eyeing him, may have said, "Can I help you?"

"Thank you," replied the typically polite and soft-spoken Ted Hall. "Could you direct me to the Amtorg office?"

"Who're ya lookin' for?" asked the worker in unmistakable idiomatic New York English.

"I don't really know," replied Ted, not sure how to proceed.

Then, knowing he had to be back at Los Alamos by October 29, which was fast approaching, he decided to take a gamble and lay his cards on the table, saying, "I'm a scientist working on a top-secret superbomb project out in New Mexico, and I want to tell someone in the Soviet Consulate about it. The Soviet Union needs to know about this project."*

Ted told Joseph Albright and Marcia Kunstel that the man he spoke with at Amtorg grew visibly nervous as he was talking, but replied that while there was nobody at Amtorg who could help him, there was a man—a Russian journalist and author who had connections with the whole Russian community in New York—who might be able to steer him in the right direction. The man took out a slip of paper and wrote down the name and address of Sergei Kurnakov.

While Hall and Sax were each disappointed at being provided with the name of a writer/journalist instead of a Soviet official, when they got back together and realized they'd both been given the same name, it seemed considerably more encouraging. And in fact, while they didn't yet know it, Kurnakov was *exactly* the person they needed to see.†

After the victory of the Bolshevik Revolution in 1917 and the end of the civil war in 1922, a span of time during which the former tsarist calvary officer had fought on the losing side with the White Russian counterrevolutionary forces, Kurnakov had, for his own safety, moved to the United States. Over time, though, he had come around to supporting the new Soviet Union and, rather remarkably, became an important figure in the NKVD, the Soviet spy apparatus in the United States, which in 1941 was put in charge of foreign espionage.

Despite what the Communist government considered to be a suspicious political past, Kurnakov (code name BEK) showed himself to have a knack for spotting and vetting potential informants and spy candidates for the Soviet Union's expanding U.S. spy organization. So when Ted showed up for a visit at his lower Manhattan apartment, it was not surprising that Kurnakov buzzed him in to talk.

Ted reportedly opened up immediately to Kurnakov and, according to Soviet spy cables decrypted and made public decades later, impressed him with his detailed description of the Manhattan Project underway at

---

* This conversation is a fictional reconstruction based on what Ted said transpired and the knowledge that it was an American New Yorker he met upon exiting the elevator.

† As it turned out, Hall and Sax both lucked out with their first efforts. Napoli was an agent with the NKVD but didn't want to acknowledge it, and the man at Amtorg who suggested Ted go to Kurnakov, who was an NKVD recruiter, also had to have been with the Soviet spy agency or at least was a Party member. Coincidentally, when I related this story to Ted's Cambridge physics friend and colleague Emeritus Prof. Mick Brown, he mentioned that his father-in-law had worked at Amtorg during the war and had later immigrated to Canada because of harassment from HUAC. I jokingly said it would be funny if his wife's father had been the man who directed Ted to the NKVD spy recruiter Sergei Kurnakov, and he laughed, saying, "Well I guess it could have been possible."

Los Alamos. In a cable to Moscow about that meeting dated November 12, 1944, Kurnakov said that the nineteen-year-old walk-in volunteer spy was "characterized by political development, broadmindedness, and exceptionally sharp intelligence."[2] "Politically developed and broadminded" were NKVD code words meaning someone was a leftist and was friendly toward the USSR and Communism (see appendix, figure D.1).

Seeking proof that Ted was actually a scientist at Los Alamos and really did have important information about the atom bomb being developed, which he wanted to offer to the Soviets out of an idealistic desire to ensure some kind of postwar strategic balance in atomic weapons instead of a dangerous U.S. monopoly, Kurnakov, after first plying his surprise guest with vodka, challenged Ted to prove himself. In response, Ted handed him a report he had written about Los Alamos that listed, among other things, all the prominent scientists secretly assembled there. On that list were the names of prominent physicists from the United States and abroad, including Hans Bethe, Niels Bohr, Percy Bridgeman, Arthur Compton, Enrico Fermi, George Kistiakowski, Ernest Lawrence, William Penny, Bruno Rossi, Emilio Segrè, Geoffrey Taylor, Edward Teller, Harold Urey, and the noted mathematician John von Neumann.

But just to be certain, Kurnakov, in his report filed to Moscow by diplomatic pouch instead of by cable, noted that as a test of the sincerity of this almost too eager volunteer spy, he asked Hall why he was offering to betray his own country's secrets to the Soviet Union. He wrote,

> He told me that the new secret weapon was an "atomic bomb" of colossal destructive capacity. I interrupted him. Do you understand what you are doing? What makes you think you should reveal the USA's secrets for the USSR's sake? He replied, "The SU [Soviet Union] is the only country that could be trusted with such a terrible thing. But since we cannot take it away from other countries—the USSR ought to be aware of its existence and stay abreast of the progress of the experiments and construction. This way, at a peace conference, the USSR—on which the fate of my generation depends—will not find itself in the position of a power subjected to blackmail."[3]

It was at that point, Kurnakov wrote, that Hall, explaining the principles of the plutonium bomb, took out a neatly written report, gave it to him, and said, "Show this to any physicist, and he will understand what it's about." This was the first the Soviet scientists would learn of the implosion system.

Kurnakov, whose father had been a scientist, knew he had the real deal, and he knew that Soviet physicists at work on the struggling Russian bomb project, seeing that high-powered list of U.S. bomb makers and the report on the plutonium bomb's design, would clearly recognize that a major atomic bomb project was underway in the United States. But as a low-ranking NKVD "illegal" agent (one lacking the protection from arrest afforded by diplomatic status, meaning that being caught spying could have serious consequences), he was not allowed to even acknowledge the *existence* of a spying operation. As a result, without identifying himself as a spy, he promised to pass the information along to appropriate people at the consulate, along with word that Ted Hall had a friend, who he also had met, willing to act if necessary as a courier/contact when Ted was back at Los Alamos.

After that meeting, Hall and Sax were at a loss about what to do. Kurnakov had not let on to them that he was with the NKVD, and Ted had to get back to his post at Los Alamos on time to avoid any suspicions about his trip. And yet they still didn't know if they would be accepted as spies or even if the consulate would receive Ted's information from Kurnakov. It seemed all they'd managed to do was to meet a loquacious old Russian exile writer!

They decided it was time for Sax to visit the consulate, as he had originally planned, on the pretext of asking for information about his Russian relatives. The following day, he went there.

As Ted recounted to Albright and Kunstel, upon entering the consular building, Sax met a clerk named Anatoli Yatskov (code name ALEKSEJ). Fortunately for Sax, Yatskov was himself an NKVD spy and the very one who, because of his scientific background, had been tasked with developing sources to report on the U.S. atomic bomb program.

Yatskov, however, was troubled by the whole thing. It would break all the rules of spycraft for him to take on these two young men as spies without a thorough vetting. And yet, as fate would have it, Ted and Savy were coming to the NKVD's attention and volunteering to provide information about the U.S. atomic bomb project at moment of crisis for the Soviets. They had just recently lost touch with Klaus Fuchs (who had come to the United States with the British Mission, first being posted in New York but then shifted to Los Alamos, and had not contacted them since leaving Manhattan). This left the NKVD without a source working inside the Manhattan Project bomb laboratory. Moscow and the New York *Rezidentura* were desperate to obtain one. Yatskov took from Sax another copy of the same document Ted had provided to Kurnakov and, without making any commitment, sent him on his way.

Worse yet for Yatskov, time was really getting short: Ted had told Kurnakov that he had to be on a train back to Santa Fe in two days, and once he left New York there would be no way to reach him. There was simply no time for a real vetting of this potential recruit, much less for training him in basic spy craft. Nor was there time to alert Moscow NKVD headquarters of the situation and receive instructions on how to handle it.

What Yatskov did know—and *could* check out, thanks to an NKVD contact at U.S. Communist Party headquarters—was that Sax's mother, Bluma, was a U.S. Communist Party member (a "FELLOW COUNTRYMAN" in NKVD code) and that both Sax and Hall were "GYMNASTS," the code term applied by the NKVD to people who were or had been once active in Communist front youth organizations: the Young Communist League, in Sax's case, and the American Student Union, in Hall's (although, as a young high school student, he likely had no idea it was a Communist front organization).

In discussions involving Yatskov's boss, Stepan Apresyan, a Soviet vice-consul who was also the New York NKVD station chief (code name MAY), it was decided locally that *losing* Ted Hall was a bigger risk than that he and Sax were actually double agents working for the United States, so they asked Kurnakov to check both young volunteers out further without their meeting (and putting in jeopardy) higher-up NKVD people directly. This was quite a bold move, given that Yatskov and Apresyan were working in an agency under the ultimate direction of Soviet People's Commissar for Internal Security Lavrentiy Beria, a ruthless man who dealt with failure the same way he dealt with betrayal: by a bullet to the head or a push out of a high window.

But there was little alternative. The NKVD in New York could not just pick up a phone and call the Soviet state security compound Lubyanka or get on a computer and send an encrypted message. Phones were presumed to be tapped, and computers didn't yet exist. They had instead to send a cable, using a complicated manual encryption process of multiple layers that took considerable time to compose, and would then have to wait for a reply, a process that could take days, or use a secure diplomatic pouch, which would take longer still. Nor would there be any way to contact Ted once he was back at Los Alamos (as had happened with Fuchs only a few months earlier). Any arrangement would have to be between him and Sax, and would itself take time, as even the use of pay phones around the Los Alamos area was too risky.*

---

* It's interesting to note that the NKVD's fear of using telephones was a U.S. phenomenon. Robert Williams, author of the first biography of Fuchs, remarked to me that in Britain, Soviet spies routinely communicated by pay phone, but not in the United States. That fear of phone use in the United States led to some of the problems that arose for the NKVD U.S. spy network, such as their losing contact with

With the situation right down to the wire, Kurnakov himself went to the vast and ornate lobby at New York's Penn Station to give Hall the word, hanging around as inconspicuously as possible as Ted, his father, and his new stepmother ate a farewell meal together at a local restaurant outside the station on 31st Street. Ted later recalled being shocked and concerned when he entered the station's huge, echoing hall with its clacking flip board schedule board showing arriving and departing trains and saw a seated Kurnakov beckoning to him. While his parents looked on, confused, Hall walked over to Kurnakov, who broke to him the welcome news that he and Sax had been accepted into the NKVD fold. Ted was left to concoct a hasty explanation for his brief encounter with the much older gentleman, who he clearly seemed to know. Adding to his embarrassment, Ted recounted to Albright and Kunstel that as he headed for his train, Kurnakov stood up at attention and saluted his new recruit![4] Luckily for Ted, he had to board the train immediately and didn't have to come up with a hasty explanation to hand his father and stepmother for *that* gesture!

On November 12, two weeks after that fateful meeting, Moscow received a message from the NKVD in New York, one of the first to be decrypted by SIS decoders several years later, reporting that two young men, including one working as a physicist at Los Alamos, had offered to spy for the Soviets. In a lapse of security likely caused by the need for haste in getting instructions from Moscow—one that would later nearly cost Ted and Savy their freedom and even potentially their lives—that cable cited both men's actual names, slightly misspelled as Teador Kholl and Savil Saks, as their code names of MLAD ("Youngster") for Hall and STAR ("Old One") for Sax, had not been assigned yet. Hall was described as a nineteen-year-old graduate of Harvard and the son of a furrier, making identifying him later as Theodore Hall, Manhattan Project scientist, a piece of cake for the FBI six years later. It was a breach of security that rendered the NKVD's diligent future use of only their code names in subsequent communications pointless.

Ted arrived back at Los Alamos on October 29 a man with two identities: Ted Hall, atomic scientist, and MLAD, Soviet atomic spy. His friend Saville Sax, now STAR, was his courier.

Fuchs, who, even when traveling away from Los Alamos, was not able to safely contact his handler or the *Rezidentura* in New York.

11

EDWARD HALL AT WAR IN BRITAIN

Shifting Targets

The enemies of your enemies are not always your friends, but they can still be useful.

—James D. Sass

By the middle of 1944, Ted Hall's brother, Edward, had largely completed the work he had been doing for the last several years, which consisted primarily of repairing damaged returning bombers to get them back into the air campaign against the Third Reich. After having overseen that repair operation, his last task in helping in the fight against Nazi Germany was to organize teams to assemble the crates of wooden parts shipped from the United States for the construction of giant gliders that were to carry troops before D-Day behind enemy lines along the French coast, where they could conduct operations like destroying German communications, bridges, and so on.

His work done, with bombers by that point not facing as much opposition and damage over German skies, Ed got new orders in September: He was to report to the headquarters of the 363rd Tactical Reconnaisance Group at Villa Double, at the airport of liberated Paris. His assignment was to convert P-51 Mustang fighter bombers into F-6 spy photo-recon planes so that pilots could focus on flying and spotting potential bombing targets instead of trying to write notes about what they were seeing along with the coordinates, usually on a knee and in pencil.

The front lines on the western front were ill-defined, and Hall writes that on a drive by Jeep to U.S. headquarters in Luxembourg to obtain the needed equipment for the plane alterations, he and three other officers ended up driving into an area still controlled by German troops:

> This proved to be a pleasant trip, and on the first evening we bought excellent meals at a farmhouse in Longwy in Eastern France. We continued on, noting that the road was now littered with burned-out German vehicles. As we approached Luxembourg City, many of the vehicles were red hot. We felt something was wrong with our orders, but decided to proceed. We found out later that the orders sending us to Luxembourg had been cancelled and then reissued a week later. We had left Paris too soon.
>
> As we approached Sandweiler, we noticed that the sentries were wearing gray uniforms. Evidently, they saw our brown ones. They rapidly retreated into the base, and we very rapidly sped away. . . . In a few minutes, we entered Luxembourg City. We were immediately approached by the standard gang of kids asking for chocolate and chewing gum, which we distributed the best we could. . . . After a few failures, we found a man willing to discuss our dilemma in French. He recommended that we proceed to the offices of the Luxembourg FFI [French Forces of the Interior], the resistance group now more or less running the city as the Germans decamped. These people had been expecting the Americans and welcomed us with open arms.[1]

Unable to locate the aerial photography equipment he was hoping to receive, Hall requested to be returned to England to requisition it. Flying back to headquarters, though, he found his mission had been changed, and he was assigned to the Directorate of Technical Services (DTS). The twelve officers assigned to the unit—several of them, like Ed, engineers by training—were tasked with studying and analyzing equipment, primarily captured German equipment, to see what could be learned from it. "At this time," he writes, "London was being attacked by V1s and V2s. We gathered whatever parts and information were available and analyzed these to determine the best methods to render them harmless."[2]

The unit was also assigned to go over and analyze the Allied bombing target map, and Ed writes, "We concluded that targets selected at that time were not optimized. In general we had been attacking railway yards, manufacturing plants, submarine pens, and occasionally (and largely unsuccessfully) bridges. Where possible, we also attempted disruption of communication systems."[3]

At that point, with German rocket attacks on Britain having nearly ceased and the Technical Services assignment wrapped up, Ed found himself moved back to France to a site in a former girls' school at Saint-Germain-en-Laye to do intelligence work—technical intelligence. As he explains,

> I was briefed on why I had been so hastily transferred and what I was to do. By this time the Germans were in full retreat and the Air Corps, curious about what new and startling advances they had made, had sent civilian "experts" to previously German occupied facilities to ferret out this information.
>
> For some mysterious reason, the majority of those delegated for this work were stock-and-bond salesmen. The reports they turned in to headquarters were replete with information such as the height of smokestacks, sanitary conditions in the rest rooms, and the general health of employees. These reports had somehow drifted into the hands of Gen. Henry H. Arnold, commander of the Army Air Corps, who became livid. He demanded that these people be removed immediately from technical intelligence and be replaced with engineers. The machine records section of the Air Corps listed as engineers only the officers assigned to the Directorate of Technical Services in London. Hence my pressing [transfer].[4]

At Saint-Germain, as the new unit was organized into technical groups, Hall was assigned to be chief of propulsion, tasked with looking for advanced aircraft and rocket engines on German sites. His friend Al Deyarmond was named chief of airframes. Hall writes,

> As our troops advanced, targets of apparent technical interest were submitted to our headquarters for study. When they were found, significantly, they were slated for visitation. Since engines and airframes of interest were frequently found together Al and I spent a good deal of time roaming the German countryside together. A jeep and a driver were provided.[5]

Hall says that nothing very significant turned up during those searches, but it was clear that a subtle shift was occurring even as the war continued to rage in Germany on both fronts, East and West. As he writes,

> After some months of this activity, as the war wound down, intelligence activities heated up. The United States Strategic Bombing Survey, consisting of a series of civilian "experts" and engineers, meandered over the countryside gathering data, equipment and people. The Air Corps established Project Lusty, in which officer and civilians acted in similar fashion. In general the object was to report on, or gather, technically interesting material, and send

one copy to the Royal Aircraft Establishment at Farnborough, England, and one to Wright Patterson AFB in Ohio.[6]

No copy of such details was sent to America's other wartime ally in Europe, the Soviet Union. This was, in fact, the beginning of the shift in the emphasis of U.S. intelligence activity, as the Office of Strategic Services (OSS), FBI, MI5, and MI6 turned their focus and their energies from Germany to the USSR.

Ed writes about "perhaps the most interesting of these wild forays"—this one just after the conclusion of the war—involving Logge Dora, a rocket factory that had been carved out of a mountain near Nordhausen in the Russian-occupied zone of eastern Germany. Most of the underground plant had been moved in the later part of the war from Peenemunde, a rocket facility where the V-2 was developed, to escape heavy Allied bombing of that location. Hall, who, according to his official U.S. Air Force biography,[7] had been attached to a special U.S. Army unit (almost certainly an OSS operation) as a technical adviser because of his expertise in rocket and jet engines, notes that he sought the assistance of the German officer who had run the facility during the war. He writes,

> German General [Rudolf] Hermann was in charge of operations. Near the entrance to the facility were several heaps of human bodies and some nearly dead slave laborers. I discussed my mission with the British officers in command and with General Hermann. He spoke English well and had, in fact, lived in the US for many years. I carried out my orders with no difficulty, including the dispatch of several V1s and V2s to the US. Before I left, Gen. Hermann asked me to take him in my jeep on what he promised would be an interesting journey.
>
> I agreed, and we followed a paved road into the heavily treed mountains. Some miles from Logge Dora we turned off onto a dirt road descending into a meadow, large areas of which were covered with V1s, V2s, and engines. General Hermann told me that as the transport system of the Third Reich had collapsed, government inspectors at the plant had insisted that production schedules be maintained. Consequently the plant's output was simply trucked to this meadow and dumped.[8]

On his return to Nordhausen, Hall directed the removal of equipment likely to be of interest to the United States and Britain and then led in the destruction of equipment that was left, pointing out the critical items to destroy and making sure the damage would render it useless to arriving

Russians. His official air force biography says Ed also aided in the interviewing of captured German scientists, using his expertise to help determine which ones should be sent to the United States, where they could help with the planned U.S. development of modern jet aircraft and rockets. While he doesn't identify the unit he was assigned to, this would appear to have been part of the controversial Operation Paperclip program, which secretly spirited several hundred Nazi rocket scientists and engineers out of Germany, including from the Soviet-occupied eastern zone, into the United States and out of the clutches of both Nuremberg Trial investigators and Red Army troops, as the Soviets were also trying to bring captured German scientists back with them.

Amid what he called the "confusion" of the war's end following Germany's surrender on May 7, 1945, Ed Hall was dispatched to the Royal Aircraft Establishment at Farnborough, England, to discuss the German aircraft equipment he and others on the technical intelligence team had sent from Germany and to attempt to catalogue it all.

All this time, from September 1944 through the end of the war in Europe, Ed was scooping up parts, plans, and scientists in Germany to help prepare the United States for what the War Department and the U.S. national security establishment were foreseeing as an era of epic conflict—perhaps nuclear conflict, or preemptive nuclear conflict—with the Soviet Union. Interestingly, his younger brother, Ted, was at that same time contemplating and then actually volunteering to becomes an asset, or spy, for the Soviets to help them develop their own atomic weapon so as to prevent the very military superiority that Ed was helping the Pentagon to try to achieve.

Ted's motivation was a conscious realization that his own country was likely to become a major threat to world peace and humanity's survival even as a horrific global conflict against fascism was still raging, and a growing conviction that he had to do something to prevent that threat. In his brother's case, Ed was like a driver on a one-way street, crossing an intersection to find himself facing a one-way arrow pointing the other direction: He was still driving his beloved American vehicle, but it was suddenly threatening the other vehicles on the road.

12

THE VENONA
DECRYPTION PROJECT

I never wanted it to get anyone into trouble.

—Venona cryptologist Meredith Knox Gardner[1]

Between 1940 and 1948, many, if not most, of the written messages between the Moscow headquarters of the NKVD and its operational offices in Western nations, and notably the Soviet *Rezidentura* in New York City during and for a few years after World War II, were transmitted over commercial telegraph services. The Soviets felt confident doing this because they had devised a complicated code system that was so artful and multi-layered, based on groups of randomly generated sets of numbers on a thick pad of pages changed and destroyed daily, that it was deemed by them to be uncrackable.

Initially, this system worked, in part because the FBI and the SIS, fore-runner of today's vastly larger National Security Agency (NSA), as well as Britain's intelligence service, were preoccupied with trying to crack the German and Japanese spy codes. But by 1943, intelligence began to focus on the Soviet code after the Federal Communications Commission (FCC), which was monitoring U.S. airwaves looking for secret Nazi transmissions, detected undecipherable messages originating from the Soviet consular buildings in New York and San Francisco. The FCC couldn't read them, of course, but they were recorded, saved, and sent on to the top-secret U.S.

Army SIS, which decided on February 1 of that year to set up a team of people devoted to cracking the Soviet spy code.

The program, called Venona, was set up in Arlington Hall, a former girls' school in northern Virginia taken over through an eminent domain court order by the Pentagon. As many as three hundred or more young people, most of them women because of the wartime male labor shortage and because the job involved a lot of typing, began poring over the thousands upon thousands of intercepted copies of Soviet spy cables, trying to figure out a way to crack the code.

The Soviets knew their inventively coded messages could and would be spotted, but they were supremely confident those messages could not be decrypted and so continued to use commercial wire services to transmit them. As such messages originated from their embassy and consulates— especially the New York consulate—they also weren't worried about the senders being arrested as spies (where they could be pressured to reveal other spies and informants to avoid punishment); at worst, they might be deported. The encryption system was based on the one-time use of pads of randomly selected sets of numbers in a booklet containing thousands of such random numbers. The sender of the message would clue the receiver of the message to what page of the code book should be used to decode it. The system was thus as secure as the code book, which was closely guarded. Only one page was used one time, and even if a page was not destroyed and was discovered, it would be of no use to code breakers because the random numbers on it would never be used again.

It might have worked, but the Soviet spies, increasingly busy and over-worked as they built up their network in the United States, particularly tar-geting the Manhattan Project, got sloppy and began reusing code pages, in some cases using coded versions of the actual names of U.S. volunteer spies or couriers, or of their spouses. This is what happened in the case of Ethel Rosenberg, whose name eventually was deciphered in a partially decrypted cable.* (In an interesting coincidence, which apparently had no connection to the uncovering of his spying, after earning his engineering degree in 1939, Julius Rosenberg began working in 1940 with the U.S. Army Signal Corps Engineering Laboratory in Monmouth, New Jersey. While the SIS, which

---

* It's been credibly argued by Robert and Michael Meeropol and others that, far from identifying her as a spy, the naming of Ethel in the same cable that used a spy code name for her husband proves that she was *not* a spy, because she did not have a spy identity in cables. Of course, naming her in that same cable in connection to her code-named husband was an error regardless, as it clearly linked her to Julius, rendering the use of his code name pointless.

would later be trying to crack the Soviet spy code, was a part of the same Army Signal Corps, Rosenberg and his workplace had no direct connection to the secret SIS Venona decoding project in Virginia, though it was the organization where he did a lot of his own spying work.)[2]

For a long time, the Venona Project at Arlington House remained stymied by the complexity of the Soviet spy code, but with the use of the old code book obtained by the FBI in an Amtorg "black bag" job, along with the work of a diligent SIS analyst who used it to decipher coded shipping manifests, they started making limited headway.

Finally, a polymath university language teacher named Meredith Knox Gardner, who had a remarkable gift for languages (he learned Japanese in three months after being hired on by the SIS), used the old Amtorg code book to work out the decryption of a spell table of the Latin alphabet. On December 20, 1946, he began using that breakthrough to try to decipher a spy cable that turned out to be a list of names of the top scientists working on the Manhattan Project. By chance, it was the very list Ted Hall had provided to Sergei Kurnakov as proof of his bona fides as a scientist at Los Alamos.

In a further twist of fate, the first spy cable ever to be decrypted identifying a spy by their real, if misspelled, names—actually, two spies in the Manhattan Project—was one dated November 12, 1944. (See appendix, fig. D.1.) Sent to Moscow headquarters from the NKVD's New York *Rezidentura* located in the Soviet Consulate, it reported on a young physicist who was volunteering to provide atomic bomb information from inside a tightly guarded mountaintop Manhattan Project site in New Mexico. While encoded, that cable broke an NKVD rule by listing the names of Theodore Hall and Saville Sax (both misspelled), along with their respective code names, MLAD and STAR.

It would take Gardner until early 1950 to decrypt just the first part of that spy cable—but what he decoded and translated was enough for the SIS to rush to the FBI with the stunning news of an identifiable physicist spy inside the project at Los Alamos, including information about the identity of his courier.

Fully translated in April 1961,[3] the cable is nothing less than a full report to Lubyanka by the local *Rezidentura* on its decision to accept Ted Hall's offer to become a volunteer spy and to use Saville Sax as his courier. The eleven-year delay between the successful decryption of its first revealing sentence in 1950 and the deciphering of the rest of such an important message indicates how difficult the Soviet code actually was, and why Soviet spymasters were so confident of its seeming impenetrability. In full, it reads:

> BEK [Sergei Kurnakov] visited THEODOR KhOLL, 19 years old, the son of a furrier. He is a graduate of HARVARD University. As a talented physicist he was taken on for government work. He was a GYMNAST [code word for someone who had joined a Communist front organization] and conducted work in the Steel Founder's Union [this appears to have been an erroneous conflation of Hall's and Sax's work experience by Kurnakov]. According to BEKs account HALL has an exceptionally keen mind and a broad outlook, and is politically developed [sympathetic to the Soviet Union]. At the present time H. is in charge of a group at "CAMP 2" [Los Alamos]. H. handed over to BEK a report about the CAMP and named key personnel employed on ENORMOUS [the atomic bomb]. He decided to do this on the advice of his colleague SAVIL SAKS, a GYMNAST living in TYRE [New York]. SAX'S mother is a FELLOW COUNTRYMAN [code for Communist Party member] and works for Russian War Relief [a CP front organization]. With the aim of hastening a meeting with a competent person H. on the following day sent a copy of the report by S. to the PLANT [ZAVOD; code for consulate]. ALEXSEJ [Anatoli Yatskov] received from S [Saville Sax]. H. [Theodore Hall] had to leave for CAMP 2 [Los Alamos] in two days' time. He was compelled to make a decision quickly. Jointly with MAY [Stepan Apresyan] he gave BEK consent to feel out H. to assure him that everything was in order and to arrange liaison with him. H. left his photograph and came to an understanding with BEK about a place for meeting him. BEK met S. (in our automobile). We consider it expedient to maintain liaison with H. through S. and not to bring in anybody else. MAY has no objection to this. We shall send the details by post.[4]

It was this cable's information with its clear identification of Hall and Sax as volunteer Soviet spies that caused FBI director J. Edgar Hoover to activate his counterintelligence team of agents in FBI offices across the country. They began a nationwide search to locate and build a case against the first spy identified as having worked inside America's supersecret atomic bomb project and his courier.

This cable, kept secret along with the several thousand others that had been painstakingly decrypted and then translated from Russian into English, when finally released publicly by the NSA in 1995, sent a frisson of excitement through the U.S. and British news media. It also sent a shockwave through the Hall household, as well as among Ted and Joan's circle of friends and associates at Cambridge University, in the small town of

Newnham just outside the university campus where they lived, and certainly along the one-block street of row homes lining Owlstone Road where the Halls' home was located.

Meanwhile, concerned about leaks, the SIS (which by then had undergone several name changes and expansions, in 1945 becoming the Army Security Agency, or ASA, and later, in February 1952, the NSA) and the FBI, at least until about 1948, were tight-lipped about their possession of crates of NKVD cable traffic (some thirty-two thousand pages) from the war period and some of the early Cold War years. Even Harry Truman, who became president on April 12, 1945, after Franklin D. Roosevelt died suddenly of a cerebral hemorrhage while sitting for a portrait, was kept in the dark about the cables until well after his election to a second term in 1948. The CIA did not learn of the cables until 1952 and only gained access to them in 1953. One of the great ironies of all this internal secrecy was that the British master spy Kim Philby, who was a member of the British counterintelligence agency MI6 and had been a Soviet spy since 1939, learned about the SIS's possession of encrypted Soviet cables and its progress in cracking the code long before even Truman did—and of course he informed Soviet intelligence of what he'd learned.

For all the SIS's efforts to keep the Venona decryption project secret, the NKVD and its sister military spy agency, the Main Intelligence Directorate (GRU), had in fact already learned that the SIS code breakers at Arlington Hall were in the process of cracking their secret code as early as 1944. Lauchlin Currie, a close personal aide on economic policy to FDR but also a Soviet agent, reported to his controllers in mid-1944 that the United States was "on the verge of breaking the Soviet Code."[5] (Currie, named as a spy by U.S. Soviet spy Elizabeth Bentley when she defected from the NKVD in 1945, consistently denied the accusation but was eventually identified as a spy in a released decrypted Venona cable in 1996, three years after his death.)

It could be that Soviet intelligence services, with a hot war raging against the German Wehrmacht in their country, failed to react quickly to change their code system out of overconfidence that their code would withstand efforts to crack it. Or perhaps they deliberately kept using it, but carefully, to pass false information to the United States, eventually switching to a different code system and thus finally letting on that they knew they'd been "busted." But in any event, by 1945, William Weisband, an NKVD spy who became a U.S. citizen in 1938 and had been conveniently assigned by the army to the Russian translation unit at the Venona Project's Arlington House, was able to warn the Soviet intelligence services that the United States had succeeded in being able to at least start decrypting coded messages.

Gardner later recalled that he once noticed Weisband, a popular guy who had the run of Arlington House, looking with interest over his shoulder just as he was making his big breakthrough, deciphering the names of the key physicists and other scientists working at the Manhattan Project in 1945, not long after he had succeeded in discovering the key to the Latin alphabet in a stolen spy code book.[6]

Not that all this mattered in the case of Ted Hall and Saville Sax. The important spy cable in which their actual names appeared was, of course, composed and sent well before Weisband's discovery of the breach and his reporting of that discovery to his NKVD handlers. And by April 21, 1950, just nine months after the Soviets tested their own plutonium bomb (a virtual carbon copy of the "Fat Man" bomb dropped over Nagasaki), the ASA had put the incriminating cable into Hoover's hands.

13

THE "GRAUBER INCIDENT"

Ted Seriously Risks Blowing His Cover

There are very few important rules in life: One is Tell the truth, and the other is Don't rat on your friends.

—Kurt Vonnegut (as stated to the elder son of Julius and Ethel Rosenberg, Michael Meeropol)

When Ted Hall returned to Los Alamos in late October 1944, it was as a volunteer spy for the Soviet Union. He had crossed that Rubicon by providing information about the Manhattan Project and the plutonium bomb, a transgression that, even happening at a time when the USSR was a U.S. ally in the war, could have earned him a long prison sentence—or even, as would happen with the Rosenbergs in 1951, a death sentence—were he to have been charged with espionage, prosecuted, and convicted.

In 1998, a year before he died of kidney cancer, Ted made a video at the suggestion of his attorney Benedict Birnberg, who thought he should explain what he did "for the historical record." In the video, he was asked by his wife Joan if he was afraid when he decided to become a spy. "No," he replied, thinking about that time and chuckling at the seeming absurdity of his youthful bravado. "No, I wasn't afraid."[1]

In fact, by early 1945, less than three months after returning to Los Alamos from his meeting with Soviet NKVD agents in Manhattan, Ted had felt confident enough in his decision to become a volunteer Soviet spy that he made the risky attempt to recruit another spy inside the Manhattan Project.

This effort, which could have proved a disaster for him, instead caused apoplexy among his Soviet handlers at the *Rezidentura*, especially Leonid Krasnikov (code name ANTON), the head of the atomic spying operation, and in turn led to a scolding by Krasnikov's superiors in Moscow NKVD headquarters for his failure to properly school his young spy recruit in the rules of spy craft. Former KGB employee Alexander Vassiliev, now a Russian expatriate journalist and commentator living outside London, spent considerable time poring over temporarily opened NKVD atomic spying files during the brief period of Gorbachev-era glasnost in the early 1990s. He published those notes, which included considerable information from the NKVD side about Ted Hall and Saville Sax, in a series of three books called the Yellow Notebooks. Notebook #1 begins with the cable sent from the Soviet Consulate to Moscow on November 12 reporting on Kurnakov's first meeting with Ted Hall.[2] Later, he records a cable sent in January of 1945 to Moscow by Krasnikov. It reads,

> Anton [Krasnikov] reports the following incident, recently disclosed by Star [Saville Sax]: At the beginning of 1945 [early January], in a conversation between Mlad [Ted Hall] and his fellow student—Roy Grauber*—who also works at the Preserve [Los Alamos] and lives with Mlad, Grauber expressed displeasure at the fact that the English and Amer. gov'ts were keeping work on E [E for *Enormos*, the NKVD code word for the atom bomb] in strict secrecy from the S.U. [Soviet Union] and added that, given the opportunity, he would inform our representatives [the Soviets] about the project. Mlad hinted that he had taken some steps in this direction and, in turn, asked what Roy intended to do, practically speaking, to realize his wish. Roy got scared, started taking back everything he had said, and two weeks later he even moved out of Mlad's room, and has since stopped being his friend. Mlad says he is convinced that Grauber will not inform on him, b/c his beliefs are close to Star's and Mlad's, though he is incapable of taking decisive action when there is risk involved. The fact that he moved out of Mlad's room shows that he wants to stay away from "dangerous acquaintances." This incident was not reported in the first telegram because Star only told about it recently. His tardiness in notifying us of this extremely important incident has already been brought to his attention. Anton thinks that this incident resulted from a lack of direct work on educating Mlad, as well as his inexperience and youth. Before finding out about this incident, Anton had passed on to Mlad a number of practical suggestions during Star's previous trip. There were not

---

* Glauber's last name is misspelled Grauber in the cable, either because Sax had it wrong in the telling or because the author of the cable from the *Rezidentura* reporting belatedly on the incident copied it wrong.

enough of them, however. Therefore, Anton proposes setting up a meeting between Mlad and our operative in order to conduct a detailed tutorial on the principles of our work and of personal conduct. Furthermore, Anton requests permission for Leslie [code name for Lona Cohen, an American master spy/courier working for the NKVD] to travel for a meeting with Mlad, which should take place in Sernovodsk [code name for Santa Fe] on 21 July of this year. Anton grounds his proposal to use Leslie for this instead of Star on the following reasons: 1) The competitors [American intelligence] at the Preserve [code name for Los Alamos] apparently have Star on file as someone who corresponds with Mlad, and if his name comes up repeatedly at the Sernovodsk visitors' desk, it could arouse suspicion. 2) It would be difficult for Star to account for a second visit to Sernovodsk after the explanation he gave on his last visit, a short while back, when he was questioned upon getting off the bus. 3) It would not be difficult to justify Leslie's visit, b/c she received a note from a doctor about the need for her to take a long vacation. Her vacation starts on July 10th. On instructions from the station, Leslie bought a ticket to Denver for July 14th. She was told nothing about the purpose of the trip.[3]

A second cable from ANTON, dated July 4, 1945, has the chastened Krasnikov attempting to shift the blame for the near disaster onto his subordinate Anatoli Yatskov (ALEKSEJ), who was Cohen's handler and had approved the plan to have her meet Hall in Santa Fe. It reads,

> The reason for the incident with Glauber, which should be regarded as Mlad's exposure, is the complete inadequacy of Aleksey's work with the agents on cultivating En-s [for ENORMOS, the Soviet code name, often also spelled ENORMOZ, for the U.S. atomic bomb]. It has been proposed to conduct an educational discussion with him. Approval for Leslie to visit Mlad. In connection with the Glauber incident—impossibility of setting up a meeting between Mlad and our operative.[4]

Glauber, who went on after the war to finish his physics training, earning a doctorate from Harvard and later becoming a tenured professor there with an endowed chair, never did report either to Los Alamos security or to the FBI that his friend, Harvard classmate, and roommate Ted Hall had admitted to him that he had become a spy, contacting the Soviets about his work on the bomb. Although Glauber did, according to Hall's recounting of the incident to Sax, request and get permission to be moved to a different dormitory, he apparently never related anything of the conversation to anyone else. Glauber did join fellow Los Alamos veteran and fellow Harvard student recruit Frederic de Hoffmann in arranging for a dinner reunion with

Ted and his new wife, Joan, at a fancy restaurant in Chicago in 1947 during a train stop there as he and de Hoffmann were traveling from Berkeley to resume their studies at Harvard. That friendly get-together, at which Joan recalls the three young Los Alamos veterans laughed and talked, recalling their time there while virtually ignoring her, makes it clear that Glauber had never really ended his friendship with Ted.

Their friendship was a bond that likely saved Ted Hall from a very early investigation and arrest and—because he was in uniform—a court-martial for espionage before the war had even ended. Glauber, who received a Nobel Prize in physics in 2005, would later get two more opportunities to betray his friend, but he stayed true to those bonds and didn't denounce or report Hall, as will be recounted later.

Here is part of the FBI report dated April 28, 1951, filed by the FBI's New York City office after two agents visited and questioned Glauber at his family's home in New York on March 29, less than two weeks after Chicago agents interrogated Ted and Saville:

> Dr. Roy J. Glauber, 15 W. 47th St., NY City, was interviewed on March 29, 1951. Glauber states that while at Harvard University, he had very little to do with Saville Sax. He said that Sax and Hall were quite friendly while at Harvard. Glauber was able to identify a picture of Saville Sax and Theodore Hall but he could not identify a picture of Yakovlev [a reference to Anatoli Yatkovlev, the alias of a Soviet Consul in New York, but actually Anatoli Yatzkov, NKVD officer in charge of the NKVD's atomic spying effort].[5]

This first questioning of the future Nobelist took place because early investigation of Hall and Sax had disclosed that Glauber had shared a dorm room with them at Harvard the semester before Hall and Glauber began working at Los Alamos. The agents had no awareness in 1951 that Hall had mentioned to Glauber his providing Los Alamos secrets to Soviet intelligence agents, which the FBI only learned about from a Soviet spy cable translated a decade or more later. (Even the first cable identifying Hall and Sax by name wasn't fully decrypted until 1961.)[6]

The second occasion would come almost fifteen years later, on January 26, 1966. That's when FBI special agents James T. Sullivan and Michael J. McDonegh from the Boston bureau office visited Glauber at Lyman Laboratory on the Harvard campus, where Glauber had his lab.

14

KLAUS FUCHS

The Young German Communist Who Spied in Both the British and the U.S. Atomic Bomb Projects

Spying is waiting. Spying is worrying. Spying is being yourself but more so.

—John le Carré

The journey toward an atom bomb really started in 1917 in the United Kingdom, where New Zealand physicist Ernest Rutherford, working at Victoria University (later the University of Manchester), became the first scientist to split the atom. Another British physicist, James Chadwick, a student and later colleague of Rutherford's, discovered the neutron, a neutrally charged particle found in the nuclei of atoms, the number of which creates different isotopes of the same element and also makes possible a nuclear fission chain reaction in a few isotopes of hydrogen, uranium, and plutonium, making those latter two elements the heart of both atomic bombs and nuclear reactors.

The political rise of Adolf Hitler and his fascist National Socialist Party to political supremacy in Germany and the advent of German rearmament gave an urgent push toward developing an atomic bomb in Britain as well as the United States. In a March 1940 memorandum that echoed the one Leo Szilard had drawn up for Albert Einstein to sign and send to President Franklin D. Roosevelt nearly a year earlier, UK physicists Otto Frisch and Rudolf Peierls, both refugees from Germany working at an atomic research center at Birmingham University, explained in detail how a quantity of refined U-235, an isotope of uranium, could be used to create a superbomb.

They predicted that such a weapon would produce an explosion as hot as the sun that could destroy the entire center of a city. In the key two paragraphs of that lengthy document, they warned,

> We have no information that the same idea has also occurred to other scientists, but since all the theoretical data bearing on this problem are published, it is quite conceivable that Germany is, in fact, developing this weapon. Whether this is the case is difficult to find out, since the plant for the separation of isotopes need not be of such a size as to attract attention. Information that could be helpful in this respect would be data about the exploitation of the uranium mines under German control (mainly in Czechoslovakia) and about any recent German purchases of uranium abroad. It is likely that the plant would be controlled by Dr. K Clusius (Professor of physical Chemistry in Munich University), the inventor of the best method for separating isotopes, and therefore information as to his whereabouts and status might also give an important clue. At the same time, it is quite possible that nobody in Germany has yet realized that the separation of the uranium isotopes would make the construction of a super-bomb possible. Hence it is of extreme importance to keep this report secret since any rumor about the connection between uranium separation and a super-bomb may set German scientists thinking along the right lines.
>
> If one works on the assumption that Germany is, or will be, in the possession of this weapon, it must be realized that no shelters are available that would be effective and could be used on a large scale. The most effective reply would be a counter-threat with a similar bomb. Therefore it seems to us important to start production as soon as possible, even if it is not intended to use the bomb as a means of attack. Since the separation of the necessary amount of uranium is, in the most favourable circumstances, a matter of several months, it would obviously be too late to start production when such a bomb is known to be in the hands of Germany and the matter seems, therefore, very important.[1]

Instead of being sent directly to Prime Minister Neville Chamberlain, the way Einstein's letter had been addressed directly to President Roosevelt, the memo instead went up a chain from Professor Mark Oliphant, who had already organized an atomic research team at Birmingham University, through a series of government officials before finally reaching 10 Downing Street. By that May, Winston Churchill had replaced Chamberlain at that address as Britain's new prime minister. Churchill approved the establishment of a scientific team called the MAUD Committee (a code word using the name and home region of Nils Bohr's children's caretaker).[2] That committee, in secret, began identifying and hiring physicists to explore the feasibility of creating a uranium superbomb.

Among the scientists hired early by what eventually became code-named the Tube Alloys project was a young German refugee, a brilliant physicist named Klaus Fuchs.

Fuchs, born on December 29, 1911, in Rüsselsheim, Germany, was raised by modern, progressive-minded parents—his father a prominent Quaker minister with pacifist and socialist beliefs, and his mother, the daughter of a liberal German army officer. The third of four children (an older brother and sister and a younger sister, all leftists) Klaus too eventually adopted a far more left political perspective than his parents. Attracted early to socialist ideas, the young Fuchs began his study of physics as a student at the University of Leipzig, where his father held a position as a theology professor. Shortly after his father moved the family to Kiel, Fuchs moved on to the University of Kiel. While there, he joined first the German Social Democratic Party (SPD) and later that party's paramilitary arm, the Reichsbanner Schwartz-Rot-Gold, which was regularly engaging in street battles with both Nazi brownshirts and Communists. Before long, Fuchs broke with the SPD over his opposition to that party's support of Field Marshal Paul von Hindenberg for Reichspresident instead of the Communist candidate Ernst Johannes Fritz Thälmann. Because Fuchs openly campaigned for Thälmann and against von Hindenberg, he was expelled from the SPD following von Hindenberg's victory.

At that point he joined the Communist Party of Germany (KPD). That change of party membership set him on a course he could not have imagined at the time. Because he was a militantly active Communist (including engaging with comrades in street battles with local fascists), when the country's capital building, the Reichstag, burned down in what Hitler's Nazi Party declared to be a Communist Party act of political arson, Fuchs found his name on a list of people to be rounded up and arrested. Whatever its actual cause, the fire, coming as it did at a time of political turmoil, was a shocking incident that sent tremors through German politics (similar to what followed the 9/11 attacks on New York's World Trade Center and the Pentagon or the attempted insurrectionist invasion of the U.S. Capitol Building in Washington on January 6, 2021). Fuchs was advised to flee the country, warned that he could be executed if caught. He later told people he had narrowly managed to escape arrest and go underground only because when the Gestapo came to his family's home in Kiel one morning, he happened to already be on an early morning train headed for Berlin, where he had recently enrolled at that city's Kaiser Wilhelm Institute for Physics.

With the Gestapo hot on his trail, Fuchs left Germany quickly in July 1933, escaping to Paris and arriving on September 21 in England, probably, according his biographer Robert Chadwell Williams, "with the help of Willi Munzenberg's giant International Workers' Aid organization," one of a number of Communist front groups Munzenberg had set up.[3]

Once safely in the United Kingdom, Fuchs didn't make any great secret of his membership in the KPD. Indeed, at the time, many German Communists who escaped Hitler's Gestapo by crossing the English Channel remained openly active there. The small Communist Party of Great Britain was not feared by the British public in the way its sister party was in the United States and has never been illegal—even at the height of the Cold War—since its founding in 1920, with some of its members openly active within the ranks of the British Labor Party. And with the rise of fascism in Germany, at least from Hitler's rise in the early 1930s until the Molotov-Ribbentrop Pact of August 1939, Communism and Russia had some anti-fascist appeal among ordinary Britons.

That is not to say that the British secret police—who, like the FBI, have always been more attuned to the political concerns of the corporate elite of the country, regardless of the party in power—were happy about Fuchs's choice of a country in which to seek asylum. Indeed, Williams writes that MI5 had begun a file on Fuchs in 1933, even *before* he fled Germany and while he was still a student activist in Kiel.[4] That file was based on a report sent to them from a German agent in Kiel working for the British spy agency MI6, which detailed Fuchs's KPD activities.

It was Fuchs's Quaker connection that got him into the country's good graces. Upon his arrival in England, he had registered with the Quaker Bureau there, and a Quaker who became aware of that alerted a well-to-do Brit, Ronald Gunn, who had known and admired Klaus's father Emil. He agreed to sponsor Klaus. Gunn, knowing of Fuchs's physics training, which was already significant by 1934, persuaded Neville Mott, a twenty-nine-year-old physicist teaching at the University of Bristol, to take on Fuchs as a research assistant. Mott was already raising funds to build up Bristol's physics program and was pleased with the German expat physicists he had already hired. German physicist Hans Bethe, who would later became a major figure in theoretical physics, a Nobel laureate, and an important contributor to the Manhattan Project was at that time Mott's research assistant.

Williams writes that Bethe, who died in 2005, recalled the young doctoral student Fuchs at Bristol as "a brilliant, quiet and unassuming member of Mott's laboratory." Fuchs stayed there, living at the Gunns' home, until 1937, when he received his doctorate and moved to the University of Edinburgh, where he began working in the lab of German physicist Max Born on a one-year research position that was renewed into 1939.

In 1936, while he was at Bristol, the German Consul and later the German Embassy refused requests to renew Fuchs's passport because, as they notified the British, he was a "Marxist." But the British Home Office assured Mott, Fuch's adviser, that he needn't worry about Fuchs being deported to the clutches of the waiting Gestapo. They would, they assured him, simply honor his expired passport and have his residency visa extended each year as long as he remained in Mott's lab.[5]

After Fuchs successfully defended his thesis at Bristol, he was recommended for a one-year postdoctoral research position at Edinburgh University in the lab of another German Jewish exiled physicist, Max Born. He began working there in July 1937 and was invited by Born to stay on for a second year into 1939 based on the quality of his work. During that time, his visa continued to be renewed annually using his expired German passport.

At that point, though, things suddenly turned sharply more difficult for him. In early 1939, still living year-to-year in Britain on an expired and unrenewable German passport, he applied for naturalization as a British citizen. However, the war broke out in early September before his case could be considered. Meanwhile, in August, just weeks before the German invasion of Poland, Hitler and Stalin had signed a non-aggression pact. Under the terms of that pact, the Soviet Union participated in the attack on Poland, grabbing an agreed-upon part of eastern Poland when the country was invaded from the west by Germany. As a result, Britain, which had a mutual assistance treaty with Poland, found itself at war with Germany and, by extension, in a relation of distrust and enmity, if not war, with the Soviets. Accordingly, Fuchs, along with many other German Communists with refugee status in the United Kingdom, found himself suddenly reclassified as an enemy alien.

Stalin's non-aggression pact with Hitler was clearly an attempt by the Soviet leader to buy some time to prepare the ill-equipped and unprepared Red Army for what the Soviet leadership correctly assumed would be an eventual attack by virulently anti-Communist and militarily powerful Nazi Germany. But besides embarrassing and confusing Communists in the United States, Britain, and other countries around the world, who were similarly finding themselves viewed more negatively, the pact put Russia on the side of the enemy from the British government's perspective. Stalin's pact with Hitler was viewed as treachery by Britain. Forget "the enemy of my enemy is my friend"; almost immediately, Fuchs, because of his Communist record, became a suspected enemy, even as the German Gestapo were locking up and killing his friends and comrades there, even imprisoning his own father and brother.

At first, Fuchs's new enemy alien status meant he simply had to report regularly to local police in Scotland. Then, on May 12, 1940, he, along with many other enemy aliens, was sent to an internment camp on the Isle of Man, a barren island situated between northern Scotland and Northern Ireland designated as a self-governing Crown Dependency of Britain. There, refugee German Communists were thrown together with German Nazis. In July, they were all put on a freighter and shipped off to Canada, where Fuchs was interned at a Canadian army camp outside Quebec City and later moved to even worse quarters, with 720 men crammed into shabby railroad shacks that had only five faucets and six latrines in total.[6]

As the year progressed, the attitude in Britain toward its detained German Communist refugees softened, with even the anti-Communist Churchill admitting that "many enemy aliens had a great hatred of the Nazi regime and it was unjust to treat our friends as foes."[7] As Williams notes, "Churchill realized that anti-Nazi German refugees might well serve Britain's security interests rather than threaten them."[8]

Fuchs's internment nightmare ended on December 17, 1940—while Germany and the Soviet Union were technically still observing their non-aggression pact—when he arrived back in England and was released with the approval of the British Home Office (akin to the U.S. Department of Homeland Security, it handles immigration, passports, counterterrorism, etc.). This reprieve was likely due in part to intervention by well-connected friends and especially his mentor at Edinburgh, Max Born.[9] A month later, Fuchs was back at Edinburgh University, where, as was the case at a number of Britain's top university physics departments, there was a hive of activity, with people beginning to do research into an atomic bomb. This was in response to the work of the MAUD Committee, which was drawing up its plan of action: the MAUD Report, issued in March 1941.[10] In May 1941, Fuchs was invited by Rudolf Peierls to join the new Tube Alloys Project, which had been so named in hopes of avoiding any suspicion that there might be some kind of atomic bomb project underway.[11] Peierls even allowed Fuchs to help him with some calculations on the critical mass of U-235 for the MAUD Report while he was still waiting for a security clearance from MI5 after his return from exile and detention in Canada.

Unfortunately for that secrecy plan, the British intelligence agencies MI5 and MI6, the Home Office, and even the Tube Alloys Project itself were, from the outset, penetrated by Soviet spies. One of the most important of these, in terms of the information provided, was Fuchs himself, who began spying for the Soviet Union almost immediately upon beginning his work on the Tube Alloys Project.

Like Hall would three years later (although much more easily than Hall because of his KPD history and connections), Fuchs took the initiative and contacted Jurgen Kuczynski, the head of the German Communist Party in England, who connected him with Simon Davidovich Kremer, secretary to the military attaché in the Soviet Union's London embassy. Fuchs told Kremer he was willing to spy on the British atomic bomb project, declining an offer of compensation.

There's an odd irony in this connection. Because Peierls was the one who invited Fuchs onto the top-secret British Tube Alloys Project, some spy hunters later suspected that Peierls, another German refugee physicist, was a Soviet spy, though no evidence ever was developed to prove or even suggest that.[12] Nor did either Fuchs, after he was caught by MI5, or KGB files temporarily opened following the Soviet Union's collapse, suggest anything pointing to Peierls.

Peierls's invitation to Fuchs did, however, have a perverse impact in the Soviet Union. The Soviets would have known, through their agent Kremer, that the hiring of this known young Communist onto the British Tube Alloys atomic bomb project—which, as noted earlier, was being deliberately and carefully kept completely secret from the Soviet Union—did *not* originate from a Soviet mole inside that project. They knew, after all, that Peierls wasn't working for them. So it could well have appeared possible to Soviet intelligence that his surprising inclusion, as a known Communist, on the British bomb project and his later inclusion in 1943 as part of the British Mission of scientists invited to the United States to help with the Manhattan Project meant that Fuchs had become a double agent. In an era when paranoia was running rampant, could the information he was supplying them about British and U.S. bomb research and design actually be *disinformation* designed to lead Soviet scientists astray on their own bomb development efforts?

Such fears in Moscow intelligence circles, and even among Soviet bomb project scientists, would have been heightened in 1944. That's when, after leaving the New York City part of the Manhattan Project, where he had been working on gaseous diffusion of U-235, Fuchs was transferred to the main bomb development and construction operation at Los Alamos. There he would be focusing on the theoretical issues of the plutonium bomb. This was a good development, from the Soviet perspective, but there was an unexplained and worrisome gap of almost six months during which Fuchs simply vanished from any contact with his NKVD handlers, the most important of whom was Harry Gold, the Swiss-born immigrant chemist and Soviet spy based in Philadelphia who acted as a handler/courier for both Fuchs and later at least once for David Greenglass, brother of Ethel Rosenberg. That had to have alarmed the Soviets, who had no way of confirming that he ever reached New Mexico.

In fact, according to journalist Alexander Vassiliev, it is clear that Fuchs himself volunteered to spy for the Soviet Union. In the opened files from the Soviet military spy agency GRU to the KGB, Vassiliev found a note explaining it:

> F [Fuchs] was recruited for intelligence work in England in Aug. 1941 by our operative, former military attache secretary [Comrade] Kremer, on a lead from Jurgen (brother of our illegal [not having protected diplomatic position] station chief in England, "Sonya" [code name for Ursula Kuczynski]). The latter was living in London at the time and was one of the senior workers of the German Comparty [Communist Party] in England, Kremer knew him through official connections. F. agreed to work on an ideological basis and would not accept payment.[13]

Fuchs's contributions to the Soviet bomb project during his period in England were enormous, but they would be surpassed by what he provided after he went to Los Alamos in August 1944. All that was happening just as Ted Hall, unaware that Fuchs was a spy for the Soviets, was thinking he needed to become a Soviet asset himself because, to his knowledge, the Soviets were being left completely in the dark about the U.S. project.

TED'S SPYING BEGINS
IN EARNEST

*I thought it would be a good thing, something that was called
for. . . . It was just something that fell to my lot, so to speak. . . .
At a certain point I stopped dithering and decided to act.*

—Ted Hall, explaining his 1944 decision to
volunteer as an atomic spy for the USSR[1]

When Ted returned to New Mexico from his successful "family leave"
trip to New York and made his way back up the Hill to Los Alamos,
things were hopping, though Ted Hall was unaware of it. The U.S. Army
security unit responsible for maintaining the secrecy of the Manhattan
Project at Los Alamos was just in the midst of trying to build a case against
Joseph Rotblat, a Polish senior physicist and expat living in the United
Kingdom who, like Klaus Fuchs, had arrived in Los Alamos as part of the
British Mission team of scientists from the UK Tube Alloys atom bomb
project.[2] He was suspected by the Army Counter Intelligence Corps (CIC)
of being a spy, in part because as (by his own admission) "something of a
rebel," he had gone to visit the daughter of a friend who he had learned was
in Santa Fe for medical reasons. While he had informed James Chadwick,
the head of the British Mission to Los Alamos, of the visit in advance, he had
skirted informing security officials, explaining later that he didn't want the
young woman "pestered" by security people. That decision to bypass the
rules heightened concerns about an earlier issue: Rotblat was already under

suspicion and had been initially rejected for admission to the United States, even though he was an invited and trusted member of the British Mission to Los Alamos, because he had not yet become a British citizen. Rotblat had been allowed into the United States only through the intercession of Chadwick, who later also had to confirm that he'd been notified about the unauthorized visit.

Rotblat was the only scientist working on the Manhattan Project to take the step of walking away from it on moral grounds, a fact that surely led the U.S. counterintelligence operation to enhance their monitoring and investigation of him. (After first being barred from leaving the country and even the Los Alamos compound, he was eventually allowed to return to Britain with the stipulation that he not inform anyone at Los Alamos of the reason for his departure. As this came well after his decision to leave, that was closing the barn door well after the proverbial horse had left. The United States also confiscated a shipping crate containing his papers.)

Ironically, while Rotblat—who went on after the war to become a founding member of the Pugwash Conference on Science and World Affairs, an early nuclear disarmament organization—was *not* in fact a spy for the Soviets, Klaus Fuchs, another member of the British Mission, who arrived at Los Alamos in August on his own, *was* an atomic spy and had already been working for the Soviet Union as a spy for several years while in Britain. But unlike Rotblat, Fuchs had by that time received British citizenship and had signed a loyalty oath before he was hired onto the Tube Alloys Project. As a result, there was much bureaucratic security monitoring work going on concerning the non-British citizen Rotblat, while the British citizen Fuchs, who only a few years earlier had been locked up by British security officials as a Communist enemy alien in a Canadian prison camp, sailed right through U.S. immigration when he arrived in New York in 1943 with Chadwick's team. Indeed, the intense focus on Rotblat by army counterintelligence officers may well have, as he suspected, contributed to their missing both Fuchs and Hall.

There was also another Soviet spy besides Fuchs at Los Alamos, who Hall also knew nothing about: David Greenglass, the machinist brother-in-law of Julius Rosenberg and brother of his wife, Ethel. In an amazing stroke of good luck for the NKVD, Greenglass, a former Young Communist League member who had joined the U.S. Army in 1943, had been assigned by the Army, because of his skills as a machinist, to the Special Engineering District (SED) unit headed by General Leslie Groves that was posted to provide operating assistance as well as protection and security at the various sites of the Manhattan Project. And so, beginning in July 1944, he was inside the Manhattan Project, though not yet a spy.

Greenglass was initially assigned to the project's Oak Ridge, Tennessee, location, where the focus of work was to develop several different large-scale systems to refine the significant quantities of U-235 and plutonium for the two atomic bombs being developed at Los Alamos. But in August, after only a few weeks there, he was transferred to New Mexico. That November, in what would be a fateful decision for him, Julius Rosenberg convinced the NKVD in New York to take on Greenglass's wife Ruth. A Young Communist League member since 1942, she said she would be "honored" to be able to help serve the Soviet Union. Assigned the code name WASP, Ruth then agreed to travel to Santa Fe in November at the NKVD's urging to ask her husband to join her as an atomic spy for the Soviet Union. It was a proposal that Greenglass, a Communist Party member himself, assented to readily. Ruth also agreed to return to New Mexico in February to rent an apartment in Albuquerque and to find a local job there, taking advantage of a policy allowing spouses of project staff to live there, some one hundred miles away from Los Alamos, to facilitate family visits. She landed a job as a typist.

It's worth at least speculating about whether Ted Hall, had he known about those two other committed spies already working in the Manhattan Project, would have decided to become a spy himself. In an unaired portion of an interview taped in 1998 for a BBC program, Ted offered an explanation of his decision to engage in espionage:

> Top scientists were going to the White House saying not to keep the bomb a secret from the Russians, but they were not being listened to. A number of scientists [at Los Alamos] raised the question, what kind of terms are we going to be on with at the end of the war if we exclude the Russians? What will be the consequences if it *isn't* shared? In fact some extremely eminent scientists worried about this question and said that the knowledge should be shared. Niels Bohr was, I think, the most prominent and wasn't listened to.
>
> These two ideas coexisted within my head: One was "It's a lovely world, we've seen the light and we're getting through with the Second World War and things are going to be good." And then off in the corner there was this little question, "But suppose it isn't like that? What if there's a disintegration to disharmony between the nations after the Second World War and what if a capitalist system generates another Nazi Germany? Maybe the United States might turn into something like that?"[3]

A year earlier, Joan Hall recorded a statement from Ted explicitly stating his belief that that he had no choice but to become a spy, since nobody else seemed to be taking effective action to prevent the postwar monopoly on atomic bombs that the United States was hoping to obtain. Recalling that at the time he and Sax had volunteered to spy for the USSR, it was a powerful ally in the war against Nazi Germany, he said,

> I wasn't acting against the intentions of the US people. I felt myself to be part of a broad democratic front. These actions were undertaken at a time before the beginning of the Cold War, and I saw myself as part of the political front insisting on peaceful and harmonious relations between the peoples of these states [the US and USSR]. . . . I thought it would be a good thing, something that . . . the situation called for. It was just something that fell to my lot, so to speak. I thought it was not a particularly dangerous thing to do—there was some danger connected with it—but that it would close off one avenue of possible postwar development that should be sealed off, prevented. The bad guys might prevail . . . so I just saw what I was doing myself as helping to seal off a danger [a US atomic monopoly] which was there but probably wouldn't happen anyhow. I thought that by taking this step I could still further reduce the possibility of the bad guys taking over. . . . At a certain point I stopped dithering and decided to act.[4]

The thing is, Ted *didn't* and *couldn't have* known at that time about the other spies for the Soviet Union working practically alongside him, because the NKVD tried to be very meticulous about keeping their spies separated from each other, for example, using different handler/couriers for each spy in the project and never sharing spies' actual names or even code names with other spies. (We now know there were at least eight of them inside the U.S. bomb project:[5] four working for the NKVD, two for the NKGB, and one whose agency is inconclusive.)* This siloing of spies was done so that the discovery of one spy or courier would not lead to an unraveling of the entire NKVD atomic spying effort. Thus, even after the war ended and the Manhattan Project was closing down, when Fuchs was assigned to teach four lectures on hydrodynamics at Los Alamos to younger workers still at the Los Alamos site and actually had Hall *working* for him as an assistant—responsible for copying down, for all the registered students and auditors in

---

* Other Soviet spies, like John Cairncross and Kim Philby, reported on the U.S. atomic bomb project, but they were not scientists working *inside* the project. Others, like Hall's couriers Saville Sax, Lona Cohen, and Harry Gold, while never inside the project, played key roles in delivering information from the insider spies to locations like the *Rezidentura* in the Soviet Consulate in New York City, for delivery to Moscow.

the class, all the formulas Fuchs wrote in chalk on the blackboard—neither Hall nor Fuchs ever knew the other was a fellow Soviet spy.

So committed to the Communist cause was Fuchs that later, when he was released nine years into a fourteen-year sentence for revealing state secrets and returned to his home in East Germany (by then a Soviet satellite, the German Democratic Republic), he went on to help the USSR and China build their atomic and hydrogen bombs, remaining a Communist until his death in 1988. Indeed, as his biographer Robert Williams told me during an interview in 2022, "Fuchs was the only physicist to help develop the atomic and hydrogen bomb for four countries: Britain, the US, the USSR and China."

Meanwhile, Julius and Ethel Rosenberg went to their deaths in the electric chair in 1953 rather than confess or rat out other spies in the United States or friends in the Communist Party in a deal that would have granted them reprieve from execution.[6] Lona Cohen and her husband, Morris, after getting caught by MI5 in Britain and sentenced in 1961 to twenty and twenty-five years, respectively, for atomic spying, were released to the USSR in a prisoner swap in 1968, after which they worked in Moscow training new spies for the KGB. Neither of them ever outed another spy in an effort to obtain a lighter sentence. In other words, these were all dedicated Communists who had unhesitatingly done what they could to help the Soviet Union regardless of how many others were also doing so and regardless of the personal risks they were taking or punishment they were receiving.

In contrast to that powerful conviction, Ted, as late as October 1943, after his interview for the Manhattan Project at Los Alamos, wrote a letter to his brother in which he said, "I carried a few study projects through this summer, in the effort to develop a consistent philosophy. I will have to carry many more through before I can feel I have one that I can act on: my views are changing too rapidly. I cannot regard myself as a member of any political, philosophical, religious, etc., sect. I do not feel prepared to pick my team."[7] Certainly not the words of the "committed Communist" some atomic historians have claimed he was as a sixteen-to-eighteen-year-old at Harvard and as he headed off to help create the atom bomb. I could, of course, be wrong, but I doubt Ted would have felt the need to become a spy if he thought others were already doing it. He knew what he was doing was dangerous, but he accepted the risk to prevent a postwar U.S. monopoly on the bomb, thinking at the time that he was alone in taking that precarious but, in his view, necessary step.

Asked for her opinion in 2022, ninety-three-year-old Joan Hall told me, "I do not think Ted would have provided information about the bomb to the Soviets if he had known others were already doing it." She added, "Ted was not an ardent Communist, or supporter of Stalin. He was just trying to prevent the US from having an atomic monopoly because he didn't trust how the government would use that power."[8]

But because he believed it fell to him to help enable creation of a counter-power also possessing the bomb (one that could stand against any use by the United States of the weapon he was helping to create), he ended up making a contribution more impactful than what he could have possibly imagined at the time.

The key reason his espionage contribution was so critical had to do as much with his timing as it did with the actual information he provided about the bomb project.

The last word the NKVD had received from their spy Klaus Fuchs in the critical year of the U.S. atom bomb's development had been in late July 1944, when he was still working in a branch of the Manhattan Project located at Columbia University in New York and was living in that city. That last communication from him was to tell his courier Harry Gold that it appeared he might be getting transferred back to the Tube Alloys Project in the United Kingdom. In fact, however, he was ultimately sent, as he had hoped, to join the rest of the British Mission team in Los Alamos, arriving there on August 14, 1944. The problem was that Gold had missed an August 5 appointment with him, at which Gold would have learned about his surprise transfer to Los Alamos. The two could have arranged them for a connection once Fuchs arrived in New Mexico. Instead, because of that missed meeting, the two men had no way to contact each other, as Gold didn't know where Fuchs was. When Gold traveled to Fuchs's New York apartment a few days after the missed appointment, he was given the incorrect news from neighbors that Fuchs had "left for England."[9] During a later visit to Cambridge, Massachusetts, where Fuchs's sister Kristel Fuchs Heineman lived with her husband, Robert, Gold found them away on vacation. Visiting again in late October, Gold was told by Kristel that she hadn't heard from her brother but thought he had returned to England.

Returning to Cambridge once again in November, Gold had better luck. This time, Kristel said she had heard from Klaus, who had phoned her from Chicago, where he told her he had gone on "business from New Mexico." A relieved Gold reported back to the *Rezidentura* that Fuchs had told his sister he'd be traveling to her home with plans to stay there for two weeks over the

Christmas holiday. (Project workers at that time were allowed to have two weeks' family leave per year.) Fuchs also told his sister he planned to make a short stop in New York after his visit to her. Reporting on all this, Gold added that he had been "so happy with this news that I stayed for lunch."[10] He gave Kristel a note for her brother, saying that if he went to New York, he should "call the phone number of Hudson" with news of his arrival.

Christmas came and went, however, with no word from Fuchs. It wasn't until the second week of February 1945 that Fuchs finally arrived at his sister's home in Boston and made the prescribed call to "Hudson" (actually the NKVD New York *Rezidentura* agent Anatoli Yatskov, who immediately rushed to Philadelphia and alerted Gold of the reconnection). Eventually, on February 16, Gold returned to the Heineman home in Cambridge and found Fuchs there. In a long, relieved note to Yatskov, he wrote that Fuchs had explained apologetically that his planned leave for Christmas had not been granted and that February was his first opportunity to visit his sister. He informed Gold that the Los Alamos project had ballooned from the twenty-five hundred to three thousand people there when he first arrived in August to forty-five thousand, and that a factory to mass-produce atom bombs was being set up, adding, "They are expected to go into full-scale production in three months—but K [Klaus Fuchs] was hesitant about this date and said he would not like to be held to it."[11] A plan was proposed for Fuchs to meet Gold in June, when he said he would have details of the bomb that was being prepared for a test explosion.

Fuchs's long and worrying absence had understandably left the Soviet spy organization and its congenitally paranoid chief, Lavrentiy Beria, wondering if perhaps their most important spy inside the U.S. and British atomic bomb projects had actually been "turned" to become a double agent. The information about the complex implosion system, so baroque in its construction—with its multiple tampers being blasted into a small sphere of sub-critical plutonium, all of which had to detonate and strike the plutonium sphere within nanoseconds of each other and at similar pressure to produce a massive explosion—seemed an over-the-top engineering nightmare. Could it, they wondered, all have been disinformation designed to send Soviet scientists off into a costly and time-wasting dead end?

As an indication of how concerned about this Beria was, Joseph Albright and Marcia Kunstel write in *Bombshell* that the dreaded Soviet spymaster Beria, on receiving the latest new information on the U.S. bomb project from Leonid Kvasnikov, head of the New York *Rezidentura*'s scientific and technical unit, warned, "If this is disinformation, I'll send you off to the basement," a reference to the location in the Lubyanka headquarters where Beria sent people to be summarily executed. On another occasion, when the head of the overseas directorate of the NKGB proposed giving a decoration to Kvasnikov for his work on atomic bomb intelligence, Beria scolded him, saying it remained to be seen whether Kvasnikov deserved a reward or a punishment.[12]

Fuchs's suspiciously long disappearance and the inability of the Soviet spy network—either the NKVD or the military NKGB—to locate him, or even to communicate with each other, had a kind of "Keystone Kops" aspect to it. Much like Ted Hall, Fuchs had originally volunteered on his own initiative, and because of his German CP membership and connections, he was much more easily accepted as a spy inside the British Tube Alloys Project virtually from its start by the GRU—the Soviet military intelligence operation in the United Kingdom—in 1941, before the U.S. Manhattan Project had even begun. He continued with that arrangement until late 1943, when he became part of the high-powered British scientific mission that transferred to the United States to integrate their work with the Manhattan Project, which was vastly larger and vastly better funded.

While most of the mission, led by the British Nobel physics laureate James Chadwick, went straight to Los Alamos, Fuchs was initially assigned to the uranium gaseous diffusion research project operating at Columbia University in Manhattan. He remained there (in good contact with Soviet intelligence located at the Soviet Consulate in New York City) until August, when he was transferred by the British Mission to the Theoretical Division at Los Alamos and put to work on the implosion system for the plutonium bomb. At that point, because of the missed meeting with Gold, with phones there limited and monitored and mail opened and inspected, there was no word from him and no way to contact him. By October, the NKVD was getting frantic. Without Fuchs—and without knowing if Fuchs was even there—the Soviets had *nobody* inside the American bomb project at Los Alamos.

It was in the midst of that panic that an acne-plagued teenage atomic scientist, supposedly straight from New Mexico, walked in unannounced, claiming to be a Manhattan Project physicist wanting to become a volunteer spy. Ted's detailed sketches and accompanying explanation of the implosion-based bomb design, as well as information about the large number of eminent physicists at the location, gave Beria, who knew that neither Hall nor Fuchs knew the other was also a Soviet spy, more confidence in Fuchs and made Hall's claim to be a real physicist with real bomb information seem credible, since they were saying much the same kind of things.* The information from Hall also gave Igor Kurchatov, the young head of the Soviet bomb program, more details about the implosion process as well as the confidence he needed to go directly to Stalin—not a person one would want to make mistakes with. Kurchatov told the Soviet leader that the bomb project needed to set aside the uranium bomb, for which they could not hope to make sufficient U-235 in that time, and to focus on creating a plutonium bomb, employing all available speed, resources, and scientific talent. Stalin responded favorably to that approach, telling Kurchatov to move ahead with his suggestion of deferring efforts to create a uranium bomb, given the difficulty of quickly obtaining sufficient U-235. He assured Kurchatov that whatever he needed to produce a plutonium-based bomb, the project would receive. As a result, the Soviets went on to build their first bomb in record time—four years after the U.S. bomb rather than the eight to ten years Western scientists predicted it would take—and at vastly less cost than it took the United States to make it, because they didn't have to design it too.

A young Russian pianist of my acquaintance, now living in the United States, offered a good explanation for why the United States failed to discover anything about the Soviet bomb project and ended up caught completely unawares when they demonstrated the results of it on August 29, 1949. In a conversation we had back in 2019 when she learned I was planning to write this book, she recounted to me how her father had told her that her grandfather had been attracted by a Soviet government call for people to accept offers of free land to work in the impoverished and underpopulated region in Urals on the edge of Siberia. It was a call that produced a flood of tens of thousands, bringing with them tractors and building equipment by train, with the stated goal of making that remote region into a vibrant, modern industrial and agricultural area. As it turned out, her father explained to her, the call for farmers and workers, while genuine, was at the same time a perfect cover to allow the Soviet government to also, without arousing U.S. suspicion, ship all the massive equipment and masses of scientists, engineers, and workers needed to build up their own version of the Manhattan Project, with a nuclear research center, facilities to refine U-235, a bomb testing site, and the like, all without notice. That was, of course, much easier to do in those days, when the United States didn't have the benefit of satellite

---

* And Hall wasn't just a "junior" spy. Assigned a white badge, he had full access to all parts of Los Alamos and was a team leader on the implosion system.

imaging or even U-2 spy plane overflights. The subterfuge worked, developing the region around the atomic bomb project and creating an atomic bomb at the same time.

One good indication of the importance of Ted's espionage work after he returned to Los Alamos from his meetings with NKVD contacts comes from the KGB files, read through for the first time during the brief glasnost years in the early 1990s by KGB veteran Alexander Vassiliev. One such note, from the New York *Rezidentura* to Moscow headquarters on February 1, 1945, listing its American sources and agents, included the names "MLAD" and "STAR" (Hall and Sax). It notes that MLAD had only been "with us since Oct. '44," and that he "has not been tested at work yet nor has he been studied." But in a February 28 memo to Beria, then a politburo member and overall head of Soviet intelligence and secret police, Vsevolod Merkulov, who headed the NKGB in Moscow from 1943–1946, "spoke about Hall" and "included specific details about Los Alamos." He also "discussed such matters as the plutonium implosion concept." That information, at that point, according to the authors of *Spies: The Rise and Fall of the KGB in America*, "likely came from Hall," who was right at the heart of the plutonium bomb development process, because at that point the NKVD still hadn't heard from Fuchs since July 1944.[13]

But Ted had a lot more important information to pass on, and now that Soviet intelligence had the confidence that two key atomic spies, both working on the plutonium bomb and both unaware that the other was also a spy for the same agency, were saying much the same thing, their information was taken very seriously indeed.

The next trove of information from Hall came via Sax, who was encouraged to go to New Mexico to meet with him. The meeting was arranged using a code the two friends had worked out on their own while still in New York. Like the Harvard intellectuals they both were, they used two similar editions of Walt Whitman's *Leaves of Grass*, and the numbers the poet had assigned to his verses, to convey rendezvous information. It was a code book that few FBI agents or even SIS code breakers, none likely aficionados of Whitman's poetry, would have dreamt of. To look the part, Sax traveled from Boston to Albuquerque and back by bus, using as justification for the journey the fabricated story that he was interested in applying to grad school at the University of New Mexico to study anthropology. Sax took notes from his conversation with Hall, which he wrote onto a newspaper using milk as ink, since it would show up when heated but would otherwise remain invisible. The information provided covered details of what different divisions of the project at Los Alamos were working on, including details about several methods of uranium separation. At that meeting, Sax also heard from Hall about his botched attempt to recruit his friend Roy Glauber, though he didn't mention that to his contact in the *Rezidentura* until June.

Meanwhile, in part likely because of concerns about Sax's lack of professionalism, in part because he told them he was planning to return to Harvard as a student, and also because, with several spies now operating at Los Alamos and time running short, they wanted a professional courier, the NKVD decided to replace Sax as Hall's courier. For this important assignment, Lona Cohen, an experienced American spy and courier, was called back to work as a spy courier after being elected by fellow workers to be union shop steward at the Aircraft Screw Products company on Long Island where she was working. The thinking was that as a young and attractive woman, she would attract less attention than either Gold or Sax when meeting with the young Hall at a rendezvous in Albuquerque.

16

THE SUCCESSFUL TRINITY
TEST OF THE "GADGET"

Now we're all sons of bitches.

—Kenneth Bainbridge, after the Trinity Test blast

On the warm but overcast evening of July 16, 1945, most of the top scientists of the Manhattan Project had gathered some 250 miles south of Los Alamos in the appropriately named Journado del Muerto (Journey of Death) Desert on the U.S. Army's Alamogordo Bombing and Gunnery Range. Waiting in several concrete bunkers arrayed about six miles from ground zero around a hundred-foot-tall steel tower that held a huge hanging 5.4-ton steel ball covered in a web of thick electrical cables, they were preparing to witness the next morning's test of their creation—the product of almost three years of crash development: the "Gadget."

Their hope was that the complex implosion system they had devised and constructed, using twenty perfectly timed explosive charges, would compress a tiny 3.2-inch diameter sub-critical-mass ball of plutonium-gallium alloy weighing just 6.19 kg into an even tinier and denser but critical mass. That, it was hoped, would produce by far the biggest man-made explosion in history—an atomic bomb.

While they waited tensely for the test, these senior scientists were placing bets on what the size of the explosion would be. Their estimates ranged from physicist Norman Foster Ramsey's prediction of complete failure and scientific director Robert Oppenheimer's cautious and pessimistic bet of a 0.3

kiloton "fizzle" to Edward Teller's high-end bet of 44 kilotons. That's not counting those few who thought it possible—though unlikely—that the blast could set off a chain reaction in the nitrogen that is the major component of the earth's atmosphere, destroying the state of New Mexico or perhaps all life on earth—a catastrophic prospect that physicist Enrico Fermi darkly tried to get the assembled scientists to also wager on the likelihood of.*

Ted Hall, who had played a seemingly small but critically significant role in making certain the plutonium bomb would work, said he was "pretty sure" that what had been dubbed by Oppenheimer the "Trinity Test" would be successful. But instead of watching it from a relatively nearby bunker, he was posted miles away, waiting with several other GIs sent from the Special Engineering District military unit based at Los Alamos by General Leslie Groves to wait beside one of a number of strategically placed Army trucks. As a U.S. Army draftee, Hall was part of the SED and had been assigned to one of a number of rescue teams tasked with racing out to evacuate to safety some of the area's local, mostly indigenous, natives should the winds change without warning and blow radioactive fallout over occupied areas.

In an interview clip from 1998, Hall laughingly recalled that while hanging out in the dark and waiting for a passing storm to clear away before the detonation, he and other SED soldiers with him entertained themselves by debating "whether marriage as an institution would survive or soon fade away."[1]

After an unanticipated weather-related delay of almost one and a half hours, the bomb was detonated just before sunrise, at 5:29 a.m. Silently, a blinding initial flash of light many times brighter than the noonday sun lit up the entire basin of Alamogordo and its surrounding mountains before quickly fading as a huge shock wave and deafening roaring sound swept outward at the speed of sound toward the observers, followed by a searing wind. A towering mushroom cloud of boiling dust and radioactive fallout also quickly billowed up to thirty-eight thousand feet above ground zero. The shockwave of what was later determined to have been a blast measuring 24.2 kilotons (the equivalent of a staggering 24,200 tons of dynamite) was reportedly felt as far as 160 miles away and broke windows as far away as 120 miles in every direction.[2]

The test was, that is to say, a resounding success. William Lawrence, a *New York Times* reporter transferred temporarily in 1945 to the Manhattan

---

* Hans Behte, head of the Theoretical Division at Los Alamos, did calculations ahead of the test that proved that there was no possibility of such a disaster.

Project at the request of General Groves, was on hand for the test. He recalled that after the explosion, "A loud cry filled the air. The little groups that hitherto had stood rooted to the earth like desert plants broke into dance, the rhythm of primitive man dancing at one of his fire festivals at the coming of Spring."[3]

Oppenheimer, scientific head of the Manhattan Project and the man often referred to as the "father of the atomic bomb," recalled more soberly thinking, rather romantically, of a line from the Hindu *Bhagavad Gita* after the successful detonation of the Gadget: "If the radiance of a thousand suns were to burst at once into the sky, that would be like the splendor of the mighty one." Later, though, he was heard by fellow scientists to utter another, more ominous line from that same Hindu scripture, which has, for better or worse, become his legacy: "Now I am become Death, the destroyer of worlds."[4]

After that initial euphoria and melodrama, Kenneth Bainbridge, director of the Trinity Test, reportedly turned to Oppenheimer and said, bluntly and more appropriately, "Now we're all sons of bitches."[5]

Most of those who witnessed the test returned to Los Alamos as heroes, where they joined in parties and celebrations featuring plenty of cheering, dancing, and drinking. In a recording made a year before his death,[6] however, Ted said that he didn't feel at all like celebrating that day. Instead, he repaired to his barracks, where he turned on his portable record player and listened to 78 rpm recordings of his favorite Mahler and Beethoven music, darkly pondering the grim future that his and the other scientists' work had set in motion as well as the importance of the latest information about the U.S. bomb project that he would be delivering to a NKVD spy courier in a matter of days.

Meanwhile, although Germany had surrendered unconditionally on May 7 without building an atom bomb after all, the war against Japan in the Pacific and in China and Southeast Asia was still raging. President Harry Truman and his key advisers were anxious to put the bomb to use before Japan spoiled things by surrendering, which the country's emissaries were reportedly desperately attempting to do. Gone was the original premise for the creation of the Manhattan Project: building the bomb as a counter to hopefully prevent any use of a feared German atomic bomb. Gone, too, was the idea that the U.S. bomb would be a more or less defensive weapon. Japan had no atom bomb and no program to develop one beyond one physicist with no financing who was looking into the possibility. Truman's intention was to use his new atomic bombs on Japan, killing largely civilians, ostensibly to terrorize the government into surrender and avoid having to fight a land battle on Japan's home territory—but more importantly, as General Groves let on during a dinner with senior scientists, as a warning to Joseph Stalin and the Soviet Union that there was a new world order and the United States would be in charge of it.

The idea of using the bomb on Japan, a non-nuclear nation, had been opposed by many of the scientists who had worked on its development at Los Alamos. Leo Szilard, the same physicist who had initially urged his former teacher Albert Einstein to convince President Franklin D. Roosevelt that he should establish a project to develop the atomic bomb, wrote an impassioned and well-reasoned appeal to Truman on July 17, a day after the Trinity Test, urging him *not* to use it on Japan. Seventy Los Alamos scientists readily signed onto it as it was circulated.

Szilard wrote,

A PETITION TO THE PRESIDENT OF THE UNITED STATES

July 17, 1945

Discoveries of which the people of the United States are not aware may affect the welfare of this nation in the near future. The liberation of the atomic power which has been achieved places atomic bombs in the hands of the Army. It places in your hands, as Commander-in-Chief, the fateful decision whether or not to sanction the use of such bombs in the present phase of the war against Japan.

We, the undersigned scientists, have been working in the field of atomic power. Until recently we have had to fear that the United States might be attacked by atomic bombs during this war and that her only defense might lie in a counterattack by the same means. Today, with the defeat of Germany, this danger is averted and we feel impelled to say what follows:

The war has to be brought speedily to a successful conclusion and attacks by atomic bombs may very well be an effective method of warfare. We feel, however, that such attacks on Japan could not be justified, at least not until the terms which will be imposed after the war on Japan were made public in detail and Japan were given an opportunity to surrender.

If such public announcement gave assurance to the Japanese that they could look forward to a life devoted to peaceful pursuit in their homeland and if Japan still refused to surrender, our nation might then, in certain circumstances, find itself forced to resort to the use of atomic bombs. Such a step, however, ought not to be made at any time without seriously considering the moral responsibilities which are involved.

The development of atomic power will provide the nations with new means of destruction. The atomic bombs at our disposal represent only the first step in this direction, and there is almost no limit to the destructive power which will become available in the course of their future development. Thus a nation which sets the precedent of using these newly liberated forces of nature for purposes of destruction may have to bear the responsibility of opening the door to an era of devastation on an unimaginable scale.

If after the war a situation is allowed to develop in the world which permits rival powers to be in uncontrolled possession of these new means of destruction, the cities of the United States as well as the cities of other nations will be in continuous danger of sudden annihilation. All the resources of the United States, moral and material, may have to be mobilized to prevent the advent of such a world situation. Its prevention is at present the solemn responsibility of the United States—singled out by virtue of her lead in the field of atomic power.

The added material strength which this lead gives to the United States brings with it the obligation of restraint and if we were to violate this obligation our moral position would be weakened in the eyes of the world and in our own eyes. It would then be more difficult for us to live up to our responsibility of bringing the unloosened forces of destruction under control.

In view of the foregoing, we, the undersigned, respectfully petition: first, that you exercise your power as Commander-in-Chief, to rule that the United States shall not resort to the use of atomic bombs in this war unless the terms which will be imposed upon Japan have been made public in detail and Japan knowing these terms has refused to surrender; second, that in such an event the question whether or not to use atomic bombs be decided by you in the light of the consideration presented in this petition as well as all the other moral responsibilities which are involved.[7]

Szilard's petition, which included many prominent project scientists, was given to General Groves, who was asked to deliver it to the president. The letter was not likely to change Truman's mind about using the bomb on Japan, but Groves, who wanted badly for the bomb to be used, made sure of that by, without informing the author and signers, accepting it with no intention of delivering it, and he never did.[8]

The die had already been cast. President Truman wanted the bombs to be used. Indeed, on the day the letter was composed and circulated for signatures, just one day after the successful Trinity Test, the already completed and ready-to-use "Little Boy" uranium bomb was being loaded from a dock in San Francisco onto a U.S. Navy vessel bound for Tinian Island in the Pacific, the takeoff point for the B-29 bomber *Enola Gay* on its already scheduled bombing run to the doomed city of Hiroshima three weeks later. The parts for the heavier "Fat Man" plutonium bomb (basically the "Gadget" with its cables encased in a sleek, blimp-shaped steel shell with fins at one end), were later flown out on several planes to be assembled on Tinian, along with parts for a second plutonium bomb.

The age of nuclear war was about to begin with a flash.

LONA COHEN REPLACES SAVILLE SAX AS COURIER

Both these reports [from spies Fuchs and Hall] contained a 33-page design of the bomb [that] . . . became the basis for our own program of work on the atomic project over the next three or four years.

—Pavel Sudoplatov

By July 1945, a variety of uranium enrichment systems—gaseous diffusion, electromagnetic separation, liquid thermal diffusion, and centrifugation—run by the Naval Weapons Lab and various other sites that were part of the Manhattan Project had collectively produced 50 kilograms of enriched uranium at a concentration of 89 percent fissile U-235. It was shipped off to the bomb-making facility at Los Alamos along with some uranium that was enriched to only 50 percent U-235. When combined, the resulting 64 kilograms of uranium in the nearly five-ton bomb was 85 percent U-235, enough to go critical in the gun-type design of what became named "Little Boy," the bomb that would be dropped by the *Enola Gay* on Hiroshima on August 6. Given the simplicity of its design—a hollow cylinder of sub-critical U-235 propelled by a nitrocellulose chemical blast into a stationary sub-critical solid cylinder located at the other end of the "barrel" to produce a critical chain reaction fission blast—it was deemed unnecessary to test that bomb; in fact, project scientists and Pentagon strategists considered it a better bet for the untested uranium bomb to explode as designed than the more complex plutonium bomb, which is why the 5.4-ton "Fat Man" plutonium bomb was the second to be used.

This is also the reason the plutonium design was the first nuclear weapon exploded in history in the Trinity Test: It was the one that required prior successful testing to know it could even work if used as an act of war.

There is some question about who delivered the message from Ted Hall that the United States was about to test the atomic bomb known in NKVD code as ENORMOZ. In *Bombshell*, Joseph Albright and Marcia Kunstel, noting that reactivated courier and master spy Lona Cohen (code name LESLIE) recalled making two trips in 1945 to connect with Hall, argue convincingly that it was her on those trips, both eventful and significant and not the kind of thing one would forget. On her first trip, she claimed, she did not actually meet Ted Hall, but she nonetheless returned to New York with a packet of papers from him. On the second, she clearly returned to New Mexico in August, after the two bombs had been dropped on Japan, and met him in person for the handoff.

Alexander Vassiliev, the ex-KGB employee who obtained access to opened KGB atomic files in the post-Soviet glasnost era, claims that based upon the files he was able to examine, it was Sax who made a trip out to New Mexico in April or May and brought back information from Hall, stating, according to a report to Moscow headquarters filed two weeks later by Leonid Kvasnikov (ANTON), that there was work underway near Carlsbad, New Mexico, to prepare "the place for the practical testing of the ENORMOZ bomb." That same report by Kvasnikov said the source, MLAD, had listed most of the sites around the United States and Canada where the U.S. bomb project was being conducted.

That cable from Kvasnikov reads:

From: NEW YORK
To: MOSCOW
No: 79   26th May, 1945

TO: VIKTOR
Reference your No. 3367.
MLAD's material contains:

(a) A list of places where work on ENORMOZ is being carried out:

1. KHEMFORD [Hanford], State of Washington, production of 49 [Plutonium]

2. State of NEW JERSEY, production of 25 [U-235] by the diffusion method, Director Urey [UREJ]

3. BERKELEY, State of CALIFORNIA, production of 25 by the electron-magnetic method Director LOURENS [LAWRENCE]

4. "Novossroj," administrative center for ENORMOZ, also production of 25 by the spectrographic method. Director COMPTON

5. CHICAGO, ARGONNE [ARGONSKIJ] Laboratories—nuclear research. At present work there has almost ceased. Director Compton.

6. "THE ZAPOVEDNIK" [RESERVATION or Los Alamos], the main practical research work on ENORMOZ. Director "VEKSEL."

7. Camp [two words or letters not recovered] base in the area of CARLS-BAD, State of NEW MEXICO, the place for the practical testing of the ENORMOZ bomb.

8. MONTREAL, CANADA—theoretical research.

(b) A brief description of the four methods of production of 23spectro-graphic5—the diffusion, thermal diffusion, electromagnetic and spectro-graphic methods.

The material has not been fully worked over. We shall let you know about the contents of the next letter.

ANTON [Kvasnikov][1]

Whether that first major trove of information from Los Alamos, including detailed information about the construction of the plutonium bomb, was picked up in New Mexico and delivered to New York by Sax or Cohen is not so important here. What matters is that it clearly originated from MLAD (Hall). And whether Cohen's trip to meet Hall in Albuquerque around the time between the dropping of the two bombs on Hiroshima and Nagasaki and the Japanese surrender in mid-August was her first or second visit to New Mexico, that trip to Albuquerque was the one where Hall delivered his most important and detailed information about the design of the U.S. plutonium bomb.

Once Manhattan Project scientists had successfully tested the bomb on July 16, 1945, the Soviets urgently wanted all the information they possibly could get to hasten a crash program to obtain their own bomb. Albright and Kunstel say that Cohen was accordingly sent back to Santa Fe to obtain what she could from Hall, while Harry Gold, Klaus Fuchs's courier, was dispatched to get what he could from both David Greenglass and Fuchs.

Sending Gold to see *two* spies at Los Alamos, not to mention sending Lona Cohen, who had knowledge of other spies in the United States, to meet with Hall, were both serious breaches of NKVD rules about not having couriers working with more than one spy. It was a shortcut in a crisis that ended up ensnaring Greenglass and the Rosenbergs when, four years later in late 1949, Fuchs's name turned up in an early decrypted Soviet spy cable and, after being informed of that by the FBI, MI5 picked him up and questioned him intensely. To protect his sister Kristel from arrest in the United States, Fuchs ultimately agreed to confess to his spying and identified a photo of his courier, Harry Gold, which in turn led to the discovery of Greenglass at Los Alamos, and thence to Ethel and Julius Rosenberg (although the FBI claims it had enough information from its own detective work based upon Venona decrypts to figure out who Fuchs's courier was without that late-in-the-game identity confirmation from Fuchs).

To avoid suspicion on her August run, Cohen, a true master of spy craft, took lodgings not in Santa Fe or Albuquerque, but in a workingman's boarding house in a small New Mexico spa town called Las Vegas, located one station stop before Santa Fe. The plan was to meet Hall on the University of New Mexico campus in Albuquerque—a three-hour, 120-mile bus ride away—a few days later. When he failed to show up at the scheduled meeting, she decided to try again a week later. After a third failed effort, according to an official KGB historian, instead of giving up to avoid raising suspicions by repeated visits to Albuquerque, she decided to give it one more try before returning to New York empty-handed. That risky fourth appearance at the same location was the charm, and she spotted him, a bit late but carrying a shopping bag with a fish tail hanging out of it—the prearranged signal.

There are multiple versions of how Cohen received what Hall had brought for her and whether it was seven pages or thirty-three pages long, but these versions—one from Lona herself; one from her handler, Yatskov; one from her husband, Morris; and one from the head of the Soviet Union's secretive Administration of Special Plans—all agree with what Hall told Albright and Kunstel: that he and an initially annoyed Cohen strolled around the campus posing as lovers and talking for about half an hour while, warming up to Hall, she reportedly teased him about attractive young coeds as they passed, asking a red-faced Ted if he'd like to "spend time with them." More seriously, he said she warned him that things could get "pretty hot" and that he should know that the Soviet intelligence network "didn't forget and would get him out of harm's way" if need be.[2] Eventually Hall passed her a tightly wrapped sheaf of papers containing detailed schematic plans for the plutonium bomb and its implosion system design as well as an explanation of the Ra-La experiments that had led to the design including of the plutonium core called the "pit" and the explosive used to produce the symmetrical explosion required to produce the implosion around it.

While the stories vary from there, all accounts of Cohen's departure from Albuquerque refer to a Kleenex box she had brought along to support her alibi that she was visiting New Mexico for relief from "chronic bronchitis." On arriving at the station, she found it crawling with security agents scrutinizing everyone before allowing them to board the train. The bombings of Hiroshima and Nagasaki having just happened, concern about security at Los Alamos was soaring. Thinking fast, she put the Kleenex box to good use. I will give two versions here of what would become a major part of KGB lore.

The first version is from General Pavel Sudoplatov, who likely got the nail-biting story of Cohen's escape from Anatoli Yatskov or his boss in the United States, Alexander Feklisov, or perhaps from Cohen herself, but who also, having been jailed for a number of years following the death of Stalin, wrote his version in a self-justifying book, meaning he could have embellished "his" success. As he told it,

> On one of her trips [to New Mexico], August 1945, she traveled to Albuquerque shortly after the first atomic bomb was dropped on Hiroshima. She anxiously awaited a contact [Hall/MLAD], who gave her a "thick wad" of tightly written pages that were "priceless" to Moscow Center [NKVD headquarters].
>
> As she left the security-infested town, she demonstrated her tradecraft. Carrying a suitcase, a purse, and a box of Kleenex tissues, she arrived at the railroad station just as the train was supposed to leave. She dropped her suitcase and started rummaging nervously through her purse, searching for her ticket. She handed the Kleenex box to the conductor to hold while she looked for and found her ticket. Delighted, Lona boarded the train leaving the box of tissues with the conductor. "I felt it in my skin, that the conductor would return the box of Kleenex, and indeed later he handed it to me." When Yatskov [Lona's handler, codenamed JOHNNY from the New York Consulate and *Rezidentura*] met her in New York City, Lona told him, "You know, Johnny, everything was all right except for one thing. The police held those materials in their hands."
>
> The Kleenex box contained a detailed description and drawing of the world's first atomic bomb.[3]

Other versions more credibly say that the people checking her bags— to one of whom she handed the tissue box containing the plans for the plutonium bomb—were security officers, not train conductors. Here is Yatskov's version, as published in *Bombshell*, attributed by the authors to an article by Yatskov published in an "internal KGB newspaper."

Adopting the role of a disorganized, flustered young woman, Yatskov related, she acted as if she'd lost her ticket:

> As luck would have it [Lona's] ill-fated ticket disappeared somewhere. Others also arrive at the station well ahead of time. But she . . . does not belong to the category of "other" people. . . . Nerves get rattled by petty things. . . . Her purse she deliberately hung on her arm, put a little suitcase on the ground, and only a box remained in her hands and deliberately hindered her search. . . . The woman was obviously marking time, which was pressing in on her. A lot of stuff—a suitcase, a big bag, and a big box with Kleenex paper tissues. She could not open the zipper on the bag. It got stuck. They tried to help her, like servants. Nervously she tore at the zipper and it jammed. And the time was running.
>
> Without hesitation, self-confident HELEN [her code name] handed the box with the tissues to one of the checkers, found the ill-fated ticket, at the same time answered the questions they posed, and was directed into the car with the ticket, the handbag and little suitcase, as if she'd forgotten her box. That's how she explained it later: "I felt in my bones that the gentleman himself must remind me about this box."

As Albright and Kunstel complete the tale, "That is exactly what the gentleman did, recounted Yatskov. The guard on the platform hailed Lona and handed up to her the Kleenex box in which she had hidden the documents." Relating the tale to Yatskov upon her safe arrival with Hall's documents, she said it "had been in the hands of the police."[4]

And so Lona Cohen was safely away from New Mexico with the plans that would a few months later seal the deal for Stalin's go-ahead of Kurchatov's proposal for the Soviet atomic bomb project's all-out push to create its own plutonium bomb.

Explaining the tremendous significance of Ted Hall's information delivered by Lona Cohen, Sudoplatov wrote in his memoir that Cohen's Kleenex box had contained a "33-page design of the [plutonium] bomb that was similar to what had been provided by Fuchs." This matching information ultimately formed the major part of a summary Sudoplatov's Department S forwarded to Beria and Stalin in September 1945. He added that the information "became the basis for our own program of work on the atomic project over the next three or four years."[5]

That Albuquerque rendezvous with Hall was the last time Cohen served as a courier to Los Alamos, but it was not the last time she was sent to meet Hall, as will be explained later.

Eventually, after the MI5/Special Branch arrest of Fuchs and the subsequent arrest of the Rosenbergs, Moscow decided things were getting too hot for the Cohens to remain in the United States. They left their apartment at 178 East 71st Street on Manhattan's East Side in a hurry at night in mid-1950, reportedly on orders from an NKVD officer, even leaving the lights on so that any FBI agents possibly surveilling their apartment wouldn't know they were splitting. They made their way south, crossing the poorly monitored border into Mexico using fake travel documents produced by the NKVD, and ultimately got to safety in Moscow. Later, from a base in Poland, they conducted some missions abroad for the KGB, but always outside the United States, using fake identities and passports. While in Moscow, Lona received additional spy training as a radio operator and cipher clerk. Later, apparently not ready to give up their spy work on behalf of the Soviet Union, the two dedicated American Communists adopted the identities of Helen and Peter Kroger, purportedly two immigrants from Canada via New Zealand, on which country's passports they moved to the town of Ruislip in West London, England. There, Morris bought an antiquarian bookstore as cover, from which they ran the KGB operation in London. The town was located conveniently near Britain's main Royal Air Force base.

Arrested as spies by MI5 in 1961 after being exposed by a Polish intelligence officer who was a double agent, they were both convicted of espionage and violating the country's Official Secrets Act, with Lona receiving a sentence of twenty years in prison and Morris getting a stiffer twenty-five-year sentence. Amazingly, they were convicted by a jury under their false identities as the Krogers. Only after that, but before they were sentenced as spies, did the court and prosecutor learn that they were the Cohens, who had been atomic spies in the United States. Judicial embarrassment may explain, at least in part, the harshness of their sentences, which were considerably worse than the fourteen years given to Fuchs, though it also may have had to do with their steadfast unwillingness to divulge to MI5 or MI6 any information about any of the spies they ran or served as couriers for during their several decades as Soviet agents.[6]

At least as far as Ted Hall was concerned, his secret had stayed safe with them.

The Cohens didn't actually serve out those long prison terms, as they were pardoned by Queen Elizabeth II and traded in 1969 to the Soviets in

SPY FOR NO COUNTRY

exchange for two British spies arrested and held in the USSR. Returned to Moscow, they became Soviet citizens, working as trainers of young KGB recruits until their retirement on KGB state pensions. Both received the Order of the Red Banner and were named Heroes of the Russian Federation. They are buried in the KGB's Novokuntsevo Cemetery.

18

THE CONTROVERSIAL ATOMIC BOMBING OF JAPAN

As the bomb fell over Hiroshima and exploded, we saw an entire city disappear. I wrote in my log the words: "My God, what have we done?"

—Capt. Robert Lewis, copilot of the bomber *Enola Gay*[1]

Many scientists and other employees at Los Alamos joined the huge majority of American citizens across the country and around the world in cheering the successful detonation of two atomic bombs on Japan over the course of three days from August 6–9, 1945, despite the incineration of hundreds of thousands of Japanese civilians. The mood of national jubilation continued when, on August 12, Japan agreed to accept the surrender terms drawn up two weeks earlier at the Potsdam Conference attended by U.S. president Harry Truman, Soviet general secretary Joseph Stalin, and British prime ministers Winston Churchill and Clement Attlee (who replaced Churchill after his Labor Party won control of the British parliament in an election held during that July 17–August 2 summit). After all, the war, which had killed or injured more than half a million American troops, was finally over, and it appeared as if the U.S. atom bombs had contributed to the war's ending. Even Robert Oppenheimer shared in the rejoicing.

But that mood of celebration didn't last long for many of the scientists who had helped make the bomb. It was, in that sense, not a repeat of the extended celebration that had followed the success of the "Gadget" in the

July 16 Trinity Test at Alamogordo, which morphed into a headlong rush to get the two operational bombs intended for use on Japan completed and transported safely and intact across the Pacific to within bombing range of the two Japanese targets.

The big difference, of course, was that no one was killed by the Trinity Test (at least not by the actual bomb blast, though there is evidence that cancers, some no doubt fatal, birth defects, and stillbirths from fallout downwind from the explosion did result among the mostly indigenous people of the Tularosa Basin in New Mexico).[2] But the scientists who had designed and built those bombs didn't need to wait for the after-bombing damage assessments to understand the horror that had befallen the nearly half million people living in the two leveled cities because of their work. Nearly half of the bombs' casualties were killed in a flash, while the other half died over the following weeks and months from the radiation damage to their bodies. Many of the surviving men, women, and children were left maimed, scarred, crippled, and/or doomed to eventual cancers and genetic damage, leaving many of the wounded envying the dead.

As Paul Ham, author of the book *Hiroshima Nagasaki: The Real Story of the Atomic Bombings*, writes in a commemorative article in *Newsweek* magazine dated August 5, 2015, seventy years after the night that the *Enola Gay* B-29 flew from Tinian Island with its deadly "Little Boy" cargo to the first doomed civilian target city of Hiroshima:

> As the facts of the destruction of Hiroshima and Nagasaki filtered back to Los Alamos in August and September, the earlier exuberance of the Manhattan Project's scientists and engineers turned introspective and, by stages, morose. Some found themselves reflecting guiltily on what they had done.
>
> The nuclear reckoning preoccupied the experts in ways they had not foreseen: The "questionable morality" of dropping the bomb without warning "profoundly disturbed" many, and their moral qualms deepened after Nagasaki, observed Edward Teller. "After the war's end," he wrote, "scientists who wanted no more of weapons work began fleeing to the sanctuary of university laboratories and classrooms."[3]

That new gloom and sense of guilt also weighed increasingly on Los Alamos scientific director Oppenheimer. Ham writes that later, on October 16, his own last day at Los Alamos and as project science director, Oppenheimer, at a farewell gathering in his honor, addressed the assembled Los Alamos workforce (all of whom, including himself, had received from the White House a Certification of Appreciation scroll). He told them,

It is our hope that in years to come we may look at this scroll, and all that it signifies, with pride. Today that pride must be tempered with a profound concern. If atomic bombs are to be added as new weapons to the arsenals of a warring world, or to the arsenals of nations preparing for war, then the time will come when mankind will curse the names of Los Alamos and of Hiroshima.[4]

The widespread sense of horror, dismay, and guilt up on the Hill in the days and weeks following the bombings sprang from questions about why cities with large numbers of civilians had been targeted rather than a demonstration of the bomb on an unoccupied target, or at least on a genuine military target—and even on why the bombs were used at all, since Japan was already effectively finished as a military threat.

People also wondered why there was such a rush after the Hiroshima bomb to hit Japan with a second bomb on another city, resulting in the deaths of hundreds of thousands of civilians within the span of three days. After all, that country's major cities were already so thoroughly destroyed by August 5 that the Pentagon had been sparing even relatively small ones from firebombing with its incendiary bombs to make sure there were still a few suitable undestroyed targets to demonstrate the uranium and the plutonium bombs on. Instead of being answered or explained satisfactorily, these questions have continued to fester as time has gone by and as government lies and misinformation about the bombings have been uncovered.[5]

Truman, introducing the American public abruptly to the reality of the new nuclear age with its first nuclear lie (the first among many to come), declared in a January 6 national radio broadcast, "My fellow Americans, the British, Chinese and United States governments have given the Japanese people adequate warning of what is in store for them. The world will note that the first atomic bomb was dropped on Hiroshima, a military base."[6]

It was the beginning of an era of propaganda and disinformation about nuclear weapons and the U.S. government's intentions for them. Of course, Hiroshima was not just a military base, but rather a city of 360,000—similar to Cleveland today—at the time the bomb was exploded one thousand feet over its urban center. There were an estimated forty thousand soldiers in the area, but the bomb wasn't dropped on the base but rather the city's center.[7] More than two hundred thousand people are estimated to have died from that one bomb, either instantly or from burns or radiation effects after the bomb, nearly all of them civilians, including children on their way to school. After Japan surrendered, Truman claimed in a subsequent announcement that the two atomic bombs the United States had dropped on Japan, by allegedly causing the Japanese government to cry uncle, had saved the lives of twenty thousand American troops predicted to die in an anticipated invasion of Japan slated for November.

Japan was portrayed by apologists for the bombings as a warrior-culture nation whose soldiers would rather fight to the death and die with honor than surrender to an enemy invader. The truth, however, was that the country was tired of war, its navy and air force were destroyed, and much of its army was trapped in China and Korea with no way to get home or even to move from one island of the Japanese archipelago to another. By early August, Japan was on its knees, was facing an approaching winter with no food or fuel, and was suing for peace—and since the United States had cracked the Japanese diplomatic code, Truman knew all the details of that frantic effort before dropping the bombs.[8] All the United States had to do was keep the country blockaded and surrender was inevitable.

In a 1963 memoir, Dwight Eisenhower, a top U.S. general during the war, recalled a conversation with U.S. Secretary of War Henry Stimson before the bombs were dropped:

In 1945 . . . Secretary of War [Henry] Stimson visited my headquarters in Germany [and] informed me that our government was preparing to drop an atomic bomb on Japan. I was one of those who felt that there were a number of cogent reasons to question the wisdom of such an act. . . . During his recitation of the relevant facts, I had been conscious of a feeling of depression and so I voiced to him my grave misgivings, first on the basis of my belief that Japan was already defeated and that dropping the bomb was completely unnecessary and second because I thought that our country should avoid shocking world opinion by the use of a weapon whose employment was, I thought, no longer mandatory as a measure to save American lives. It was my belief that Japan was, at that very moment, seeking some way to surrender with a minimum loss of "face." The Secretary was deeply perturbed by my attitude, almost angrily refuting the reasons I gave for my quick conclusions.[9]

After lying that the Hiroshima target was a "military base," Truman added a second lie, claiming that its selection had been made "to avoid civilian casualties."[10] In fact, the city was picked not because it had some forty thousand troops in its jurisdiction, but because the surrounding hills were expected to "contain and focus" the power of the blast and because its concentrated population of nearly ten times that many civilians meant the bomb would kill vastly more people and demonstrate the awesome destructive power of America's new superweapon.[11]

The truth was that the decision about which two cities to hit with the completed atomic bombs at the Pentagon's disposal was based upon what target cities would best demonstrate "the destructive capacity of the bombs." As most of Japan's major cities had already been destroyed by a brutal six-month campaign of aerial bombardment with conventional bombs, and especially incendiary bombs designed to create massive firestorms of the mostly wooden structures in them, a list of "finalist" targets had been carefully protected from attack. That list included Kyoto, Hiroshima, Kokura, Niigata, and Yokohama, as well as secondary targets like Nagasaki, which had the bad luck of having clearer skies on August 9 when the second B-29 bomber arrived at its primary target of Kokura, which was obscured by clouds, leading to a last-minute switch in targets. As Amy Briggs wrote in an article about the targeting decisions in an article in *National Geographic*, far from being based upon "minimizing civilian casualties," the main considerations in selecting the two target cities were: "First, the cities needed to be large, wider than three miles with sizable populations; second, they needed to have 'high strategic value,' meaning military installations of some kind; and third, they needed to have escaped the U.S.'s ongoing firebombing campaign begun in March 1945."[12]

Dropping the bomb on Hiroshima at 8:15 a.m. on a weekday, meanwhile, ensured that many of those people would be out on the street heading to school and work and not in shelters, homes, or offices when the bomb was detonated high in the air. In a retrospective on the decision to pick Hiroshima as a target, aired on the seventieth anniversary of the bombing, NPR reporter Geoff Brumfiel explained,

> The [military] target committee decided the A-bomb had to kill. At the time, American bombers were already firebombing many cities, killing tens of thousands. So, they decided this bomb would not just kill—it would do something biblical: One bomb, from one plane, would wipe a city off the map. It would be horrible. But they wanted it to be horrible, to end the war and to try to stop the future use of nuclear bombs.[13]

As the tally of the number of dead from the atomic bombings mounted, so too did Truman's assertions about the number of American soldiers' lives saved by the two bombs. This inflation in "saved American lives" ultimately had Truman making the absurd claim of "half a million American lives saved"—a figure that had no basis in reality but clearly sought to belatedly justify the horrendous Japanese civilian death toll of close to 320,000 from the two "demonstration" bombs dropped on Hiroshima and Nagasaki.[14]

Many historians have concluded that the real reason the bombs were used was to intimidate the Soviet Union, so that the U.S. atomic monopoly could be used to win concessions from Moscow even without having to use the bomb on that country or its military. Popular U.S. mythology has it that the Nagasaki bomb was dropped three days after Hiroshima because Japan was taking "too long" to surrender. In fact, however, as the report of the Atomic Heritage Foundation in partnership with the National Museum of Nuclear Science and History states,

> The decision to use the second bomb was made on August 7, 1945 on Guam [one day after the Hiroshima bombing]. Its use was calculated to indicate [falsely] that the United States had an endless supply of the new weapon for use against Japan and that the United States would continue to drop atomic bombs on Japan until the country surrendered unconditionally.[15]

The reality was that after "Fat Man" destroyed Nagasaki, there was not another completed atom bomb in the U.S. nuclear "stockpile." A bomb identical to that second bomb—another plutonium weapon given a generic classification as a Mark III by the War Department—was completed at Los Alamos on August 14, but it couldn't have been delivered to a target in Japan for at least another few weeks. Because of its limited range with such a load, a B-29 couldn't even deliver the 4.5-ton "Fat Man" plutonium bomb to Tinian; instead, it had to be delivered to its initial assembly point in the Pacific by ship, as the next bomb would have had to be. In the end, the third bomb was not shipped out of the country to the western Pacific at all because of Japan's acceptance of the Potsdam surrender terms on December 10, and it would not be until late December of that year that a second Mark III would join the U.S. atomic "stockpile." Such was the slow early pace of U.S. bomb construction, which was still being done by hand and was also dependent upon the availability of not just plutonium but also polonium, used for the initiator at the center of the fission "pit."[16]

Historian and political economist Gar Alperovitz, in *The Decision to Use the Atomic Bomb*, his magisterial history and analysis of the U.S. decision to use its new atomic bombs on Japan, makes it clear that the U.S. military and government, and President Truman himself, were well aware even before the Trinity bomb test at Alamogordo in mid-July that Japan wanted to surrender.[17] In fact, Alperovitz shows that Truman and Secretary of State James Byrnes, who had earlier been trying to push the Soviets to enter the war against Japan, had by then reversed themselves and were secretly pressing Chinese Nationalist Party leader Chiang Kai-shek and his negotiator in Moscow, Soong Tse-wen, to stall on reaching any agreement with Stalin over the terms of a Japanese peace deal—not admitting, of course, that this was so that the United States would have time to use its atomic bombs on Japan.

In other words, Truman, who later claimed using the bomb saved American lives, actually allowed the fighting between U.S. and Japanese troops in the Pacific and Chinese and Japanese forces in China to continue for weeks longer than it had to so that the new weapons could be used in action against real targets. The Hiroshima bomb also killed twelve unfortunate American soldiers who were being held as POWs in Hiroshima when it was dropped—something that was not publicly announced by the U.S. government until late March 2016, when President Barack Obama mentioned them in a speech during a historic first visit to the city by an American president.[18]

It's hard to find information about how many American soldiers, airmen, sailors, and merchant seamen died during that last month of combat waiting for the bombs to be demonstrated, but that number of pointless casualties was likely in the thousands, as hostilities continued until August 15, when the emperor formally called for an end to them. The U.S. Army alone records 469 U.S. war casualties in July and August 1945, likely mostly soldiers killed in the Pacific theater fighting against Japan, since the European theater fighting had ended on May 7, 1945.[19] But this number does not include Marines, sailors, and merchant seamen, who combined were taking far more casualties than the army in the Pacific war. Fighting between U.S. and Japanese forces continued even after August 15 because of poor communication, with the last American to die being an Army photographer named Sergeant Anthony J. Marchione, hit by fighter gunfire on August 18 while riding in a B-32 Dominator bomber flying a damage-assessment photo mission over Japan.[20]

This intentional delay in encouraging and accepting a Japanese surrender on the part of the Truman administration likewise gives the lie to later claims by Truman and others that the two atom bombs also saved millions of Japanese lives that might have been lost by continued ruthless U.S. incendiary bombing of Japan's cities and by a planned U.S. invasion of the Japanese homeland.

Left unsaid too is the reality that while waiting for the two bombs to be completed and delivered to Tinian Island and not accepting a Japanese surrender, the United States needlessly killed tens of thousands more Japanese civilians with its conventional incendiary bombing campaign, which caused firestorms nearly as deadly in Japan's largely wooden cities as were the atomic bombs. (To illustrate the deadliness of incendiary bombings and the resulting firestorms caused by them, between 80,000 and 130,000 Japanese civilians were killed during a massive bombing of Tokyo that began on March 9, 1945, when two thousand tons of incendiary bombs were dropped on the city over forty-eight hours, incinerating sixteen square miles in the worst deliberate firestorm in history.)[21]

Alperovitz quotes Secretary Byrnes's own memoir, *All in One Lifetime*, explaining that the U.S. goal by late July was "to encourage the Chinese to continue negotiations after the adjournment of the [late July] Potsdam Conference. I had some fear that if they did not, Stalin might immediately enter the war. . . . On the other hand, if Stalin and Chiang were still negotiating, it might delay Soviet entrance and the Japanese might surrender. The President was in accord with this view."[22]

Given that Japan's surrender was not really in question—and it's hard to argue with the judgement of Eisenhower, the nation's top commander, a five-star general who had access to all the latest intelligence related to the course of the global war—it seems clear that the real "target" of the only two atomic bombs ever dropped in wartime was not the cities of Hiroshima and Nagasaki, which played no role in Japan's ability to continue fighting U.S. forces, nor was it the political and military leaders and Japanese emperor Hirohito. It was the Soviet Union.

Stalin and the Soviet government declared war on Japan just two days after the Hiroshima atomic bombing and a day before the second atom bomb struck Nagasaki, sending nearly a million Red Army troops streaming into Korea and Manchuria and crushing Japan's Kwantung Army, which had been seriously depleted of men and weapons sent to fight the Americans and Chinese forces over the course of the prior year.

Thanks to his atomic spies in the United States, including Ted Hall, Stalin well knew about America's supposedly secret atomic bomb project and so appeared surprisingly nonplussed when Truman, at the Potsdam Conference of the wartime allies in July, cockily broke the news about the successful Trinity Test. The Russian leader also likely knew that the United States did not have a stockpile of more such bombs—knowledge that would have given him the confidence to successfully have his forces back Kim

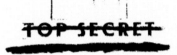

TOP SECRET

USSR

Ref. No: ███████

Issued: ██ 25/4/1961 *)) i*

Copy No: 204

DECISION TO MAINTAIN CONTACT WITH THEODORE HALL (1944)

From: NEW YORK

To: MOSCOW

No: 1585   12 Nov. 44

To VIKTOR.[i]

BEK[ii] visited Theodore HALL[TEODOR KhOLL],[iii] 19 years old, the son of a furrier. He is a graduate of HARVARD University. As a talented physicist he was taken on for government work. He was a GYMNAST[FIZKUL'TURNIK][iv] and conducted work in the Steel Founders' Union.[a] According to BEK's account HALL has an exceptionally keen mind and a broad outlook, and is politically developed. At the present time H. is in charge of a group at "CAMP-2"[v] (SANTA-FE). H. handed over to BEK a report about the CAMP and named the key personnel employed on ENORMOUS.[vi] He decided to do this on the advice of his colleague Saville SAX[SAVIL SAKS],[vii] a GYMNAST living in TYRE.[viii] SAX's mother is a FELLOWCOUNTRYMAN[ZEMLYaK][ix] and works for RUSSIAN WAR RELIEF. With the aim of hastening a meeting with a competent person, H. on the following day sent a copy of the report by S. to the PLANT[ZAVOD].[x] ALEKSEJ.[xi] received S. H. had to leave for CAMP-2 in two days' time. He[b] was compelled to make a decision quickly. Jointly with MAY[MAJ][xii] he gave BEK consent to feel out H., to assure him that everything was in order and to arrange liaison with him. H. left his photograph and came to an understanding with BEK about a place for meeting him. BEK met S. [1 group garbled] our automobile We consider it expedient to maintain liaison with H. [1 group unidentified] through S. and not to bring in anybody else. MAY has no objection to this. We shall send the details by post.

No. 897   [Signature missing]
11th November

Distribution   [Notes and Comments overleaf]

First Venona Soviet New York–Moscow spy cable decryption from November 12, 1944, naming Theodore Hall and Saville Sax as volunteer Soviet spies. *National Security Agency*

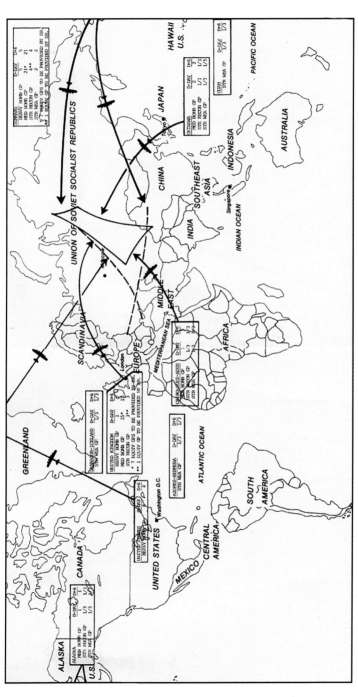

Operational bombing plan map for a "nation destroying" U.S. surprise preventive atomic blitz on the Soviet Union, using more than four hundred bombs on more than seventy Soviet cities, as well as major cities in Eastern Europe, China, North Korea, and North Vietnam. Originally planned for 1950–1951 but pushed back to 1954 because of inadequate numbers of bombers to deliver the bombs. *National Archives*

Edward Hall (left) and Ted Hall in the mid-1980s, during a visit by Ted and Joan to Ed and his wife, Edith, at their Pacific Palisades home. *Courtesy of Sheila Hall*

Entrance and security checkpoint of Los Alamos, circa 1944. *Manhattan Project Archives*

Saville Sax in 1947 in Chicago. *Photo Courtesy of Boria and Sarah Sax*

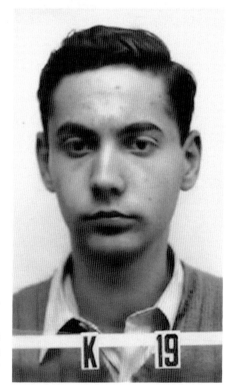

Ted Hall at age eighteen in his Los Alamos Manhattan Project ID badge photo, taken in January 1944. *Manhattan Project Archives*

The completed "Gadget" plutonium bomb, whose design and construction Ted Hall played a major part in. It was the first atomic bomb, exploded in the Trinity Test at Alamogordo, New Mexico, in a 21-kiloton blast that sent smoke and fallout 38,000 feet into the atmosphere and broke windows in a 120-mile radius, announcing the dawn of the nuclear age on July 16, 1945. *Manhattan Project Archives*

The "Fat Man" (left) being prepared for its mission to destroy a Japanese city in early August 1945. It became the second, and last, nuclear bomb to be used in war for the ensuing seventy-eight years. On the right is a model of the virtual copy made by Soviet scientists and engineers, the "First Lightning," successfully detonated at a desert test site in Semipalatinsk in the Kazakh Socialist Republic on August 29, 1949. *Manhattan Project Archives*

Joan Hall at age seventeen, when she met Saville Sax and Ted Hall at the University of Chicago, circa 1946–1947. *Courtesy of Joan Hall*

Joan Krakover Hall, ninety-three, in her home in Newnham, Cambridge, June 2022. *Film still from* A Compassionate Spy, *2022*

Nagasaki after the dropping of the second U.S. atomic bomb, the "Fat Man," three days after the atomic bombing of Hiroshima. This photo was taken by U.S. Marine Lieutenant Arthur Vidich, head of the first military unit to be dispatched to the bombed area shortly after the dropping of the bomb (to search for weapons). He commandeered a Japanese plane and pilot to fly him above the city to take the first photos of the scene from the air, which his family discovered after his death. His photos are now available at https://nagasakiafterbomb.blogspot.com/2015/08/a -photo-documentary-of-nagasaki-after.html. A noted sociologist who taught for forty years at the New School for Social Research and died in 2006, Vidich, after witnessing the destruction caused by the bomb, "remained forever opposed to its further use," his oldest son, Charles, said. *Courtesy of Charles Vidich*

Klaus Fuchs, the brilliant young German Communist refugee physicist who spied for the Soviets on the British "Tube Alloys" bomb virtually from its beginning, and then on the U.S. Manhattan Project from 1944 to the end of the war, most of the time working at Los Alamos before becoming head of the theoretical physics department of the British Atomic Bomb Project at Harwell in the United Kingdom until he was identified, arrested, and jailed in 1950. Image on Fuchs's ID badge in 1944. *Manhattan Project Archives*

Il-Sung's Communist partisans' claim to half of the Korean peninsula and to insist on the USSR's regaining the southern part of Sakhalin Island and the Kurile Islands, which Japan had conquered from Russia in the humiliating 1904–1905 Russo-Japanese War. In making those demands and then using the Red Army to grab those territories, Stalin, it must be pointed out, was acting in accord with the February 1945 Yalta Agreement, reached earlier with Roosevelt and Churchill, under which the Soviet leader had promised, in response to a U.S. request, to join the war on Japan within three months of Germany's surrender and to assume control over part of Manchuria and the former Russian territory conquered by Japan at the beginning of the century. Indeed, his declaration of war against Japan on August 8 was in compliance and right on schedule with that agreement.

Writing an article in a publication of the National Archives, Pad Kumlertsakul explains that throughout the war, the Soviet Union and Japan operated under the terms of the Soviet-Japanese Neutrality Pact reached on April 13, 1941. But, in keeping with his verbal agreement with the Allies that the USSR would break out of that pact and join the war against Japan once Germany had surrendered, Stalin began shifting large numbers of Red Army troops and equipment to eastern Siberia to prepare to join the war against Japan.

Kumlertsakul writes that the August 8 Soviet declaration of war "sent shockwaves through Japanese policy makers: just before he left Moscow for the [July Potsdam] Conference, Stalin had received a personal message from the Japanese Emperor, asking him to act as intermediary between Japan and the United States. The Soviet betrayal was an important factor in forcing Japan to surrender."[23]

By the night of Tuesday, August 14, the Japanese government had sent to Washington a letter of surrender. As Kumlertsakul writes,

At 10:00 on August 14, as the situation deteriorated, the Emperor declared before his cabinet at the Imperial Conference: "The military situation has changed suddenly. The Soviet Union entered the war against us. Suicide attacks can't compete with the power of science. Therefore, there is no alternative but to accept the Potsdam terms [of surrender]."

The American Secretary of State Mr. [James F.] Byrnes considered, on behalf of the Allies, that it amounted to satisfactory acceptance of the terms of the Potsdam Declaration.

While the Emperor had an audience with his cabinet, a military coup was attempted by a faction let by Major Kenji Hatanaka. The rebels tried to seize control of the imperial palace to stop the Emperor announcing the surrender, but they failed and the coup was crushed shortly after dawn.

At noon on Aug. 15, Emperor Hirohito's voice was heard on national radio for the first time. He announced the Japanese surrender.[24]

It should be clear from this recounting that from a military and political perspective, the only two atomic bombs ever used in war, the "Little Boy" on Hiroshima and the "Fat Man" on Nagasaki, had little to do with the end of World War II, which would have ended anyway with the entry of the Soviet Union in the war against Japan. Far more than it feared more atomic bombs being dropped on its territory, Japan's emperor and government feared having large parts of the country being overrun by the Soviet Red Army.

We don't know whether Ted was at that gathering of Los Alamos employees listening to Oppenheimer on October 16, and we don't know what his reaction was a month earlier to the detonation of the two first operational bombs produced there—one constructed with his direct involvement—on two Japanese cities. In September 2022, his wife, Joan, said, "Ted later developed a very strong feeling of revulsion about it. He was not a man who focused on analyzing himself. He did the things he thought needed to be done, but while he did have strong feelings, he did not talk about those things. I know he wanted the project to succeed for various reasons when he was working on it, but he was horrified about the bomb's actual use."[25]

What Ted Hall clearly realized after the Hiroshima and Nagasaki bombings was that the U.S. government under President Truman, in using its new superweapon on Japan—a country on its knees and with no similar weapon or any capability of further threatening the United States—not to defeat that already defeated nation but rather to intimidate the Soviet Union, had proven him right in his decision to share information about the atomic bomb with the Soviets. He had concluded in mid-1944 that the United States, with a monopoly on the atomic bomb, would pose a dire threat to the other nations of the world. His fear that the United States would use its devastating power to dominate the globe unless prevented by another nation with a similar weapon was not misplaced.

If Ted Hall had had any nagging doubts that his concern about the malevolent capacity of the U.S. government to misuse the atomic bomb might have been unfounded or overwrought, the leveling of those two Japanese cities surely put an end to them.

19

TED LEAVES LOS ALAMOS FOR CHICAGO AND MEETS JOAN KRAKOVER

There's something I have to tell you . . .

—Ted Hall to Joan Krakover after she
accepted his marriage proposal

With the war finally over in mid-August 1945, many of the senior scientists, in a mini-diaspora, headed home to their jobs, many at universities around the country and in the United Kingdom and other countries of Europe. Younger scientists, including Ted Hall's friends and colleagues from Harvard who had been hired along with him—Frederic de Hoffmann, Kenneth Case, and Roy Glauber—went off to pursue doctorates; some, like Ted's friend Sam Cohen, who later invented the neutron bomb, continued in the field of nuclear weapons research.

Those like Ted, who were still in uniform, found themselves stuck in their Special Engineering Division posting at Los Alamos, waiting for demobilization and for new opportunities to work or study. In the meantime, to keep those people busy and to help the younger scientists to advance themselves in their studies, General Leslie Groves set up a temporary "Los Alamos University"—basically an ad hoc physics department where courses in advanced physics could be offered by the considerable talent still assembled on the Hill. In a memo, Groves said the purpose would be "to give the younger staff members a chance to learn some of the things that they had missed in the war years, about the actual development of the bomb at Los

Alamos and about recent scientific progress."[1] The faculty list of the pop-up college, which included such notable scientists as Hans Bethe, Enrico Fermi, Klaus Fuchs, George Kistiakowski, Rudolf Peierls, Bruno Rossi, and Victor Weisskopf, would have rivaled any top physics program in the nation's elite universities.

Hall availed himself of two of the courses, enrolling in Weisskopf's class on nuclear physics and a course on hydrodynamics taught by Peierls, the senior scientist in the British Mission to Los Alamos. Hall volunteered and was accepted by Peierls to be a kind of teaching assistant, with the responsibility of compiling the lecture notes for each day's teaching for distribution to class auditors and later preservation in the Los Alamos Library. As it turned out, Peierls left earlier than expected to return to Great Britain, and he delegated four of his most advanced lectures to a younger colleague in the British Mission, the brilliant German exile and (by that point) British citizen Klaus Fuchs. As Joseph Albright and Marcia Kunstel write in their book *Bombshell*, "As far as can be determined, neither Ted Hall nor Klaus Fuchs knew the other was a Soviet spy," even though after each of the four lecture classes Fuchs gave, Hall met with Fuchs to check all the formulas he had copied down from the blackboard.[2]

While Ted was taking those classes and writing down notes on Fuch's lectures, he was also working in the soon-to-be disbanded Manhattan Project's theoretical division, where Edward Teller was also working. Teller, for the last two years of the war, had been busy on a project of his own—developing what he called the "Super"—a bomb that would be orders of magnitude more powerful than the fission bomb, based upon hydrogen fusion, the same process that powers stars. Teller, a Jewish Hungarian immigrant and naturalized U.S. citizen, had a reflexive antipathy towards Communism and Russia, and was quick to tell colleagues that he feared the Soviet Union after the war would be "as dangerous as Germany had been," as he reportedly told Bethe at the time.[3]

Under Teller's leadership, Hall and his Harvard colleague de Hoffmann worked on a problem Fermi had raised with Teller's concept of a hydrogen bomb based upon deuterium, an isotope of hydrogen containing a neutron in its nucleus in addition to the single positively charged proton in the most common isotope of that element. The problem—a technical issue—was that no one had ever calculated the "cross-section" of the deuterium neutron, which was necessary to know to predict the probability of its being struck by another passing neutron—a collision essential to the creation of a fusion chain reaction and ultimate explosion. That, in turn, made it impossible to know how hot the core of a proposed hydrogen bomb would have to be for fusion to occur. (The hotter the core, the more collisions over a set period of time.) Hall and de Hoffmann's work on that issue didn't result in a paper, but another bit of research, not specifically related to the fusion bomb, did lead to one, on which Teller listed Hall as the lead author ahead of de Hoffmann.*

When Ted decided to apply to the doctoral program in physics at the University of Chicago, he received letters of recommendation from two key scientists at Los Alamos: Robert Oppenheimer and Edward Teller.

Oppenheimer's letter, one of many he wrote for young Los Alamos scientists, stated,

> According to your Group Leader [Rossi] you are to be especially commended for work done as a scientific assistant. You have participated in the construction and testing of special detecting equipment and you have been responsible for carrying out a number of difficult measurements in the field of nuclear physics. You have performed your work with great intelligence and care. You have given proof of a sound scientific background, of experimental ability, and of keen interest in scientific research.[4]

Teller's letter is unavailable, but we do know that as a professor in the physics department at the University of Chicago, he provided desk space in his office to Hall—an unusually generous offer for a senior professor to make to a young grad student who at that point was just working on his master's degree. It was something that caught the attention of the FBI when, aware of Teller's ongoing research into producing a thermonuclear bomb, they learned in early 1950 that Hall had been a Soviet spy at Los Alamos.

Before he left Los Alamos in March 1946, Hall continued to work on his helium research with Philip G. Koontz, another scientist at both Los Alamos and the University of Chicago and an associate of Fermi. That collaboration also resulted in several papers. The first, distributed just within the Los Alamos lab in mid-February 1946, two weeks after Teller had packed up his books, paper, and Steinway grand piano and departed to take up a professorship in the physics department at the University of Chicago, was a report on the neutron spectrum of ultra-cooled parahydrogen. The cover page

---

* In scientific papers, the standard procedure is to list the lead author or senior researcher of a group publication first rather than listing the authors alphabetically, though on some occasions, when there is no obvious principal researcher, the names can be listed alphabetically, and without any notice offered explaining the exception.

said, "Work done by Ted Hall, F. deHoffmann, Edward Teller, written by Ted Hall, F. De Hoffmann."[5]

Two other papers, also classified, circulated at Los Alamos two weeks later, both coauthored by Hall and Koontz. One paper described the ionization chamber they had developed to study neutron bombardment of liquid helium and nitrogen; the other attempted an explanation of experimental peculiarities discovered in helium cross-section measurements. Both were as close as Hall came to working on fusion issues, which Teller had been unsuccessfully pushing for since 1942 and which had led to his being pushed away by Oppenheimer from such research activity until years later. (As early as 1942 before the Manhattan Project was created, at planning sessions for the project led by Oppenheimer, Teller reportedly was already promoting the idea of a fusion bomb.)[6] But because of issues that arose between Teller and Hans Bethe, who was head of the theoretical division where he and Hall were assigned, Teller was moved by Oppenheimer, at Bethe's request, out of the theoretical division to a separate group that was looking into a hydrogen bomb. Not much happened with that work until the Soviets exploded their first plutonium bomb in 1949, after which Truman ordered a new crash program to develop the hydrogen bomb.

These dates are important because of speculation that Hall continued to spy for the Soviets after the war.

A big problem with that theory is that by early June 1946, Hall, while still at Los Alamos, had lost his security clearance for atomic bomb–related research and was ordered to leave the hilltop compound where he had lived and worked for two years. Hall recalled the incident to Albright and Kunstel, saying that he was never given an explanation for the action. The *Bombshell* authors note that no further action was taken against him and there was no interrogation or visit from military security (he was still in uniform) or the FBI, although he was "on record" as having been receiving at Los Alamos leftist literature like the weekly magazine *In Fact*.[7]

There was also the incident brought up by Los Alamos security dating back to 1944, when his brother's British wife, Edith Shawcross Hall, wrote a joking letter to Ted. It said, "I hear you're working on something that goes up with a big bang. Can you send us one of them for Guy Fawkes Day?" That letter, spotted by Los Alamos military censors, led at the time to an interrogation of Ed in Britain, though the matter seemed to blow over when he and Edith explained that it had been a joke. Edith told security investigators that when she asked her husband what his younger brother was doing in New Mexico, he had said it was "something to do with rockets."[8] (The false story about the work at Los Alamos offered to locals in nearby Santa Fe was that the vast pool of scientists, engineers, and support staff behind the security fence at Los Alamos atop the mesa were working on "electronic propulsion systems.")

Ted told Albright and Kunstel that he had naturally assumed, when he was called into the office of Los Alamos legal officer Major Ralph Carlisle Smith in the spring of 1946 and was informed about the lifting of his security clearance and the order for him to be promptly transferred by train the next day to another Manhattan Project site in Oak Ridge, Tennessee, that he was going to be questioned about his secret meetings with Saville Sax and Lona Cohen and perhaps court-martialed.[9] But those secret liaisons never came up, and he found himself instead loading and unloading trucks of soda bottles and laundry for two weeks at Oak Ridge waiting to be sent on to Fort Bragg in North Carolina, where he was demobilized on June 24, 1946.

There is no indication of any other suspicions about Ted within the U.S. Army security apparatus. Although he lost a stripe on his sergeant's badge over the same issues that led to his losing his security clearance, he received an honorable discharge and a military decoration for his work on the Manhattan Project—a unit citation from President and Commander in Chief Harry Truman for the achievements of the U.S. Army's Special Engineering Detachment at Los Alamos, of which he was a part. Nor is there anything in Ted Hall's lengthy FBI file, which begins with a document dated April 25, 1950, suggesting earlier spying suspicions. That five-page office memorandum on FBI stationery from E. M. "Mickey" Ladd, the bureau's head of domestic intelligence, is addressed to "The Director" (J. Edgar Hoover), and reads, in part:

PURPOSE

To inform you of further information made available by [CENSORED][10] [CENSORED] [CENSORED].

DETAILS

There has now been received from [CENSORED] described in my memorandum on this matter dated April 21, 1950.

The April 21 memorandum cited is not shown in the file, though it could be there in one of the file's many still completely (and unjustifiably) censored blank pages, but it is clear that it must have been the notification from what was then the Army Security Administration (successor to the SIS) that Hall and Sax's names had appeared in a decrypted Soviet wartime spy cable intercept by the SIS's Venona Project.

But while Ted's first brush with security officials at Los Alamos happened four years before the first Venona cable intercept exposing him as a Soviet spy was decrypted and before the FBI was alerted, it appears as though security officials at Los Alamos had, even then, seen enough of Ted's history of resistance to rules and authority and interest in politically suspect "antiestablishment" literature to revoke his atomic research security clearance, even though they didn't have any other, more serious suspicions about him worth pursuing. There was no further investigation, just a sudden ouster from Los Alamos and unexpected demobilization from the U.S. Army.

Importantly, the loss of his security clearance meant that Ted was no longer in a position to participate in secret work on anything like the hydrogen bomb even if he had wanted to, unless the U.S. Army security office or the new Atomic Energy Commission failed to alert the University of Chicago's physics program that Hall's clearance had been lifted, which seems unlikely.

Given that he hated the very idea of a hydrogen bomb, the loss of his clearance didn't matter and if anything, left him—after initial fears that the jig was up—with the sense that he might not be caught for his spying days at Los Alamos.

In any case, Hall, as a newly civilian graduate student, had other things on his mind. He was working toward master's and doctoral degrees, initially in theoretical physics and later changed to biophysics, a field that attracted him and had the added advantage of not drawing any attention to himself as a theoretical physicist. As a civilian, he was also interested in participating in political activism again—and before long, also in Joan Krakover. She was an attractive and intelligent young woman introduced to him by Sax, who had also moved to Chicago to be near his college friend and erstwhile spy co-conspirator.

Joan first met Saville Sax in 1946 at the University of Chicago, where he had enrolled as an undergraduate, having failed out of Harvard. She was seventeen and in her third year as a student in a special program for bright high-school kids run by the university. Although she and Sax became something of an item, things got complicated when her friendship with Sax led to her meeting his friend Ted, who was studying toward a PhD in physics, and she found herself attracted to him too. She became close to both young men, and they to her, leading to a kind of *Jules et Jim* situation.

In the film *A Compassionate Spy*, Joan recounts how one day when she, Sax, and Hall were relaxing on the grass in the main quad of the university campus, her head on Hall's chest and Sax's head on her thigh, she suddenly stood up, looked down at her two admirers, and said, "I love both of you, but how can I love you both?" She recalls Ted, looking up at her from the ground, saying dryly, "That sounds like quite a problem."[11]

In the end she chose Ted, marrying him later that year.

Ted's proposal, she recounts, came as a surprise. The two were lying on the dusty floor of the office where Hall, a grad student, had been offered a desk and where he kept a small record player and a big box of classical 78s they loved to listen to. While Mozart's Violin Sonata Number 24 was playing what Joan says had "become our song," Ted looked over at her and said "Joan, I love you! Will you marry me?" To this pronouncement, Joan says she immediately replied, "Yes," without a second thought, tossing out what she said was a prior promise she had made to herself "not to get tied down for ten years."

At that point Ted, who in their relationship had been a fun-loving guy, "suddenly went all serious and said, 'There is something I have to tell you.'"

Joan continues: "I said, 'Yes?' and he continued, telling me, 'Well, you know about the work we were doing at Los Alamos? It was very secret. We weren't allowed to tell anybody about it.'"

Explaining his motives, she says he told her, "It was very dangerous if the Americans had a monopoly on this weapon."

"So you're going to give information to the Russians?" she asked him.

"I did, yeah," he said.

Thinking over the unanticipated shocker that it was something he had already done, not something he was contemplating doing, she recalls asking skeptically, "Why? What good would that do?"

In response, Ted explained that he felt that it would be "a safeguard against another war if the Russians also had this weapon."

He added, "I wanted to tell you about it now before we got married, because you might want to drop out."

Joan says the news of his atomic spying didn't make her want to shy away from marriage, explaining, "I didn't want to drop out. Nothing could have made me leave him! He could have told me he shot someone in the street. I knew I would never meet anyone like that again, and I was right, too."

They married a few months later and kept their atomic secret for forty-eight years, until Ted's espionage role was disclosed publicly by the NSA in 1995.

Although Joan chose Ted over Sax as the love of her life, three years later Sax proved himself to be a true-blue friend to the couple when the FBI came after both him and Ted.

Over the years, occasionally depressed and sometimes talkative later about his own having "helped the Russians get the bomb," Sax never said a word about Ted Hall's being a Soviet atomic spy.

Ted's secret stayed safe with his friend and coconspirator until Sax's death of a heart attack on September 25, 1980, at age fifty-six.

20

THE SOVIETS' FIRST
ATOMIC BOMB

Imitation is the sincerest form of flattery.

—Anon.

On September 23, 1949, a little more than four years after two U.S. atom bombs obliterated the Japanese cities of Hiroshima and Nagasaki, President Harry Truman made the shocking announcement to the American people that the Soviet Union had just exploded an atomic bomb.

As Joan recalls in an interview in the film *A Compassionate Spy*, Ted was sitting at his breakfast table with her at their home in Chicago when a news announcer broke into the scheduled morning radio program with a bulletin announcing news of the Soviet test. On hearing the news, Joan says, Ted smiled. "I took his hand," she says. "I was so proud of him. It was like he'd done it all himself, although of course I knew that was not true. Afterwards we went for a walk."[1]

It would be years before it became clear that the bomb the Soviets had produced so quickly was a virtual copy of the plutonium bomb Ted had been working on at Los Alamos, the schematics for which he had provided to Soviet atomic scientists via NKVD courier Lona Cohen's Kleenex box just after the first bomb was dropped on Hiroshima four years earlier.

The Soviet atomic test had actually been detected by the United States days earlier, thanks to a specially adapted weather reconnaissance WB-29 carrying air-sampling equipment that had been patrolling off of the coast of

eastern Siberia. There it picked up telltale isotopes in the samples of strato-
spheric jet stream winds blowing west from central Asia. While Truman
tried to claim the United States was not surprised by the test—and retro-
spectively, many official sources have claimed that Soviet spying likely has-
tened the development of a Soviet bomb by just one or two years—the truth
was that the entire U.S. intelligence apparatus as well as Pentagon strategists
and U.S. nuclear scientists were stunned, as they had not expected the
Soviets to get their own bomb before 1953 or 1954.[2] Indeed, it's possible
that the only reason the United States had not already launched a preemptive nuclear strike on the Soviet Union before it could get its own bomb was
that U.S. intelligence didn't know about the site or the scale of the project
the Soviets had established in the Urals and the Kazakh SSR (now Kazakh-
stan) and at the time didn't have what the Pentagon argued would be the
hundreds of Nagasaki-sized bombs required to destroy the Soviet Union as
an industrial society. When the Soviets tested their bomb, the United States
still possessed only slightly more than two hundred atomic bombs and had
too few long-range B-29 bombers to deliver them all. Many had bomb bays
that were too small for the huge bombs. Furthermore, none could carry
them the distance to targets east of the Ural Mountains except as one-way
suicide runs by the crews, an idea that was proposed but rejected.[3]

Pentagon strategists had cautioned Truman that they would need at least
four hundred Nagasaki-sized bombs and sufficient upgraded B-29 bombers and new B-36 bombers to deliver them deep enough into the USSR to
assure hitting all major Soviet targets. Otherwise, they worried, there was a
risk the Soviets might respond to such a horrific attack by sending its battle-
hardened Red Army to overrun most of war-ravaged Western Europe. The
United States had already ramped up previously mothballed production
lines for the B-29 and was refurbishing older versions of the planes damaged
by wartime bombing runs, but it was still short of even those long-range
bombers retrofitted with bomb bays large enough to release the huge new
atomic bombs. And a fleet of new, longer-range B-36 bombers was years off.

Yet, as Michio Kaku and Daniel Axelrod disclose in their book *To Win
a Nuclear War*, as the United States expanded its nuclear arsenal, military
leaders were realizing using them successfully would require massive attacks
and the element of surprise. They write, "By September 1949, the policy of
striking the first blow with nuclear weapons in the event of war was sealed
into official US military policy by Truman's secret directive NSC-57."[4]

But the Russian atomic bomb forced a dramatic change in that deadly calculus. An angry and frustrated Truman learned that the United States would

not have all the bombs the Pentagon felt would be needed until 1951, while getting an adequate number of bombers to deliver those weapons, as well as bomber decoys to join in the assault, might take even longer. Meanwhile, Moscow would be making more of its own bombs, and the risk of nuclear retaliation for such an attack, even by just a few Soviet bombs being slipped past U.S. defenses, could no longer be ignored—or taken.

The Soviets had not announced their successful 21-kiloton test of "First Lightning," a copy of the U.S. "Fat Man" plutonium bomb, hoping it would go unnoticed by the United States. The fear was that it would push Washington to accelerate production of a large stockpile of bombs. They were right in that suspicion—production of U.S. atomic bombs was ramped up after that test—but as U.S. war-planning documents make clear, the effort to industrialize the production of massive numbers of fission bombs was already in the works long before the war ended. Besides, as early as 1946, Edward Teller and a group of other atomic scientists were working on developing a much more deadly and destructive weapon: the hydrogen fusion bomb dubbed the "Super." The first example of that awesome weapon—a thermonuclear bomb of 10 megatons, five hundred times more powerful than the "Fat Man" bomb—was successfully tested on November 1, 1952.

Moscow knew this and was desperately working to catch up with the creation of a fusion bomb of its own that would slam shut a critical window of vulnerability to U.S. preemptive attack. The only difference between the Soviet race to catch up with the United States on the fission bomb and the race to catch up on a thermonuclear bomb was that in that second race, instead of being four years behind, the Soviets were less than a year behind.

As Robert Oppenheimer and other early scientist critics of the Truman administration's hydrogen bomb development program had warned, while the United States could certainly get the hydrogen bomb first, the Soviets, having achieved the critically important prerequisite ability to make the fission bomb required to detonate a fusion bomb, would before long make a hydrogen bomb too. Oppenheimer and other U.S. physicists knew the Soviets had their own talented physicists, engineers, and other scientists who could develop their own hydrogen bomb without having to copy the United States. And so they did, exploding theirs—a totally different design based on work by Soviet physicist Andrei Sakharov—on August 12, 1953, just over ten months after the initial U.S. test.

The window of opportunity to destroy the Soviet Union before it became a nuclear power had clearly been missed, but so had what was probably the only opportunity to negotiate an end to a pointless and hugely expensive and risky nuclear arms race before it began—or at least before it moved from relatively small fission bombs to nation- or world-killing thermonuclear fusion weapons.

It is arguable that an upping of the ante from "little" fission bombs, whose power is measured in kilotons (thousands of tons of TNT equivalent), to the thermonuclear realm, where the explosive power of bombs must be measured in megatons (millions of tons of TNT equivalent), might, after all the carnage of World War II, have led to the reasonable expectation that the resulting stalemate would result in a ban on all such weapons. After all, with thermonuclear weapons or even just hundreds of smaller fission bombs being used in the next global war, the devastating fallout, rather than mostly a problem for the local regions around where they exploded, as was the case with the U.S. bombs dropped on Japan, would instead be a global catastrophe. Any atomic attack by one nation, even if there were no counterattack, would be a case of mass-murder/mass-suicide—a killing of the earth, or at least most higher life forms on it. As Albert Einstein warned, "I know not with what weapons World War III will be fought, but World War IV will be fought with sticks and stones."[5]

And indeed, a global movement to ban nuclear weapons was growing in the 1950s. Scientists who had been involved in the Manhattan Project (including the young doctoral student Ted Hall), kicked that movement off, forming the Federation of Atomic Scientists in 1945.[6] Its focus was on increasing public knowledge and control over nuclear weapons and preventing their spread. By 1948, when the group expanded beyond Manhattan Project veterans and changed its name to the Federation of American Scientists, it had twenty-eight thousand members.

In 1955, Einstein and the British philosopher Bertrand Russell authored a manifesto calling for an end to war and the use of nuclear weapons. Its conclusion read,

> In view of the fact that any future world war nuclear weapons will certainly be employed, and that such weapons threaten the continued existence of mankind, we urge the governments of the world to realize, and to acknowledge publicly, that their purpose cannot be furthered by a world war, and we urge them, consequently, to find peaceful means for the settlement of all matters of dispute between them.[7]

Signed by nine Nobel laureates and one future Nobel laureate—Josef Rotblat, the only physicist on the Manhattan Project to quit on ethical grounds after he learned in November 1944 that the bomb would be used on Japan and the USSR—that manifesto in 1957 became the founding charter of the Pugwash Conference on Science and World Affairs, another influential organization of scientists and other intellectuals focused on promoting disarmament and eliminating nuclear weapons. Its first chairman was Rotblat, who would go on to win the Nobel Peace Prize in 1995 for his efforts to eliminate nuclear weapons.[8] By the late 1950s and into the 1960s, the antinuclear movement moved beyond scientists and went mainstream with the founding in the United States of such groups of ordinary people as the National Committee for a Sane Nuclear Policy (SANE), which quickly grew to twenty-five thousand members, the Student Peace Union, and Women's Strike for Peace, while in the United Kingdom there was the Campaign for Nuclear Disarmament.

Awareness of this grim new reality—and of organized mass protests calling for an end to atmospheric bomb testing—was the reason President John F. Kennedy and Soviet Premier Nikita Khrushchev were nonetheless able, despite having nearly gone to war in the 1962 Cuban Missile Crisis, to negotiate a 1963 ban on fallout-producing atmospheric tests, which both men realized were destroying the earth, including their own countries, even without a war. (No doubt this was why they were also able to negotiate a peaceful end to that earlier crisis in the Caribbean over short-range nuclear missiles based in Cuba and the USSR's neighbor Turkey pointed at each other, by removing both threats.)

Sadly, instead of working together to stuff the nuclear genie back in its lamp, mutual distrust between the United States and the Communist nations of the USSR and China was so great in the late 1940s and on through the period between the 1950s and the 1980s, and the aggressive desire by the United States to cling to its postwar position of global dominance so ingrained that no serious effort to even reduce nuclear weapons began until the late 1980s.

I confess that as the author of this book, I puzzled a long time over where to place a section on the question of whether Ted Hall continued to spy for the Soviet Union after the end of World War II and whether he might have had more to do with both the Soviets' further progress on their fission bomb development and their even faster later acquisition of their first fusion thermonuclear bomb. I ultimately decided this chapter was the appropriate place for it, as the evidence, sketchy and speculative as it is, does hint at possible spying by Hall between 1948 and 1950, straddling the successful test of the first Soviet atomic bomb.

If Ted Hall *did* spy after the war ended, he never told anyone, other than perhaps his wife and, obliquely, Joseph Albright and Marcia Kunstel, the authors of *Bombshell*. And suspicions that he continued his spying have been disputed by some knowledgeable atomic historians. Albright and Kunstel seem fairly confident that Hall likely did spy after the war on at least two occasions, though they do not suggest he ever provided any information about the U.S. "Super," the hydrogen bomb, but rather only more important details about the fission bombs and their construction and about U.S. plans for attacking the Soviet Union.

The first instance of possible postwar spying by Hall, the authors claim, came in late 1948. Saville Sax, they say, had kept up his contacts with "Soviet spymasters." At the end of 1948, after he had delivered to the New York *Rezidentura* a letter from Ted telling them he was making a "clean break" from spying, Sax, according to the *Bombshell* authors, returned with an NKVD reply for Ted: The Soviets wanted him back. A meeting was planned in New York City, where Joan and Ted had agreed he would explain that they had decided he should quit spying, especially as he was now going to be a father.

Albright and Kunstel write,

> The evening of the meeting Savy and Ted departed under no particular cloud, and the two young women stayed behind in the Sax's apartment on West 176th Street near the George Washington Bridge. . . . It was late, very late when their husbands came back. Ted walked in the door, met Joan's eyes once, then silently turned and leaned his face into the wall. It was clear. He had gone back on their agreement. Initially Joan believed he still might retreat, go to the Soviets again and tell them he had changed his mind and wasn't going to rejoin their network. He didn't. The arguments plied by the Soviet agent who met Ted and Savy had been persuasive. The agent told Ted Hall that the Soviet Union was in a fight for its life in the nuclear arms race, and he was needed by the network. Despite his rebuttal that he no longer had access to secret information, the agent argued that the cause needed an ally with his background more than the American Communists needed another young activist couple.
>
> The Halls returned to Chicago to what Joan saw as a shattered life.[9]

Both Hall and Sax, as well as Joan, had all become politically active in the Progressive Party, labeled a Communist front organization by the FBI. (Ted had even been questioned about his activities by Chicago FBI agent W. Rulon Paxton, who later was one of Sax's interrogators in 1951.) And the first thing Ted said a senior Soviet spy handler who came to visit him that fall told him was to quit that political work, since spies were not allowed to do such things. Joan recalled in a 2021 interview that appears in *A Compassionate Spy* that she was as distressed by having to cut her ties with people in the left movement and the Wallace third-party presidential campaign as she was at having her wish for her husband to stay away from spying ignored.

Hall, according to Albright and Kunstel, was told by Soviet spymasters in New York that he had to buy an inconspicuous business suit, overcoat, and fedora and that for any spy work he would adopt the name "Tom," with Sax being "Sam." Meanwhile, the authors claim (attributing "good Soviet sources"), that Hall, explaining that without a security clearance he could no longer spy himself, came up with two people reportedly working in the polonium-making plant at Hanford, who he said were willing to spy but not to directly contact any Soviet spies. Hall, in other words, became a courier. But whatever information those alleged contacts brought him has remained "locked in the old KGB file bearing their code names," ANTA and ADEN.[10]

As to what information this arrangement might have been, Albright and Kunstel write,

> There is reason to suspect that in the late 1940s Hall did hand the Soviets at least one piece of secret information that made a difference in the arms race. It is now known that following one hurried trip on the New York Central Railway's Chicago–New York *Pacemaker* he met with a Soviet agent. At that same time, the Soviets are known to have sent an intelligence report on an "American innovation that allowed the mass production of atomic bombs." . . . An excerpt obtained by the authors from Russian Ministry of Atomic Energy archives shows that the report divulged an industrial process for manufacturing polonium 210, the isotope of that element that serves as the key ingredient in the triggering mechanism of a plutonium bomb.

Of this possible spying, the authors caution, "There is no evidence linking Ted Hall and his friends to any of this—either in declassified Russian archives or anywhere else, yet what else could have been significant enough to make Hall catch the Pacemaker for that wintry encounter in New York?"[11] (The reason for the lack of more solid information is that after the war, the

Soviets, alerted to the U.S. cracking of their once seemingly unbreakable code system, had changed it, so there is no more FBI documentation of Ted and Sax's—or any other spies'—actions, whether it was leaving spying, fleeing the United States, or continuing to spy, coming from the Soviet side. There's also a huge gap on the FBI side, because the bureau didn't even *start* monitoring Hall and Sax until mid-1950, and, for reasons that will become clear in chapter 26, had pretty much closed the book on prosecuting Hall in February 1952, at least until the mid-1960s.)

The second example of Ted's possible postwar spying, according to Albright and Kunstel, was likely, though not definitely, in early 1950, just weeks before the the FBI learned from a key decrypted Venona cable that Hall and Sax had been spies during the war.

The authors write that they heard or read three slightly different accounts, all from a "close confidante" of Ted's or from Soviet sources who got their information from NKVD spy Lona Cohen.[12] The information concerned a meeting in Chicago between the Halls and Cohen. All accounts of this meeting by those involved say it occurred in the Halls' home and included Lona's husband, Morris, and, in some versions, also Soviet U.S. spy chief Rudolf Abel. In one account, the three Soviet spies are said to have tried jointly to persuade Hall to resume working for the Soviet spy agency. "No more," Lona recalls Ted saying to them. "I helped you during the wartime, and now it's over." In a second version, there is no indication Ted agreed to take up spying again.

The third account the authors attribute to Vladimir Chikov, a sketchy Soviet KGB historian whose work, they caution, was "no doubt accompanied by false details added as disinformation." In this version, Hall, during the winter of 1948-1949, made his trip to New York on the *Pacemaker* express train from Chicago to New York to deliver "alarming information" that "generals in the Pentagon, with the help of scientists, had marked up a map of the Soviet Union with small flags designating targets for a future nuclear attack." That account has Chikov quoting Cohen as saying,

> Following Abel's instructions, I informed [MLAD/Hall] of the high appreciation with which Russia had received the information he had furnished. At the same time, I wanted to offer him, as a form of recompense for his services, $5000 which I had removed from a safe deposit box. He categorically refused the money, declaring with firmness that he had not acted to get some reward, but rather to prevent a world catastrophe.[13]

Significantly, this second incident, if it happened, suggests that the first suspected spying involving polonium-210 production didn't happen. If it had, how could Ted later tell Cohen and the other spies that he had helped during the war, "but now it's over"? Importantly, it also gives a different account of the information Ted purportedly raced by express train to New York to personally deliver.

The *Bombshell* authors' suspicion that Hall returned to spying in the late 1940s is undercut by journalist Ann Hagedorn, whose well-researched 2021 book *Sleeper Agent: The Atomic Spy in America Who Got Away* tells the story of American/Russian Red Army spy George Koval, a Manhattan Project engineer who wasn't identified as an atomic spy by the FBI until years after he'd already fled the United States for the Soviet Union. His spying was not known about at the time *Bombshell* was published. Hagedorn documents that Koval, who worked for the Manhattan Project at Oak Ridge and later, after the war, for the Atomic Energy Commission at a Monsanto plant in Dayton, Ohio, that refined polonium-210, was definitely the source of the information on a secret U.S. process for more rapidly producing that hard-to-obtain element—a report that apparently so excited Soviet intelligence chief Lavrentiy Beria and the country's atomic scientists that it won Koval a posthumous top honor in Russia for his work on the atomic bomb project.[14] (Polonium was critical to initiating the chain reaction in implosion core of the early plutonium bombs, and obtaining it in quantity was central to being able to make large numbers of plutonium bombs at that time.)

But could Koval have been ANTA or ADEN, who the *Bombshell* authors suggest could have been the source whose information Ted allegedly passed along to his Soviet handlers in New York in 1948–1950? Not likely, says Harvey Klehr, a coauthor with John Earl Haynes and Alexander Vassiliev of the book *Spies*. Now a retired emeritus professor of history at Emory University and a recognized expert on Soviet atomic spy history, Klehr explained in a phone interview in early December 2022 that "in 1947 and 1948, the KGB was getting complaints that they had nobody inside the U.S. atomic bomb program, and there was no mention of any ADEN or ANTA, which they would certainly have mentioned if they existed."[15] He added that such Soviet spy code names have often proved on investigation to be wrong or even to be Soviet disinformation designed to throw U.S. counterintelligence sleuths off the track of actual spies. One example of such disinformation would be PERSEUS, a "senior scientist" and supposed spy in the Manhattan Project from the beginning in 1942 who Klehr and Haynes convincingly skewer as a KGB fabrication (containing elements of the spy MLAD) to confuse U.S. investigators and throw them off track.[16]

Another fact arguing against Hall's having been a courier for Koval, Klehr says, is that Hall always worked for the Soviet state security apparatus—the NKVD or later the KGB—while Koval was always with the GRU, the country's military intelligence agency (akin to the U.S. Defense Intelligence Agency). As Klehr explained to me in a phone interview in early 2023, "Soviet intelligence did not allow that kind for crossover. Even Fuchs, when he volunteered as an atomic spy, went initially to the GRU, but when he was sent as part of the British Mission to the US, the GRU first had to transfer him to the NKVD's control." He concludes, "It's a mystery. It's certainly possible that Ted Hall continued to provide information to the Soviets but there's really no hard evidence of it."

One of Klehr's *Spies* coauthors, atomic historian and former KGB employee Alexander Vassiliev, insists there's no evidence that Ted Hall spied in the late 1940s or 1950 in the KGB archives he pored over during the glasnost period.

Hagedorn agrees with Klehr's view that because Koval was with the Soviet Union's military spy agency, he would not have been using the NKVD's Hall as a courier, but she also says he would have had no need to do that anyway, as he had his own GRU courier: an electrical engineer named Benjamin William Lassen (code name FARADAY and also called Benjamin Lassoff). Like Koval, he left the United States before the FBI net closed around him.[17] Lassen was, Hagedorn explains, Koval's courier throughout the period between Ted's arrival in Chicago in mid-1946 and his and Sax's interrogation by the FBI in March 1951.

In her book, Hagedorn also makes the point that one reason Koval was never suspected until after he had left the United States for the USSR was that he was very scrupulous about remaining a loner. He was, she says, the least likely Soviet spy to accept or turn to using a new courier, especially one from a different branch of Soviet intelligence.[18]

In a 2023 email, she added, "Though known for his charm and affability, Koval was astutely cautious, never socializing with fellow spies and steering clear of the CPUSA. By the time he had left his cover in the U.S. Army, in early 1946, the Soviet Union was obviously no longer a U.S. ally in a world war, the FBI was shifting resources to investigate Communist infiltration as the House Un-American Activities Committee revved its engines, and there had been recent defections tied to his espionage network. Soviet spies in the

West were headed toward a volatile time and he knew it—thus, his very low profile."[19]

On the other hand, perhaps the best reason to believe that Albright and Kunstel might be right about postwar spying by Hall and Sax is that they had an arrangement with Ted and Joan that if the couple agreed to be interviewed at length for a book, they'd get an advance look at the final manuscript before publication and the opportunity not to veto but to object to any part of it. The authors told me in late 2022 that "neither Ted nor Joan had any objections to the story as written."

On the several occasions I spoke with Joan about some aspect of the account of their lives and about Ted's and Sax's spying as recounted in *Bombshell*, her response was to say the book was "mostly correct" and that the only thing she and Ted didn't like about it when they read it was "the title." However, since mid-2022, when I've brought up the issue of Ted's postwar spying, she has insisted that after leaving Los Alamos Ted never provided any bomb information to the Soviets. She claimed that his continued contacts with Soviet spies from New York's *Rezidentura* during the late 1940s and early 1950s were an effort to "string them along" so they'd be available if he needed to spirit himself and his family out of the United States quickly. She dismissed "ANTA" and "ADEN" as just "friends of Ted's, now dead," who "didn't have any information to provide." Joan might have been trying to protect her dead husband's legacy, of course, but given her frailness at that point I couldn't really press her about the matter. It remains the case that she and Ted read the pre-publication manuscript of *Bombshell* and had no complaint about what the authors wrote, and neither of them complained about any factual errors when it was published in 1997.

My perspective is that Ted Hall probably did not do any significant spying for the Soviets after the war. But whether or not he continued with some spying is, in the final analysis, not that important and doesn't make such spying any worse, less understandable, or less justifiable than if it were done only while the USSR was technically a U.S. wartime ally. If any of the accounts of his alleged postwar spying are correct, they comport with the reasons he became a spy for the Soviets in the first place during the war: to prevent a U.S. monopoly on the bomb and to prevent the bomb's ever being used again after the war. The several examples of information he is alleged by Albright and Kunstel to have possibly provided to the Soviets in the late 1940s or early 1950—details about how to mass produce atomic bombs and maps showing U.S. bombing plans for the genocidal obliteration of the USSR as an industrial society—were clearly aimed at preventing a U.S. nuclear first strike on the Soviet Union. After all, even in 1950, that country was virtually defenseless against a U.S. stockpile of hundreds of atomic bombs, and the United States was actively contemplating using them to prevent the USSR from ever becoming a nuclear rival.

If one accepts Ted Hall's logic and motivation in sharing with the Soviets the plans for the plutonium bomb being developed in secret from the Soviets during the war, when the USSR was America's ally, that same logic and motivation applied after the war, when he learned that the United States was preparing for a massive nuclear attack on the USSR—an attack that would have killed millions of civilians—and gave that same target country information needed to allow it to continue to deter such a treacherous U.S. attack.

21

THE HIDDEN DANGER YEARS OF THE NUCLEAR ERA

For the first time, we know which Russian cities would have been destroyed, and why. The U.S. government has finally declassified the 1950s Strategic Air Command target list, . . . SAC listed over 1200 cities in the Soviet bloc, from East Germany to China, also with priorities established. . . . The SAC target list, compiled in 1956 . . . deliberately included civilian populations . . . and explicitly targeted "population" including Beijing, Moscow and Leningrad . . . all "population" in all cities, including Beijing, Moscow, Leningrad, East Berlin and Warsaw.

—Michael Peck[1]

Older Americans who lived through the Cold War remember it as an anxious era lasting from the Berlin Blockade of 1948, when the United States openly threatened a nuclear attack on the USSR, through the 1980s with collapse of the Soviet Union, and especially the years of the 1950s, 1960s, and 1970s, when nuclear weapons were still being regularly tested and new weapons systems developed.

I remember how exciting it was as a Cub Scout in the mid-1950s to be issued an official-looking blue Civil Defense ID card and be assigned the job of messenger, running between buildings at the University of Connecticut to deliver communications between adult Civil Defense and National

Guard officials during a nationwide nuclear war game. As I was doing my job, supersonic F-100 jet fighters from the Connecticut Air National Guard roared overhead making sonic booms as barely visible giant B-52 bombers from the U.S. Air Force's Strategic Air Command left their contrails high above.

Exciting as that all was for a young scout, it was also a terrifying time. Families built bomb shelters under their lawns or in their basements, often keeping them secret from neighbors lest they try to force their way in during a nuclear attack. Schoolchildren had to go through nuclear attack drills, practicing "duck-and-cover" exercises where we'd all hide under our school desks with our hands over our eyes to protect from the blast and shattering windows. Later, global antinuclear efforts like the Nuclear Freeze campaign also brought millions onto the streets of the United States, Britain, and many European countries, marching and protesting nuclear weapons.

I also recall, as a preteen in the early 1960s, going with my parents and younger brother and sister to visit a place where an enterprising oil and septic tank distributer located not far from Storrs, Connecticut, where we lived, was doing some creative welding work to turn simple tar-coated steel storage tanks into bomb shelters. Each tank featured a submarine conning tower–like tube atop it that included a welded-in metal ladder installed as an entrance, along with a vent pipe for air drawn from above ground through a filter that would purportedly exclude fallout. The vent apparatus was powered by an exercise bike rigged up inside the tank that also generated electricity for lighting. There were plenty of people in that field, inspecting this fellow's wares like vehicles at a used car lot. My dad, an engineer, skeptically climbed up an access ladder and went down into one of the tanks to examine where he and his family would be expected to try to survive a nuclear war. After a few minutes inside, he reappeared from the entrance tube, shaking his head. Climbing down to the ground, he said to my mom, "Dottie, there's no way I could survive down in that tank for weeks or months with three squabbling, cooped-up kids! I'd rather stay outside and face the fallout!"

We didn't get a bomb shelter installed, and I remember at the time regretting that we three kids hadn't promised dad we wouldn't bicker if he would buy the tank and install it "just in case." Years later we learned that the town's reform rabbi had bought a neighbor's house a few blocks from ours in which the prior owners had one of those tank-shelters. It was entered, he said, through a hole broken through the house's cellar wall. Not wanting to have a bomb shelter for his family on ethical grounds, he said, he had turned it into a small, underground year-round exercise pool.

Frightening as those years were, though, the really dangerous years in the nuclear era—years in which the United States was the only country with a deliverable atomic weapon—were earlier, during 1946–1950, as President Harry Truman's new and vastly better-funded and more powerful Central Intelligence Agency (CIA) quickly shifted the focus of U.S. intelligence activities from Germany and Japan to the Soviet Union, which became America's new apex enemy. During those years, in secret, Truman and his team of CIA, National Security Council advisers, and Pentagon strategists, as well as arms industry lobbyists, worked on plans to use America's new superweapon, the atomic bomb, on which the nation held a total or near-total monopoly, to prevent any other nation—most importantly the Soviet Union—from opposing U.S. global postwar dominance and from obtaining its own atomic bomb.

And it could have gotten a lot worse. On October 25, 1945, Robert Oppenheimer met with Truman at the White House to implore the man who had taken over the Oval Office from the deceased Franklin D. Roosevelt to not have the United States create the hydrogen bomb that Edward Teller was already researching. As atomic era historian Peter Kuznick, director of the Nuclear Studies Institute at American University, writes in an essay published on the website of the Arms Control Association, "When Oppenheimer met Truman for the first time . . . Truman asked Oppenheimer to guess when the Soviets would develop a bomb. When Oppenheimer said he did not know, Truman shot back that he did: 'Never!'"[2]

There was little ambiguity in such a shocking response coming from the commander in chief of the U.S. military and the head of a nation in sole possession of the most destructive weapon ever conceived by humankind—a weapon demonstrably capable of destroying entire cities in a split second. As Kuznick writes,

> Recognizing that [Secretary of State James] Byrnes and others planned to use the bomb to bully the Soviet Union, Oppenheimer feared the worst. After meeting with Oppenheimer, Secretary of Commerce Henry Wallace, the former vice president, wrote in his diary, "I never saw a man in such an extremely nervous state as Oppenheimer. He seemed to feel that the destruction of the entire human race was imminent."[3]

National security documents made public decades later show that the "father of the atom bomb" was right to worry. At the time he met the president, the United States had only one bomb in its "stockpile," but the Atomic Energy Commission, which had replaced the wartime Manhattan Project, was hard at work overseeing a program to industrialize production of the nation's new plutonium and uranium bombs, which at that point were being painstakingly and slowly assembled by hand.[4]

By the time the Soviets exploded their first bomb on August 29, 1949, the United States had upped the pace of production to more than 100 bombs per year and had a total of more than 230 available.[5] Aware of this, the Soviet Union was soon desperately trying to make more bombs of its own at the secret nuclear research and development facility called Arzamas-16 (located in the Urals and dubbed by the scientists and engineers working there "Los Arzamas").[6]

Given that it was well known that the Soviet Union had numbers of prominent physicists (as well as mathematicians, engineers, and chemists), including some who had made pioneering advances in understanding nuclear fission, it was clear that when he told Oppenheimer the Soviets would "never" get the atom bomb, Truman wasn't suggesting the USSR was incapable of creating the new weapon. He was instead stating that the United States was capable of preventing it from happening—and he wasn't talking about resorting to sanctions.

A demonstration of what the burgeoning and bloody-minded new U.S. national security state and Truman had in mind came early in 1946. That's when Stalin grew angry at plans by the United States and Britain, the USSR's erstwhile allies until World War II ended, to renege on their wartime agreement, reached while Roosevelt was president, that the oil fields in Iran would be divided up among the three victorious nations, with the USSR controlling the oil reserves lying under and across its shared northern border with Iran. As nuclear physicists Michio Kaku and Daniel Axelrod write in their book detailing the history of U.S. efforts to use its nuclear advantage to dominate the rising Soviet Union,

> In turn, the Soviets refused to withdraw their troops [from Iran], demanding concessions equal to what the British were getting. To bolster their claims, the Soviets began supporting a revolutionary movement in [the Iranian province of] Azerbaijan led by Jafar Pishevari and began rolling tanks toward their common border with Iran.

Truman was furious at this show of Soviet will. Finally, in March 1946, Truman met personally with Ambassador Andrei Gromyko and delivered an ultimatum: Either remove Soviet troops from northern Iran in 48 hours or the US will drop the atomic bomb.

"We're going to drop it on you," Truman reportedly said to Soviet Foreign Minister Gromyko.*

Remarking on a possible [nuclear] confrontation with the Soviet Union, Truman's Secretary of State James Byrnes declared, "Now we'll give it to them with both barrels." Truman later bragged that the Soviets removed their troops in just 24 hours, instead of 48 hours as agreed, causing the separatist government to collapse.[7]

A second nuclear threat from the United States came in March 1948, when the USSR shut down the land corridors through Soviet-occupied East Germany to Berlin, the former capital of Germany, which, after the German surrender, had been divided into four zones separately occupied by the war's four victors: the USSR, the United States, the United Kingdom, and France. To force the Soviets to back down, Truman, who discovered to his dismay that the United States at the time had managed to construct only thirty-five atomic bombs and had only thirty-two B-29s retrofitted to be able to carry the heavy devices and release them on targets—none of them located in Europe—played a nuclear bluff.[8] He had the U.S. Air Force ferry dozens of new and refurbished, war-damaged B-29 bombers to a military airfield in Britain. Although none of those planes filling the tarmac had even undergone the needed bomb-bay door enlargement necessary to allow them to actually release an atom bomb, and none were carrying an atomic bomb, Truman let the Soviets think he was prepared to attack them with atomic weapons if their blockade on Berlin's road-and-rail access routes were not opened to allow supplies into the western part of the city. Berlin at that time was a divided city, with the western part under U.S., British, and French occupation and control, but as the entire metropolis of West Berlin lay inside the East Zone of Germany under the control of the Soviet Red Army, those three sectors of the city were dependent for most supplies on a narrow road-and-rail corridor running from West Germany through 120 miles of Russian-held East Germany.

---

* It should be noted here that while attacking a nation that does not pose an imminent threat to the attacker, and without UN Security Council approval, is the highest of war crimes under the United Nations Charter, so is *threatening* to attack a nation absent an imminent threat and without UN sanction.

The Soviets, who assumed all the B-29s were functional atomic bombers and could be carrying and able to deliver atomic bombs, backed down and ended the road-and-rail blockade of West Berlin.

As explained in the preceding chapter, Stalin had his own surprise for Truman and the United States, which was revealed a bit over a year later: the detonation of the USSR's own nuclear bomb. That bomb, developed without any U.S. foreknowledge, was successfully exploded on August 29, 1949, catching stunned U.S. military and foreign policy strategists by complete surprise.

When the United States began ramping up production of its new atomic bombs right after the war ended, the goal, which the government tried to keep secret from both the Soviets and the American public, was not just to be able to intimidate and pressure the Soviet Union, but ultimately to destroy it if necessary as an industrial power and military rival before it could develop atomic bombs of its own.

Beyond moving to mass-produce Nagasaki-sized atomic bombs, the United States also, even before the end of World War II, began research into creating a hydrogen bomb based upon fusion—a catastrophic escalation in nuclear weaponry first proposed and promoted by physicist Edward Teller back in 1942. Unlike the atomic bomb, which was based on fission—the splitting of the heaviest radioactive elements uranium and plutonium—and was limited by various constraints in how large and powerful it could be, the hydrogen or thermonuclear bomb could be a thousand or more times as powerful as those bombs dropped on Japan. In fact, like the stars, which employ the same fusion process, the hydrogen bomb would be theoretically unlimited in its potential power. The War Department also reactivated the assembly line to begin cranking out B-29 long-range bombers and began upgrading repairable B-29s used during the war, so as to be able to deliver all those city-killing bombs it was producing deep into much of the vast Soviet Union. The War Department (rebranded euphemistically and deceptively as the Department of Defense by Congress in 1947) also began designing and producing ever more powerful, faster, and longer-range bombers, beginning with the hybrid jet-and-propeller-powered B-36, which had a ten-thousand-mile range and a bomb payload of forty tons. It went into operation in the air force in 1949.

From the moment the United States had its bomb, operational plans for a first strike on the Soviet Union were also drawn up with grisly names like Pincher (developed in June 1945, before World War II had even ended and at a time when the United States had, at most, nine bombs), Broiler

(March 1948), Bushwhacker (1948), Frolic (May 1948), Sizzle (December 1948), Trojan (January 1949), Shakedown (October 1949), and Dropshot (1949–1959). The last plan was one that was regularly updated throughout the 1950s, with each new revision featuring more targets as more atom bombs were added to the U.S. stockpile.

After 1954, when B-36 bombers began carrying the first operational hydrogen bomb, the 1.6-megaton MK-17,[9] targeting was expanded to include tens and eventually hundreds of Soviet cities as well as major cities in China and the Warsaw Pact nations as well as North Korea and Vietnam. In one of the more ludicrous of target selections, "East Berlin" was put on the list, as though somehow that Soviet-occupied sector of the city of Berlin could be wiped out without damaging the rest of the city, which included, in addition to more than a million West Germans, a large number of U.S., British, and French troops, diplomats, and civilians.

The earliest of these plans, Operation Pincher, relied on using a greater number of atomic bombs than had actually been constructed. This march toward Armageddon called for using nine atom bombs even though only two existed in June 1946. By the time of Operation Dropshot in late 1949, there were 250 bombs. The number of Soviet cities targeted in these planned attacks kept rising, from twenty-four in March 1948 (some larger cities were meant to be hit with more than one nuke, with Broiler calling for eight bombs on Moscow alone), to two hundred by the end of 1949, as the number of bombs in the U.S. nuclear arsenal kept mounting. Later Dropshot iterations used mostly thermonuclear bombs and targeted hundreds of Soviet cities, all the capitals and major cities of the Warsaw Pact nations of Eastern Europe, as well Beijing, Shanghai, and dozens of other Chinese cities, and even Hanoi in North Vietnam. (See figure D.2 in the appendix, showing an early plan to drop 180 Nagasaki-sized nuclear bombs on Soviet cities, with the targets being population centers.)

What prevented this nightmare plan for a genocidal holocaust being perpetrated by the United States on the USSR and other Communist nations was the slow pace of bomb construction and the even slower pace of new bomber construction to deliver those bombs. Those who try to claim that these plans were simply Pentagon war-gaming must explain the unexplainable: Before August 1949, when the Soviets stunned Washington experts by exploding their own bomb, those experts—scientists and policymakers alike—were predicting the war-ravaged Soviet Union would not have its own atomic bomb for eight to ten years, meaning sometime in the mid-1950s. Given that thinking, why did United States, beginning in 1945, embark on a hugely expensive crash program to mass-produce hundreds and ultimately thousands of atomic bombs and to develop a vastly more powerful hydrogen bomb? The arsenal of death they were stockpiling consisted of real nuclear bombs, not game pieces. And no other country had them, nor was any country expected to for years to come.

The U.S. atomic stockpile wasn't for nuclear deterrence in the late 1940s, either, since no other country even had a single atomic bomb until August 29, 1949. And clearly, the United States was not anticipating any kind of conventional military attack by the USSR or any other country or combination of countries for a decade, especially as it had a proven deliverable weapon nobody else had, which would deter any would-be aggressor. In the 1950s, the USSR had no significant deep-water navy, no operational transcontinental heavy bombers, and no missile subs. It had no missile that could strike the United States until 1957.

As Dan Axelrod, coauthor of *To Win a Nuclear War*, wrote to me in a response to a question about the U.S. rush to build bombs and bombers during the late 1940s,

> Americans have been told for decades that having nuclear weapons has been entirely defensive, to discourage an adversary from nuking us first and risking our retaliation. If you believe that, then you could reasonably conclude that Ted Hall made things worse by giving an adversary the opportunity to get their own nuclear weapons. In other words, he was a traitor, not just to America, but to world peace.
>
> But in the decades since the Manhattan Project and the use of the two atom bombs on Japan, we've learned much more about how Washington intended to use its nuclear monopoly and clearly that defense-only story we've been told is just not true. The US government has always recognized that nuclear superiority gives it the ability to make credible nuclear threats, even against nonnuclear countries that it wants to manipulate. Paul Nitze, a long-time US government nuclear strategist and one of Pres. Reagan's chief arms control negotiators, wrote (in 1984) that "To have the superiority at the utmost level of violence helps at every lesser level."
>
> Ted Hall presciently recognized this situation early on: that if any side had a nuclear monopoly, it would make the world less safe and more prone to military belligerence and actual attack. In the early days of US nuclear monopoly (the late 1940s), the US military made actual plans to attack the USSR, our recent WWII ally which was non-nuclear in those days. In fact, some US government advisors actually wanted to carry out the offensive strike plans. What temporarily held them back was the realization that the US had not yet stockpiled quite enough A-bombs to do a complete job of

flattening the USSR and killing millions of its people. But, just as the nuclear door was opening for them to do that job with the hundreds of US bombs coming on line needed for a successful nuclear first strike, the USSR slammed it shut with their own A-bomb test.

To the extent that Ted Hall's passing of information helped hasten the Soviet A-bomb, one can easily argue that his action actually helped prevent the start of a second nuclear war in the late 1940s and early 1950s.[10]

It would have been a very one-sided nuclear war, but to prevent that, by 1951 the Soviets also began building their own atomic bombs as quickly as they could, eliminating U.S. strategists' hope of being able to attack the Soviet Union without fearing a significant retaliatory blow, at least on U.S. bases in Europe and Asia and on U.S. allies. Meanwhile, the arms race shifted to thermonuclear weapons, the first of which, dubbed "Ivy Mike," was tested on November 1, 1952, by the United States. That first H-bomb, with a power of fifteen megatons (over one thousand times more powerful than the bomb dropped on Hiroshima), was certainly awesome, even for those scientists who had witnessed the Trinity Test or the Japan bombs' destructive results. But weighing eighty-two tons, it was of no practical value beyond proving the theory behind its construction, since no plane could possibly even get off the ground while carrying it.

The Soviets followed up with their own first hydrogen bomb less than a year later, on August 12, 1953. Probably not the result of stolen information about the U.S. bomb, the first Soviet thermonuclear bomb was based upon a completely different design worked out by Soviet physicist Andrei Sakharov.[11] It had a much lower, though still significant, blast yield of four hundred kilotons, less than one-fortieth as powerful as the U.S. hydrogen bomb but still twenty times as powerful as the Nagasaki "Fat Man" bomb. While a team of U.S. scientists led by Hans Bethe, examining the atmospheric evidence from that test, concluded the Soviet bomb had not been a true thermonuclear weapon, deriving "only" 20 percent of its power from fusion and the rest from fission, the Soviets countered by pointing out that unlike the more powerful U.S. hydrogen bomb, their first H-bomb was mission-ready and could be delivered by an existing bomber.[12] In any event, two years later on November 22, 1955, the Soviets tested their own fully thermonuclear bomb, another deliverable weapon (at least to targets in Europe or the western Pacific region) that had a blast calculated to be 1.6 megatons.

The design of the second Soviet hydrogen bomb, which was similar in design to the U.S. H-bomb, may conceivably have benefited from some information obtained from spies in the United States, but probably not much, if any. And if the Soviets did get stolen information, a likely source would have been Fuchs, who had been heading the British bomb project at Harwell until his arrest in 1950 and had heard the U.S. hydrogen bomb explained by its main inventor, Teller, in a lecture there that year. It was information he would surely have passed along to the Soviets. Fuchs, before his move back to the United Kingdom from Los Alamos in 1946, actually gathered up all the materials and information he could about both the fission bomb and the work on a fusion bomb to deliver to the Brtitish, who had been cut off at that point from the U.S. bomb project, so he was effectively spying for two countries simultaneously for a time, and no one in the British postwar nuclear project saw anything wrong with his spying on the United States *for* them.[13]

Supporters of the aggressive expansion of the U.S. nuclear arsenal after the end of World War II and the decision to develop the more powerful hydrogen bomb have always claimed that the U.S. program was (and is) purely defensive and for deterrence and is not intended for a first-strike preemptive attack. In fact, however, the Joint Chiefs of Staff at the War Department had approved a first-strike policy in dealing with the Soviet Union on July 19, 1945, just three days after the successful Trinity Test, while World War II was still on and the USSR was a key U.S. ally. This policy, JCS1496, called for "striking the first blow in a nuclear war."[14] As Kaku and Axelrod write,

> The Joint Chiefs said, "In the past, the US has been able to follow in a tradition of never striking until it is struck." In the future, the JCS said, the military must be able to "overwhelm him [the enemy] and destroy his will and ability to make war before he can inflict significant damage upon us."[15]

Skeptics of claims that the United States would launch a nuclear war should also recall that, even much later in 1997, in an era again when post-Soviet Russia was a significantly weaker nation than the United States, a group of neoconservative, fiercely anti-Russian Cold War politicians and prowar apparatchiks—including William Kristol, Robert Kagan, John Bolton, Richard Pearle, Eliot Abrams, Dick Cheney, Midge Dekter, Donald Rumsfeld, and Paul Wolfowitz—began a new organization called Project for the New American Century (PNAC). They developed a program called "Rebuilding America's Defenses: Strategies, Forces, and Resources for a New Century," which portrayed the post-Soviet United States as the world's dominant and "sole superpower." Their program called for the establishment of a "uni-polar" world dominated militarily by the United States.[16] That document stated that one of the goals of that "new world order" would be for the United States to "*prevent* [emphasis mine] any country from achieving the status" of a rival superpower. This would clearly necessitate the destruction of any attempt by another country to achieve such power. Many of those who developed that hegemonic plan during the years of the Clinton administration went on to assume important policy positions over the next decade as part of the administration of President George W. Bush.

Fortunately for the people of the Soviet Union, in the decade following World War II, the bomb Ted Hall had helped that country develop so quickly prevented the monopoly top U.S. generals and admirals had assumed they would have for a decade and caused Truman and his atomic war hawks to call a halt, or at least a hiatus, to any plans for a preventative first strike. U.S. war planners did this not because of any change of heart about the horrors of precipitating a genocidal nuclear holocaust, but because by that time there was no longer any assurance that there would not be a catastrophic response from the USSR on U.S. domestic targets or on U.S. or other NATO allies' targets in Europe.

The timing of the Soviets' obtaining their first atomic bomb was critical for another reason: By 1954, U.S. B-36 bombers were already flying around carrying 1.6-megaton H-bombs, and in 1956, the new B-52 bomber had air-dropped a new operational 15-megaton thermonuclear weapon over the Bikini Atoll—a weapon the giant new eight-engine Stratofortress *could* deliver from the United States to targets in the USSR.[17]

Since those hydrogen bombs needed to be detonated by an initial uranium or plutonium bomb, had the Soviets *not* received all the detailed information their spies (most notably Hall and Fuchs) provided, and had it instead taken eight to ten years for them to develop a *fission* bomb on their own, the U.S. ability to destroy the country completely with *hydrogen* bombs would have been vastly greater (and likely irresistibly attractive to U.S. policymakers).

A study called the Harmon Report, requested by Truman in 1949, and completed by Lieutenant General Hubert Harmon of the U.S. Air Force in 1950, when the United States was seriously planning a preventive strike on the USSR, had dismayed the president. Harmon determined that destroying even seventy Soviet cities with nuclear bombs would not, "per se, bring about capitulation, destroy the roots of Communism, or critically weaken the power of the Soviet leadership to dominate the people," but it did offer a troubling conclusion—namely, that "the advantages of [the bomb's] early use would be transcending."[18]*

Kaku and Axelrod write that faced with the "pessimistic tone" in the Harmon Report that the United States still could not, with its existing atomic bomb arsenal, "execute a decisive blow" on the Soviet Union:

> The Joint Strategic Survey Committee of the Joint Chiefs of Staff at the Pentagon informed the Pentagon that the US must build 400 atomic bombs by Jan. 1, 1953. The JSSC stated that "a military requirement exists for approximately 400 atomic bombs of destructive power equivalent to the Nagasaki-type bomb." The JSSC confidently stated that 100 of these bombs eventually reaching their targets could implement *the concept of "killing a nation."*[19]

Remember that those desired four hundred bombs were being constructed as rapidly as possible at the time this chilling excerpt was written. Indeed, for the AEC, which oversaw nuclear bomb production, the last two years of the Truman administration were a frantic time, according to Kaku and Axelrod, with 1954 viewed as a critical year—the last date by which the United States "might be strong enough to pre-empt the Soviet Union by launching a surprise attack of its own," even if the Soviet Union by then might have up to 200 nuclear bombs.[20] The authors quote a national security document from that time, NSC-68, explaining the nightmarish logic of its official policy for a preventive U.S. nuclear first strike:

> The military advantages of landing the first blow . . . require us to be on the alert in order to strike with our full weight as soon as we are attacked and, *if possible, before the Soviet blow is actually delivered.* . . . In the initial phases of an atomic war, the advantages of initiative and surprise would be very great.[21]

Kaku and Axelrod write,

> It was a race against time. On one side, Truman was pushing a crash program to build enough hydrogen bombs to execute a "decisive blow" in a possible conflict with the Soviet Union. On the other side, Stalin was demanding the

---

* As an aside, I've often been appalled that the same people who believed the Soviet people were "dominated" and oppressed by a tyrannical government were so ready to casually slaughter them by the tens of millions to destroy that government. The same mad and criminal illogic was on display two decades later in the U.S. approach to the Vietnam War, in which U.S. troops and South Vietnamese troops armed by the United States killed millions of "captive" people in Indochina in a vain effort to destroy Communist "dictatorships" in North Vietnam and Laos. It's the Vietnam War line, "We had to destroy the village in order to save it" writ large and applied to the whole population of Russia instead of North Vietnam and the South Vietnamese rural population.

development of a long-range bomber capable of mounting a retaliatory strike. The [US] military began to forecast "A-Day"—the last foreseeable opportunity for the US to mount an attack without risking direct retaliation, the day of reckoning between the US and the Soviet Union. The NSC [National Security Council] placed A-Day in 1954.[22]

Once the United States and the USSR had a rough parity in nuclear warheads and bombs and each had the planes, rockets, submarines, and other equipment needed to plausibly attack the other with hydrogen bombs during the later 1950s, the contest morphed into a grim race. On one side, the United States was spending vast sums hoping to so surpass the Soviet Union in numbers of deliverable bombs it would have a credible potential to launch a first strike and prevent any significant retaliation. On the other side was the USSR, trying to keep up, at least to the extent of posing a credible threat of responding in kind sufficient to deter such a U.S. attack. This latter contest came to be called mutual assured destruction (MAD) and it continues to this day, costing both the United States and Russia an incomprehensible amount of money that, as President Dwight Eisenhower complained in his departing letter to the nation at the end of his presidency in January 1961, could be far better used building schools and hospitals for the American people instead of for building rockets, planes, ships, submarines, warheads, and bombs.[23]

22

STILL SEEKING A REAL LOS ALAMOS SPY

Hoover felt paranoid that his job was at risk . . . [so] he rein-
vented himself as "J. Edgar Hoover, American hero" by identi-
fying a new foe to fight: Communism. The Cold War provided
a perfect backdrop.[1]

—Frank Close

On April 21, 1950, FBI director J. Edgar Hoover was informed by his chief of domestic intelligence, D. M. Ladd, of a Soviet spy cable decrypted and translated by what had by then been renamed the Army Security Agency (ASA) Venona Project. Although only the first portion of it had been decoded, those few sentences clearly identified "Theodor Kholl," the nineteen-year-old son of a Russian Jewish immigrant furrier, as a Soviet spy inside the Manhattan Project at Los Alamos.

Hoover's team of counterintelligence agents quickly confirmed, thanks to other identifying facts about the two young men mentioned in the same only partially decrypted cable, that the misspelled name "Theodor Kholl" actually referred to Theodore Alvin Hall, a teenage physicist from Harvard who had worked on the atomic bomb at Los Alamos as part of the Manhattan Project during 1944–1945, and that "Savil Saks" was Saville Sax, who had been at Harvard with Hall in 1943–1944 and became a spy courier delivering information from Hall to the NKVD in New York City. The bureau's director promptly launched a nationwide search by FBI offices as far-flung as Albuquerque, New York City, Los Angeles, San Francisco, St. Louis, Philadelphia, and Boston in 1950 to locate Hall, who had by mid-1946 left Los Alamos and been discharged from the U.S. Army, and the also identified Saville Sax, who had dropped out of Harvard.

One can easily imagine the FBI director's glee and excitement at this discovery. He had not been having great luck trying to remake himself from the dreaded scourge of mobsters he had been during the Prohibition Era and the 1930s into the scourge of hidden Communist subversives he hoped to become in the 1950s. His first big case, the capture of Communist agent Judith Coplon, an employee in the U.S. Justice Department's Foreign Agent Registration Office, came in 1948 when her name was discovered through a Venona decryption at the Signal Intelligence Service's project center at Arlington House, Virginia. Coplon, a Barnard College graduate and Young Communist League member, was arrested in early 1949 in the act of handing over some documents naming people the FBI was investigating as spies violating the Foreign Agent Registration Act to Soviet intelligence operative Valentin Gubichev. She was tried and convicted, but her conviction was subsequently overturned because an appeals court found it had been based on illegal warrantless FBI wiretaps.[2] (The ruling sounds quaint in modern America, where judges, citing "national security," routinely excuse prosecutorial excesses like torture, solitary confinement in cold cells without clothing, as well as warrantless searches and wiretaps, and the like, and where a so-called Foreign Intelligence Surveillance Court routinely rubber-stamps bureau requests for electronic surveillance.) The Coplon case had embarrassed the FBI and Hoover himself because her attorney, Archie Palmer, had been allowed to introduce an admission by the bureau that it had been bugging the phones of such notable and beloved Americans as Helen Hayes, Danny Kaye, Fredric March, Paul Robeson, Edward G. Robinson, and Dalton Trumbo.[3]

In the case of Klaus Fuchs, the second spy identified and ultimately caught, Hoover didn't even get to claim credit. This is because although the FBI was initially informed about a spy by the code name CHARL'Z in early 1950, again by the Venona Project's SIS translators, and although it was at least in part the detective work of the FBI's counterintelligence team that had figured out who that was, Fuchs had long since left the United States. Widely admired for his contributions at Los Alamos, he had returned to the United Kingdom and, completely free of suspicion that he might be a spy, had become chief of the physics department at the Harwell Atomic Energy Research Establishment near Oxford, which was where the British atomic bomb project was located. As a result, the publicity-seeking FBI director was reduced to secretly passing information about Fuchs to Britain's MI5. Thus, it was MI5 and Britain's Special Branch that ultimately pressured Fuchs to confess to his spying.

In his new anti-Communist incarnation, especially after the Soviet Union's successful atom bomb test in August of 1949, Hoover had been looking for dramatic atomic spying cases to make his name, but by early 1950 he still had little to show for the effort. Suddenly, thanks to the SIS-ASA-NSA, here was his first spy *inside* the Manhattan Project: Ted Hall, a teenage American atomic physicist, dabbler with Communist front groups, and soldier in uniform at the time of his spying for the Soviets—and with no messy phone bugging involved in identifying him. Indeed, Hall was identified by the work of the same Venona Project that had earlier identified and exposed Coplon and Fuchs and was helping uncover a network of Soviet spies headed by Julius Rosenberg (though there was little connection there to atomic spying).

In short order, Hoover's gumshoes in the FBI's counterintelligence division, working with FBI regional offices, dug up considerable information about the young Hall and Sax. Their report shows that as early as April 25, 1950, four days after learning from ASA of the Soviet cable identifying "Kholl" and "Sachs" as Soviet agents, FBI domestic intelligence chief Ladd already had sent a memo titled "Espionage-R" and stamped "Top Secret" to Hoover. It stated that Sax's mother, Bluma Sax, had "a connection with the U.S. Communist Party" and that during the war, she had been "working for Russian War Relief" (deemed a Soviet front organization).

That same FBI file memo also contained the information obtained from FBI offices around the country, including these items:

> By teletype dated April 22, 1950, the Albuquerque Division advises that Theodore Alvin Hall aka Theodore Alvin Holtzberg, was employed as a Junior Scientist by the University of California at Los Alamos from January 28, 1944 to December 28, 1944; his employment was terminated by his induction into the United States Army; Hall was then stationed at Los Alamos as a member of the Special Engineer Detachment from January 1945 to April 1946. He was denied clearance in April 1946 to return to Los Alamos as a civilian employee [CENSORED].
>
> Albuquerque has also advised that Hall was graduated from Harvard University in 1944 with a BS Degree, cum laude. His PSQ [Personal Security Questionnaire] reflects he was a member of the [Commununist Front] American Student Union from January 1938 to June 19, 1938 [when Hall

would have been age thirteen]; on this form he listed as a reference Professor Wendell Furry of the Massachusetts Institute of Technology [*sic*; he was a professor at Harvard, though he worked during the war for the Radiation Lab, which was based at MIT—ed.]. You will recall that Furry is a [CENSORED].* Hall's parents are Barnett Holtzberg born in Russia, and Rose Moskowitz Holtzberg (deceased), born in the United States.

Records at Los Alamos reflect Hall was on leave from Los Alamos in October, 1944, and visited his family at 63-03 102nd Street, Forest Hills, New York, between October 19, 1944 a, [CENSORED]

The Albuquerque Division also has advised that in June 1944, Hall was in correspondence with Saville or Savoy Sax, Lowell House, Cambridge, Massachusetts (believed to be a Harvard dormitory), concerning the change in the policy of the Communist Party and the Communist Political Association. This correspondence also revealed that Sax was leaving college permanently on June 20, 1944, and his address would be 15 West 75th Street, New York City, as of that date.[4]

The memo continues:

The reports of Special Agent [CENSORED] dated March 24 and April 4, 1944 at Boston, Massachusetts, in the case entitled American Youth for Democracy, formerly known as the Young Communist League, Internal Security—C, reflect that one Saville Sax, Harvard, was a member of the Wendell Phillips Club of the AYD in Cambridge, Massachusetts. In Special Agent [CENSORED] report in the same matter dated May 2, 1944, Sax is referred to as one of the "key people" in the AYD.[5]

The memo concludes: "[CENSORED] the investigations of Sax and Hall are being handled in one case. Separate cases will be opened later on them if subsequent developments indicate the desirability of making each the subject of an individual file."†

---

* Because Furry was known to the FBI to be a Communist, though he never admitted to membership in the Party, and although Ted was quite likely unaware of his professor's politics, this relationship would have been seen as very significant to Hoover and the FBI's counterintelligence investigators.

† This bureau decision, never changed, to combine Sax's and Hall's FBI files into one (referred to as the Saville Sax file), delayed, on grounds of the privacy exemption to the Freedom of Information Act, any public or media access to FBI information on the two spies until after *both* were deceased. As a result, none of the records were available until November 1, 1999, even though Sax's would otherwise have become available after his death on September 25, 1980. Boria Sax told me that he was told by the FBI that they had two files on his father—one he eventually received that was on the two men together, and another, vastly larger (Boria Sax claims he was informed it ran to about twenty-four hundred pages), on just his father, which he was told would take a year or longer to declassify and which he never obtained.

A third report originated in the Chicago FBI field office. Dated May 2, 1950,[6] it summarizes what is known about both Ted Hall's and Saville Sax's academic records and their various places of residence during that period. It then notes,

> An examination of the Class Report of 1944, issued in 1947, identified Theodore Alvin Hall as then associated with the Institute for Nuclear Studies, University of Chicago, Chicago, Illinois, and as being a research assistant in the Department of Physics in the Chicago Bureau, which was taking the lead in the investigation, where Special Agent McQueen was heading up the investigation, summarizes all the information on the two young spies gathered up by the initial dragnet by agents around the country.[7]

This would mark the first indication to the bureau about where Hall had gone after leaving Los Alamos. Coincidentally, Chicago is where Robert McQueen, the FBI's local bureau special agent in charge (SAC), was moved after serving with the FBI's counterintelligence division during the pursuit and frustrated prosecution of Coplon.

Certainly of interest to Hoover, the Boston report notes that Hall's adviser at Harvard was

> known to [CENSORED] then serving [CENSORED] of the Communist Party, USA, District #1 Boston, Massachusetts, and this informant further indicated that WENDELL [Furry] was reportedly associated with a group known to informant only as "H.T." but the informant believed referred to Henry Thoreau. This information provided by [CENSORED] appears in confirmation of the material provided by Boston Confidential informant . . . [who] advised on May 30, 1943 plans had been made for a field day to be held by the Young Communist League at Boston, Massachusetts, and that in connection with the announcement relating to this program TED HALL, a resident of Lowell or Leverett House, D-42, Harvard College, Cambridge, Massachusetts, was among those persons who had been invited to participate in the picnic. The Young Communist League was the predecessor to the American Youth for Democracy, both of which organizations have been included by the Attorney General as coming within the purview of Executive order #9835.[8]

Another report, originating in the New York bureau, indicated that on October 23, 1944, Sax told an FBI source that he had tried to arrange a meeting with Communist Party USA general secretary Earl Browder and that he had "important information" for Browder. (This independently obtained FBI source's information could have been a major opening for the FBI to try and get Sax to admit, without their having to rely on Venona decrypts, what he and Hall had been up to on that first trip to volunteer as spies. But based upon the FBI's voluminous files on Sax, it appears not to have been used.)[9]

But the real kicker in terms of putting Hoover's pursuit of Hall and Sax into high gear was a report from the Boston FBI office that included information obtained from various schools and universities Sax and Hall had attended, noting that Harvard records said Ted had an older brother who was, during the war, a lieutenant and later major in the U.S. Army.

It didn't take long for the FBI to learn something even more interesting: Ted's older brother, Edward Nathaniel Hall, at that point still a major in the U.S. Air Force, was working as an aeronautical engineer at a top-secret rocket engine lab located on the grounds of Wright-Patterson Air Force Base outside Dayton, Ohio, where he was designing advanced rocket motors for nuclear-capable missiles.

After almost nine months of fevered investigation by the FBI's counterintelligence unit of both Ted and Ed Hall, as well as Saville Sax and even Joan Hall's younger brother, Air Force private Philip Krakover (who, while attending flight school in hopes of becoming a pilot, had been busted by MPs during a raid on a local gay bar), Hoover, on January 6, 1951, sent an internal letter to Air Force general Joseph Carroll. The bureau director knew Carroll well, as the Chicago-based FBI agent had been working as a top aide in his office when Air Force secretary Stuart Symington had asked for the recommendation of someone to head up that new military branch's Office of Special Investigations.[10]

In that letter to his former aide and protégé, Hoover wrote,

Dear Gen. Carroll:

Transmitted herewith for your information is a memorandum concerning Major Edward Nathaniel Hall, ASN 0-434506, and Private Philip Krakover, ASN AF-16342051

Neither Major Hall nor Private Krakover has been the subject of investigation by this Bureau, and no investigation of them is contemplated. Inquiry concerning Theodor Alvin Hall, brother of Major Hall and brother-in-law of Private Krakover, was instituted upon receipt of information from a highly confidential source of known reliability that Hall has been engaged in Soviet espionage activity. . . . Investigation of Hall is continuing and you will be advised of any developments believed to be of interest.

Investigation has disclosed that Theodore Alvin Hall is a brother of Major Edward Nathaniel Hall, ASN 0-434506. Major Hall, as of September 27, 1950 was assigned to the Power Plant Laboratory, Engineering Division, Wright-Patterson Air Force Base, Dayton, Ohio, and was working on a highly secret and confidential project.

It has also been determined that Philip Krakover, [CENSORED but likely says: brother-in-law of Theodore Alvin Hall] is a Private in the United States Air Force, ASN AF-16342051, and as of October 28, 1950, was assigned to the 3726th Training Squadron, Lackland, Texas, Air Force Base.

Sincerely yours,
John Edgar Hoover
Director

Attached as an enclosure to that rather (for Hoover) personal note was a bureau report authored by J. M. Kelly, also dated January 6, 1951. That report reads,

Jan. 6, 1951

Re: MAJOR EDWARD NATHANIEL HALL,
ASN 0-434506;
PRIVATE PHILIP KRAKOVER,
ASN AF-1632051

During the course of an investigation of Theodore Alvin Hall, who resides at 6002 University Avenue, Chicago, Illinois, it has been ascertained that both he and [CENSORED but apparently the name of Ted's wife, Joan Krakover] have been extremely active in the affairs of the Progressive Party of Illinois. A reliable confidential source has advised that the Progressive Party of Illinois is actually under the control of the Communist Party. Hall was graduated from Harvard University in 1944 with a B.S. degree in physics, and is presently employed by the Institute of Radio Biology and Biophysics of the University of Chicago. Hall and his wife have been extremely active in soliciting signatures to the "Stockholm Peace Pledge" and signatures to place the Progressive Party on the Illinois ballot for the November 1950 election. On May 3, 1950, [CENSORED reference to Joan Krakover Hall] was elected corresponding secretary of the Fifth Ward (Chicago) Progressive Party, and membership meetings of that club have been held at the Hall residence.

On July 9, 1950, Hall and four associates were taken into custody by the Chicago Police Department for soliciting signatures to politicians to place the Progressive Party on the Illinois ballot and to outlaw the Atom Bomb, but were released without charges being lodged against them. Hall also has been active in the affairs of the Chicago Tenants Action Council, which organization has been described by informants of known reliability as a "Communist front organization" which is receiving active support from the Communist Party. Most of Hall's associates in Chicago have a background of past or present membership in the Communist Party or other Communist organizations.

This news, coming from his old boss and mentor at the FBI, had to have come as a shock to General Carroll. But the response from his protégé must have come as an even bigger surprise to the FBI director. (See figure D.1 in the appendix, "Letter from FBI Director J. Edgar Hoover to Air Force Director of the Office of Special Investigations for the U.S. Air Force Gen. Joseph F. Carroll.")

23

BUSTED!

*What's important at this time is to re-clarify the difference
between hero and villain.*

—FBI director J. Edgar Hoover

General Joseph Carroll wasn't the only person shocked by J. Edgar Hoover's news that an active-duty U.S. Air Force major, working on a top-secret missile project at Wright Patterson Air Force Base, was the elder brother of a known atomic spy. Just two months later, Ted Hall and Saville Sax were at least as shocked as the Air Force's intelligence chief when FBI agents approached them separately, without warning, and escorted them separately to the bureau's downtown Chicago office, without either knowing the other was there. They were held for grilling in different rooms. One pair of FBI agents showed up on Friday afternoon, March 16, 1951, at Ted's office in the physics building of the University of Chicago after first meeting with his department chair and saying that they wanted to speak with him. At the same time, another pair of agents walked up to Sax on the street.

These were "arrests" without handcuffs—an "offer you can't refuse" sort of thing—and neither young man attempted to reject the "invitation." Neither of them had hired or even consulted with an attorney at that point regarding their legal jeopardy or how to handle such a situation, nor did either man say he would not agree to be questioned without an attorney present, which would have been their right.

Not that they hadn't been dreading the possibility of being caught up in the fever of anti-Communist spy hunting that was already well underway in the United States at the time. The highly publicized trial of alleged Soviet spy Judith Coplon had taken place in 1948, and in February 1950, Klaus Fuchs, at the time the head of the Theoretical Physics Division of Britain's Harwell Atomic Energy Research Center, had confessed in Britain to spying and had been sentenced that March to fourteen years in prison. Even closer to home, in July and August 1950, first Julius and then Ethel Rosenberg had been arrested as Soviet spies. At the very time Hall and Sax were picked up and interrogated by FBI agents, the Rosenbergs were standing trial for their lives in a federal courtroom in lower Manhattan, facing the capital charge of "conspiracy to commit espionage," with the evidence presented including the passing of information relating to the atomic bomb.

Although they weren't aware of it, more than a year before the Rosenbergs were arrested, two Soviet atomic spies code-named MLAD and STAR had been the first Manhattan Project spies to be identified by name along with their code names in the intercepted and partially decrypted Venona Project cables sent between Soviet spies in the United States and Moscow NKVD headquarters. Once they had been exposed, at least to FBI investigators, as spies by the SIS code-crackers, Hoover had immediately been alerted to the breakthrough by the Army Security Agency, successor to the SIS, in late April 1950.

While keeping the information about the two young spies tightly held within the Venona Project and the FBI, Hoover immediately put bureau offices around the country on the case, with agents in Hall and Sax's hometown of New York City, Boston (which covers Cambridge, where they had both been students at Harvard), Chicago (where both were living at the time), Albuquerque (which covers Los Alamos), St. Louis (where the files of discharged service people are stored), San Francisco (where much of the bomb development program and personnel at the Los Alamos operation had been shifted after the war), and other cities. Agents were put to work trying to locate the two men and interview people who would have known them during various periods. The goal was to try to develop independent evidence about the two being spies separate from what was revealed in the secretly decrypted Venona cables. These thousands of pages of intercepted cables and the fact that the code used to keep them unreadable was being gradually and painstakingly cracked was a secret the FBI was so keen on keeping from the Soviets that even the CIA and Truman himself—and for a long time, the British MI5 organization—were kept in the dark.

This, of course, meant that at least during 1950 and into 1951, including during their interrogations of the two men, FBI agents needed to be discreet in their questioning of Hall's and Sax's friends and family and had to avoid citing the spy cables in questioning any potential witness or interrogating the two men themselves. Hall and Sax couldn't be told that they had been outed as spies in those secret Soviet spy cables, lest they alert the Soviets, who would then move their remaining spies to safety and change their code. This secrecy applied even when Hoover notified General Carroll at the Air Force Office of Special Investigations. Carroll—a man with long prior experience at the bureau working as an assistant to Hoover—certainly knew "fudge words" when he saw or heard them, as he did when Hoover, in a personal letter dated January 6, 1951, attributed the evidence that Ted Hall had been "engaged in Soviet espionage activity" not to captured and decoded Soviet spy cables but rather more cryptically to "receipt of information from a highly confidential source of known reliability."[1]

When the agents brought Hall and Sax to the FBI office on the nineteenth floor of the forty-one-story Bankers Building on 105 West Adams Street, instead of using the elegant lobby elevators, they brought their suspects one at a time in the back way from an alley, up a tall, poorly lit stairway, in an effort to make them more anxious. The interrogations, which at times got heated for both men, involved several agents, with one taking notes, in each room. Sax's interrogation lasted two hours, while Ted's ran for almost three.

According to Ted's wife Joan, the two men had discussed well in advance of that day what they would do if an arrest ever came. Her husband, she said, planned to try to be assertive, accusing his interrogators of being deceitful and "tricky," and to attempt as much as possible to avoid getting caught in a lie. Sax, who had taken courses in acting and theater, decided to pretend he had a problem remembering things like dates and places and other details— even his wedding date from just two or three years before. Both tactics seem like high-risk and amateurish approaches, but they also seem, based on the agents' reports, to have worked pretty well.

In general, the two reports[2] on the interrogation sessions of the two men, which are combined into a single twenty-one-page report (the report on the Hall interrogation starting on page two and running eight single-spaced typed pages to the top of page ten, and the report on the Sax interrogation starting immediately on page ten with the heading "<u>SAVILLE SAX</u>" and running to page twenty-one)[3] show that the FBI interrogators appeared to know a good deal from what was in the eight at least partially decrypted spy cables reporting on Hall's and Sax's actions. But without citing those cables and the information in them, they knew little that would allow them to trip the men up in lies—which are felonies when being questioned by an FBI agent, even not under oath.

For example, Hall was specifically asked if he knew Sergei Kurnakov or Anatoly Yakolev (a cover surname used by Yatskov while in the United States, where he was consul in the Soviet Consulate in New York and head of the atomic spying effort). Though he had dealings with both, which was clear from the cables, Hall denied knowing them—though he wisely admitted to recognizing Kurnakov as a Russian journalist, since Kurnakov wrote articles about the Soviet Union's war with Germany for some mainstream U.S. magazines.

Asked about his fateful trip to New York City in October 1944, Hall said he had gotten a leave to visit his family there for his nineteenth birthday, but denied remembering how he had traveled there and back, that is, whether it was by train or by plane. While admitting he had met Sax once in Albuquerque, he claimed it had been by "chance" that they ran into each other there, claiming he had gone to the town to buy records and that he hadn't been informed in advance by Sax that he was visiting the University of New Mexico to look into transferring there to pursue the study of anthropology. (An astonishing claim, given that the two had been close friends at college and that Sax knew Hall was at Los Alamos, only an hour away, making it strain credulity that he wouldn't have alerted his friend to such a purportedly innocent exploratory journey across the country to a destination so near to him.) The agents did surprisingly little, at least according to their report on the session, to challenge the credibility of those rather unbelievable claims.

The reports on the two interrogations show that both Hall and Sax were informed that they were being investigated for espionage, and both simply denied that they had provided information to the Soviet Union. When asked at the end of the three-hour grilling if agents could search his home, and being told that he need not consent to such a search without a warrant, Hall

first stated that it would be agreeable with him and then asked for time to think the matter over. After several minutes he said he would be agreeable to the search as there was nothing in his house pertaining to espionage, but that due to the fact that he did have a lot of "left wing" literature he desired to propose a condition. This condition was that the searching agents would take no list or any record of the "left wing" literature in his possession and that as each piece was found he would have permission to destroy it and that the agents would not at any later date take "cognizance" of this material.

The report adds dryly, "A search was not conducted."[4]

There were only two short questions asked of Hall regarding his older brother, Edward Hall. The first came early in the questioning, when Hall

> discussed some trouble that his CENSORED [Edward Hall] had "gotten into when he was in England in the army during World War II as a result of a letter to [Ted] HALL from "CENSORED," [clearly a reference to Edith Shawcross Hall, Ed's wife] in which she made a statement construed by the Army censors [at Los Alamos] to mean she had knowledge of the Atomic Bomb prior to its first public use. HALL stated that she did not have knowledge of the bomb and had been referring to the use of Rockets which she had read about. Ted then implied that the above episode resulted in his having some difficulty in getting out of the United States Army Service. He said it was possible at that time for persons with certain scientific backgrounds to be discharged from the Army and work on atomic projects as civilians. He could not get one of those discharges, however, although other persons did, although he continued to work on the project as a soldier.[5]

The other question relating to Ed was about Ted's relationship with his older brother. The report says that Ted told the agents his brother "had graduated from college as an engineer and was very much interested in aero mechanics." He told them Ed "went into the Army before the war and is presently doing flight research at Wright Field, Dayton, Ohio." Asked about their relationship, Ted told them he was "not in close contact" with his older brother.

After almost three solid hours of being grilled, Hall said he would "rather not continue the interview" but that he was "willing to return": "He claimed he had some personal matters to take care of on Saturday, March 17, 1951 and so could not continue the interview then, but would appear at the office at 9:30 am on Monday, March 19, 1951."[6]

The same report goes on to say HALL returned as promised three days later but didn't stay long. It reads,

> At 9:35 am he stated that after discussing the matter with his wife and Saville Sax, he felt he had nothing more to say and would not continue the interview since he distrusted the FBI. He was asked to be specific concerning his distrust and he would not explain. He stated that he had read an analysis by former Judge Landis of the first HARRY BRIDGES trial,[7] which reflected the FBI had purchased perjured testimony. This statement was refuted by the interviewing agents. He said that the FBI had lied to him but could not identify the incident. He also said the FBI has a capacity to go cleverly from

one line of questioning to another without the interviewer being aware of what is happening.

HALL stated that he had not been mistreated and that his legal rights had been specifically pointed out to him.

At 9:52, the interview was terminated.[8]

The two other agents interrogating Sax during Ted Hall's first interview on March 16 at the same time in a different room of the bureau office didn't make out any better. The report on the Sax grilling states that the agents

originally approached Sax at 2:58 on the southeast corner of 62nd and State Streets, Chicago, Illinois. He was advised there was something of importance pertaining to the national security of the United States which the Agents desired to discuss with him and he was invited to come to the Chicago Office. He immediately agreed.

After furnishing the agents with his full name and his address at 1370 East 61st Street, and being advised of his right to counsel and the fact that any statement he might make could be used against him, Sax very quickly demonstrated an appallingly poor memory. The agents wrote, "SAX stated he believes he was married about November 1949 in City Hall at Chicago. He stated he has a son BORIA who is about two years old. He said that he does not recall the date and month, but that since his son is now two years old he was probably born about March 1949."[9]

Following this stunningly imprecise recollection of rather recent important milestones in his life, the agents wrote,

It is noted that SAX stated on several occasions that he has a bad memory for face[s], names, dates and places. He says he is not entirely sure as to the order of time with respect to when he lived in certain places, when he had certain employment, or when he attended certain schools. He stated that in 1939 through 1941 he attended school in New York City. About 1942 he went to Harvard. During the period of time covered by his attendance at Harvard he stated that he was employed for a time at a rubber plant near Cambridge. He said this is the first employment he recalls while at Harvard, but it was not necessarily in 1942. SAX stated he was also employed during this time by a road construction company at Pine Bush, NY. This employment was during summer. SAX stated he does not remember the name of the rubber plant or the construction company.

SAX also advised that he was employed in New Bedford, Massachusetts, in a small machine shop which repaired fishing boats, but he could not recall the name of the company.

When the agents tried to refresh his memory, likely using Social Security records they had obtained that provided the names and addresses of places he had worked—the ones listed above and others—he said only that he couldn't recall; they could be right or not. Nor, he claimed, could he remember places he lived when he had worked at different jobs.

Rather incredibly, Sax told the agents that he decided to attend Harvard because a friend of his (whose name is censored in my copy of this FBI file, despite the passage of so many years) "suggested it was a good school."

The agents then wrote,

> According to SAX, he had one roommate at Harvard who became a lasting friend, namely THEODORE HALL. He said HALL is now at the University of Chicago where he is employed doing research work in Biology. . . . He said HALL had been an assigned roommate and he had not previously been acquainted with him.
>
> HALL, according to SAX, comes from Queens, New York City. He said that they have associated some since they were at Harvard together, where he said they first met in about the middle of 1945, but later stated this must have been in 1943.
>
> With further regard to his associations with HALL he stated that during World War II the latter was at Los Alamos. He then stated that he became acquainted with HALL about six months prior to the time Hall went to Los Alamos. He stated he corresponded with HALL who was there but that he does not think HALL was in the Army. He recalled that HALL was taking physics while at Harvard but claimed not to know the nature of HALL's work at Los Alamos.
>
> SAX stated that the correspondence between him and HALL during HALL's stay at Los Alamos was intermittent, and pertained to astronomy. He said he could recall no letters from HALL which had political overtones.
>
> According to SAX, HALL visited in New York on vacations, once or twice while he was working a Los Alamos. SAX stated that he could not really recall the time of the year or the year of HALL's visits. He said that the discussions he and HALL had at that time were "silly," since he was taking a course on astronomy and he had some theories pertaining to astronomy which he desired HALL to put in mathematical form. HALL was unable to do this. SAX said he believed he was still going to Harvard at this time but later stated he believed that visit of HALL, during the time HALL was at Los Alamos,

took place in New York. SAX stated that on those visits, HALL did not ask any favors of him, and SAX stated he did not do anything for HALL.

The report states that Sax did say he was at the Soviet Consulate in New York once or twice and that he went there

> because his mother has relatives in Russia and he wanted to find out if they were alive. SAX stated that he discovered they were not alive. . . . He denied that he was ever at the Soviet Consulate for any other reason than given above, He said that while at the Soviet Consulate he discussed nothing except the problem involving his relatives. . . . He claims he was never asked and never did furnish any information which might be of use to the Soviet Government nor did he ever act as a middle-man for the transmittal of such information.

Resuming the rather bizarre line of questioning of Sax about his relationship with Ted Hall, the agents wrote,

> To return to HALL, SAX stated that HALL had once told him he had failed to obtain security clearance, but that he did not know why.
> He said he has never seen a photograph of HALL insofar as he can recall. He says he might have seen such a photograph, however. He said he never received a photograph of HALL and that he does not recall HALL during the latter's vacations and does not recall any discussions with HALL, which would indicate who else, other than SAX, that HALL would contact during these vacations. According to SAX, HALL probably saw him in New York during the latter's vacation or vacations. He does not recall whether it was once or more than once. This was during a period while HALL was at Los Alamos, when he came east for a vacation. SAX saw HALL, during more than two days of such vacation, when they spent a couple of hours together on at least two times during at least one vacation. . . . SAX believes that HALL stayed at his parents' home in Queens, New York, and claims not to know HALL's parents and does not know whether they live in an apartment or house. According to SAX HALL probably came to see him in the afternoons and he believes they went boating in Central Park and stated no one else was along.

Asked about New Mexico, Sax was equally vague and was obviously feigning an exaggerated inability to remember:

> He thinks he saw HALL while HALL was in New Mexico, but he does not recall that HALL was in uniform at that time. SAX said he was very depressed at that time and was living in a dream world. He said he does not know when

he went to New Mexico but it was probably after the last time he flunked out at Harvard. He said his memory is very blank in this regard. He added that he only went to New Mexico to look around and that he went there because TED HALL was the only person he could rely on to get him out of his state of depression. He said he did not tell HALL he flunked out of Harvard and claimed this was the only occasion he was in New Mexico. SAX said that he was thinking of studying Anthropology at the University of New Mexico because there were Indians there. He said he got this idea from friends. . . .

SAX said he traveled to New Mexico from New York by bus, but he is not sure what line he took. He said he is not sure to which city he went in New Mexico but that the University of New Mexico was in that city. He stayed in some small hotel and that he recalls the University is on a highway going through the city . . . he believes it was either Albuquerque or Santa Fe. He said he stayed there for a couple of days, that he visited classes at the university, that he does not know what season it was except that it was mild. That he saw no one there who he knew that he did not see HALL while there but, as stated above that he might have seen HALL.

The agents wrote that they showed Sax photos of David Greenglass, Julius Rosenberg, Alfred Asarant, Nicola Napoli, Joel Barr, William Perl, Sergei Kournukoff, Max Plitcher, Morton Sobel, and Michael Sedrovich, none of whom he said he recognized. He also told them that he never saw a list of important atomic scientists and that Hall never mentioned or showed him such a list. The agents then offered public information known about the names of the people in the photographs they had shown him and asked if he recognized their identities. They wrote: "SAX stated he had not been reading the newspapers recently and that the names still meant nothing to him."

At the end of the questioning, the report states,

SAX was then invited to continue the interview at a later date when he was prepared to discuss his relationship with Soviet representatives.

He was also advised that it was desired that a search be made of his premises with his permission, and he was advised of his constitutional right not to have such a search made and that he was not under arrest. He agreed to consent to a search.

This simultaneous interrogation of Hall and Sax on March 16, 1951, plus the short visit the following Monday by Hall, when he announced his unwillingness to participate further in any questioning, were the only occasions where the FBI interrogated the two men.

This was certainly not a good candidate for an episode of the popular 1965 TV series *The FBI*, where the savvy agents always got their man!

Given that there were clear discrepancies between their answers to questions relating to Hall's October 1944 trip to New York, where he and Sax made their connection to Soviet agents, and to Sax's trip to Albuquerque, where he met and picked up important bomb information from Hall for delivery back to the New York *Rezidentura*, it is clear that the FBI had a way to move forward in their effort to pursue the case if they had wanted to use it:

They had grounds from the interviews to pursue charges of lying to the FBI, even given Sax's rather comical pretense of having almost no memory.

They could have interrogated, or just threatened to interrogate, the two men's spouses.

They also had plenty of other areas to look further into. For example, thanks to FOIA filings that revealed twelve hundred pages of FBI files of informants,[10] we know that the bureau had hundreds of people reporting to it from inside the U.S. Communist Party—some in its headquarters—at least one of whom likely would have known Sax had gone there in mid-October 1944 attempting to see Party secretary Earl Browder, which he had denied doing during his interrogation. Sax had in fact told Harold Smith, at that time Browder's personal secretary, that he "must see Browder as soon as possible because he has some information for him." No attempts to challenge his statements were put to him at his interrogation session,[11] nor was he ever charged with lying to the FBI.

Robert McQueen, who left the FBI in the early 1970s to take an appointment as an assistant judge in Lake County, Illinois, was elevated to circuit judge in 1977, where he served until his retirement in 1982. He was interviewed by Marcia Kunstel in the mid-1990s in the San Fernando Valley home where he had retired. Of that interview, Kunstel writes,

"I believed they were guilty then, and I didn't necessarily believe what they said, of course," McQueen remembered. In addition to what he knew from the secret Soviet cables, McQueen found Hall's demeanor suspicious. "That is the curious thing, that he has never expressed resentment that he was questioned about this. An innocent man usually does. 'Why are you asking me these questions?' There was not any outraged denial. Just calm, matter-of-fact statements."[12]

McQueen and the bureau's investigation of this case, judging from the documents in Sax and Hall's joint FBI file, appears to stop with not even much in the way of further monitoring, especially of Hall's activities, suggesting strongly that it was orders external to the FBI that forced a halt to the bureau's pursuit of the case. Unfortunately, further information available now and presented later in this book, much of it likely known to McQueen, cannot be considered or discussed by him, as he died in 2017 at the age of ninety-six.

Whatever the reason that counterintelligence veteran McQueen and his fellow agents were so bizarrely reluctant to press Hall and Sax about their obvious lies and evasions regarding their activities and movements in New York and New Mexico, one particular example of their lack of aggressiveness, occurring only hours after their interrogation in the Chicago FBI office, stands out.

When Ted arrived home after his ordeal, he told his anxious wife Joan about what had happened and then told her they needed to quickly scour the house for incriminating material—leftist literature, the activist list Joan maintained as membership secretary for the local Chicago chapter of the Progressive Party, letters Ted had written to or received from Savy Sax, and so on. They packed these in a suitcase and drove to a bridge over the Chicago Drainage Canal—a foul-smelling waterway filled with sewage and industrial waste that ran through the city—and in the dark of night tossed all the material over the railing and watched it sink into the black, fetid water.[13]

Oddly, though both the Hall and Sax homes were supposedly being monitored by FBI agents round the clock, there is no report in their joint FBI file of Ted and Joan being tailed by federal agents on that particular car journey to the bridge (on which they brought along their one-year-old daughter Ruthie) for an act that could almost certainly have qualified as "obstruction of justice" or as evidence of guilt of some kind had it been witnessed, even if they hadn't been caught first with the potentially incriminating material, given that Ted had been informed that they were being investigated for espionage.

There's a reason for that lapse, but it only came to light when I pored over Ted and Savy Sax's FBI files.

24

THE RED SCARE YEARS

HUAC, McCarthyism, and the Rosenberg Trial

Are you now or have you ever been a member of the Communist Party?

—Required question on many Cold
War-era job applications

War always leads to unintended consequences, and World War II was no exception. U.S. involvement in the European theater of World War II was actually relatively limited until quite late in that war. The United States officially entered the conflict by declaring war on the Axis powers only on December 7, 1941, after the Japanese bombing of Pearl Harbor in Hawaii, more than two years after the British and French had declared war against Germany on September 3, 1939. That declaration had come in response to Hitler's attack on Poland. By May of the following year, French and British armies were battling Germany's Wehrmacht. (Britain also declared war on Japan on December 7, 1941.)

Serious fighting began immediately following the Pearl Harbor attack, with U.S. and Japanese naval forces engaging in fierce battles all across the Pacific, and U.S. soldiers battling Japanese soldiers in the Philippines, a U.S. colony. In the European theater, though, the United States only first directly engaged German forces—and then only in a limited manner—in November 1942 in North Africa. While there was U.S. naval action against German U-boats in the North Atlantic, Washington didn't commit significant ground troops to battle against Nazi forces until they landed in Italy in September 1943. The U.S. Army didn't land troops along France's Channel coast, opening up a western front against the German Wehrmacht, until June 6, 1944. That was just eleven months before Germany's unconditional surrender on May 7, 1945. Meanwhile, the major military engagements by combined U.S., British, and Canadian troops against German ground forces came almost three years after Germany launched an all-out invasion of the Soviet Union. By then the best units and equipment of the German war machine had already been chewed up and were in retreat, chased and harried by pursuing Soviet Red Army and partisan forces in what General Douglas MacArthur admiringly called "one of the greatest military campaigns in history."[1]

By the end of the six-year global war, the two big European powers— Britain and France—were weak, militarily and economically. The Axis powers—Germany, Japan, and Italy—had been decimated and defeated, with Germany occupied and divided in half. Japan, with the northern Kuril Islands retaken by the Soviets, had seen most of its cities decimated by U.S. incendiary bombs and two nuclear bombs. With the major colonial powers weakened, the war's conclusion led to a wave of liberation movements in colonies and countries long dominated by Western powers in Africa, the Middle East, Asia, Southeast Asia, Latin America, and the Caribbean. These captive nations, from India, Indonesia, and Vietnam to Nigeria, Ghana, Kenya, Tunisia, and Algeria, began efforts to throw off Western imperial and colonial domination, a process that began in the late 1940s and accelerated through the decade of the 1950s.

Liberation movements often were not Communist, but were generally opposed by the United States nonetheless because of geopolitics. Since the Soviet Union frequently, sometimes even just in a token manner, supported anticolonial liberation movements and supplied small arms like Kalashnikov rifles, the United States reflexively opposed them.[2] But even when U.S. foreign policy was focused not on opposing Communist "expansion" but simply by a desire to ensure U.S. control of key resources, global markets, and free access to U.S. corporate investment, the result was that liberation movements turned in response to Moscow and later sometimes to Beijing for support. (Fidel Castro's July 26 Movement rebel force in the late 1950s and Ho Chi Minh's Viet Minh through the 1950s and into the 1960s are good examples of this. After first appealing unsuccessfully for U.S. backing or at least neutrality in their drives for independence or an end to foreign domination, both turned to the USSR and China for support because of active U.S. opposition to their struggles.)

As this new era of proxy wars between the United States and the Soviet Union—and later, to a lesser extent, China—began developing in the late 1940s, U.S. policymakers and military strategists suffered a rude awakening. Coming out of World War II as the world's undisputed sole military superpower and with the undamaged country's economy booming at a time that the rest of the world's developed nations were in actual and figurative rubble, they believed they would have at least a decade in which to basically dictate the terms of a new Pax Americana world order—longer if they prevented the Soviets from getting an atomic bomb. This rosy fantasy, however, was literally blown apart within just four years of Japan's surrender, when the Soviet Union stunned the U.S. national security and foreign policy establishment with the surprise detonation of its own twenty-one-kiloton plutonium bomb on August 29, 1949.

A little more than a month after that explosive event, China's Communists and their People's Liberation Army, under the leadership of Party Chairman Mao Tse-tung, won that country's long civil war and national liberation revolution. The sight of Mao and other Chinese Communist Party leaders standing together before a massive cheering throng in Beijing's Tiananmen Square to announce the founding of the People's Republic of China underlined the sudden, unexpected change in America's global political fortunes.

The U.S. response to these three unanticipated developments was a Cold War and nuclear arms race with the Soviet Union and an endless series of proxy wars in Third World countries and colonies. Because U.S. foreign policy, largely in the hands of key cabinet officers and White House advisers who were current or former corporate or financial executives, was focused on protecting markets and controlling resources in the Third World and "containing" the anticapitalist Soviet Union and China, the United States found itself confronting not just a nuclear-armed Soviet Union but also new Communist nations in Eastern Europe and Asia, as well as armed uprisings against pro-Western leaders and comprador neocolonial regimes in places like Greece, Vietnam, India, Indonesia, Laos, Cuba, and the Belgian Congo and other African colonies and former colonies.

The realization that the USSR had obtained its own atomic bomb so early thanks to a successful spy network operating within the top-secret Manhattan Project—a spy network that had functioned without any notice throughout the war and into the late 1940s—fueled paranoia in the U.S. government and the mass media and also among the American public that Communists might have infiltrated all parts of society and government. There were accusations that a Communist-infiltrated U.S. Foreign Service, for example, must have facilitated the Communist movement's success in China's civil war. After all, the paranoid thinking went, how could such a colossal foreign policy disaster have otherwise occurred? This kind of reductionist thought process, encouraged by government propaganda and a sensationalist media, led to an irrational fear of a "Red menace" threatening the United States and its capitalist way of life, both from abroad militarily and at home through alleged fifth-column American Communists imagined to be infesting everything from the State Department to the Pentagon, academia, public schools, trade unions, and even the Hollywood movie industry.

As this was happening, there was a resurgence of the right wing in both major parties, which had been held in check by Franklin D. Roosevelt's extremely durable wartime popularity. Upon his death early in his unprecedented fourth term, however, when Vice President Harry Truman took over the White House, the right began gaining traction, both with the public and in Congress. The 1948 presidential election had been a squeaker, which Truman ultimately won, but there were also clear signs that the incipient fascism Ted Hall had feared possible after the war was starting to rear its head in Washington and across the nation. Large corporations, including financial houses, arms makers, and others, were anxious to crack down on unions and to unwind some of the big New Deal programs of the Roosevelt era, especially Social Security and the very notion of a national health care system. Scaremongering about alleged nefarious Communists working underground in America and around the globe was one of their strategies.

J. Edgar Hoover, who for more than two decades had headed the FBI, standing out as savvy and power-hungry official in a city of power-hungry people, saw that change in the political winds and was quick to take advantage of it. As British physicist and atomic-era historian Frank Close explains, Hoover saw an opportunity and grabbed it:

> In the years after 1945, when the war against fascism morphed into a Cold War with the Soviet Union, J. Edgar Hoover began an egomaniacal war of his own. Anti-communism and subversion became *bête-noires* in the United States, and Hoover unashamedly exaggerated the threat to gain funding for the FBI. Under his direction, the Bureau pursued Americans who were not criminals, but who did not live up to Hoover's idea of an acceptable citizen. . . .
>
> He reinvented himself as "J. Edgar Hoover, American hero" by identifying a new foe to fight: communism. The Cold War provided a perfect backdrop,

even while Hoover's spying on American citizens was often indistinguishable from the totalitarian regimes he despised.[3]

So began an era of witch hunts, loyalty oaths, firings, and blacklisting of tenured professors, major directors, screenwriters, and actors, and the jailing of people who refused to "name names" in congressional hearings into alleged Communist subversion.

One ready-made institution for pursuing such witch hunts was the House Committee on Un-American Activities, more popularly dubbed with the double-entendre appellation House Un-American Activities Committee (HUAC). Established in 1938 to help root out fascists embedded in government and industry but gradually repurposed toward the end of World War II with a focus on alleged Communist infiltrators, HUAC became a permanent committee in the House of Representatives in 1946. By that time its members were concerned only with rooting out Communists from American life. They simply ignored how the U.S. government was secretly spiriting actual Nazi German scientists, who had supported Hitler's weapons development programs using slave labor from Nazi extermination camps, out of Germany and potential prosecution at the hands of the Soviets and into the United States. Once in the United States, these Nazi imports helped America with its own rocket development program, from the development of intercontinental ballistic missiles (ICBMs) and intermediate-range ballistic missiles (IRBMs) all the way to NASA's Saturn/Apollo Program.

HUAC (where an obscure California Republican House member named Richard Nixon would build his name on the national stage by pursuing State Department employee Alger Hiss and other suspected Communists in government), led directly to the rise of a powerful charlatan in the U.S. Senate. In that upper body of Congress, Senator Joseph McCarthy, a Republican from Wisconsin whose own rise from obscurity to power and influence began in 1950, relied on sensational but groundless charges that 205 Communists had infiltrated the U.S. State Department and later that 300 or more Communists had infiltrated the U.S. military.[4] Although he never managed to out any actual Reds in government, McCarthy's gift for grabbing attention, often with completely fake sensationalist claims of subversion, would engrave his name on the two-decade period of anti-Communist hysteria.

It was right at the start of McCarthy's rise in 1950 that Hoover received the first evidence of actual Soviet infiltration of the U.S. atomic bomb program. In rapid succession beginning in 1949, thanks largely to the work of the Signal Intelligence Service's Venona Program in cracking the Soviet spy code used in thousands of pages of monitored and captured Soviet wartime spy cables, Hoover's counterintelligence unit was able to use these cables to work out the identities of at least seven Soviet spies targeting that project: Klaus Fuchs, David Greenglass, Harry Gold, Julius (and Ethel) Rosenberg, Theodore Hall, and Saville Sax. Also helping in the development of that list was information some of those arrested gave up in hopes of getting leniency in their own sentencing or of sparing a relative from prosecution.

The first to go down was Fuchs, identified in late 1949 thanks to British Government Communications Headquarters (GCHQ) code-crackers and a bit of detective work by MI5, which linked him to his NKVD code names REST and CHARL'Z. FBI detective work also linked him to his identifiable sister Kristel Fuchs Heineman (code name ANT). That information was sufficient to enable the FBI to also deduce that Fuchs's courier was likely Harry Gold (code name GUS, GOS, or GOOSE), who rather quickly confessed when confronted with evidence of a Santa Fe street map found in his home during a search by agents at which he was present.[5] By that time Fuchs had long since returned from his wartime posting at Los Alamos to the United Kingdom, where his brilliant work on both atom bombs had led to his being named head of the theoretical physics department at the top-secret Harwell Atomic Energy Research Establishment, Britain's leading nuclear research center. In that high position, he was a key scientist working on (and having a good overview of) Britain's fission and thermodynamic hydrogen bomb projects. Much of the bomb information Fuchs provided to the Soviets over the years was his own work on those projects, though the charge he was convicted on was "stealing state secrets."

Rather than allowing the United States to seek extradition, MI5 went after Fuchs itself, turning to the Venona cables information, which by that point the GCHQ, Britain's version of the SIS or NSA, was also helping to decipher.

Special Branch interrogator William "Jim" Skardon (brought in by MI5 because the organization "lacked trained interrogators"),[6] with the assistance of Harwell security officer Henry Arnold, went about working on Fuchs to persuade him to confess.[7] It was a controversial process that succeeded in his case, because Fuchs was concerned about protecting his sister Kristel from U.S. prosecution. Arrested by MI5 on February 2, 1950, after an admission to Skardon on January 24, 1950 that he spied for the Soviets, Fuchs agreed to a deal negotiated between his lawyers and MI5, with buy-in by the U.S. Justice Department. Under that deal, he would plead guilty to violating the British Official Secrets Act and there would be no effort to prosecute either him or his sister in the United States. Fuchs was convicted at a quick trial and sentenced to fourteen years in jail. After nine years in a British prison, he was released in a spy swap, whereupon he moved to the new German Democratic Republic, a Communist state created from Soviet-occupied eastern Germany.

During part of his confession, Fuchs, after repeatedly being shown photographs and a surveillance film and photos, eventually confirmed that the man in them was his courier, Harry Gold, a Philadelphia chemist and Swiss immigrant to the United States, who the FBI proceeded to arrest in May 1950. Gold's arrest led to the arrest of David Greenglass, for whom Gold was also a courier, and thence, thanks to Greenglass's willingness to rat out everyone he knew to be a spy, to the arrest of Greenglass's brother-in-law Julius Rosenberg on July 17, 1950, and of his own sister, Ethel Greenglass Rosenberg, in August of the same year. Greenglass's motive in turning on his family and spying comrades was to cut a deal to keep his wife, Ruth, from being arrested as the spy she in fact was (code name WASP) so that their baby daughter would not be left without both her parents. As for the claim that Gold was betrayed by Fuchs, Close, in his 2019 book on the Fuchs case *Trinity: The Treachery and Pursuit of the Most Dangerous Spy in History*, claims that the FBI and MI5, working together with the Venona documents from the Soviet GRU, were able, as early as 1950, to make out that the code name GOOSE belonged to Gold and that the FBI didn't need Fuchs to confirm it.[8]

Because Hoover didn't get the glory for nabbing Fuchs, and because in 1950, he didn't have much else in the offing regarding atomic spying, Julius Rosenberg became a focus for the FBI and its director. While Rosenberg, an American Communist who was running a network of spies providing military secrets like the proximity fuse to the Soviets, never gave prosecutors the names of any agents, his arrest proved to be a media relations gold mine because his brother-in-law *did* talk. Prosecutors also had access to some decrypted Soviet spy cables that helped them identify other spies (even if they didn't use the cables as evidence at trial). The trial of Julius and Ethel Rosenberg for conspiracy to commit espionage during wartime (never mind that it was on behalf of a wartime ally) carried a potential death penalty, which contributed to the attention the media paid to it.

Tried in a federal courtroom in lower Manhattan, the world's media capital, and accused grandiosely of giving the Soviets "America's atomic secrets," Julius, Ethel, and their friend Morton Sobell became daily fare on the nation's front pages and on the radio. Coming just a year and a half after the Soviet Union's first atomic bomb test, and with the Korean

War raging, the trial was dubbed by the U.S. media as the "Trial of the Century."[9]

The only evidence linking the Rosenbergs to the atomic bomb were some crude and flawed drawings Greenglass, a machinist who began working at Los Alamos in 1945, made of the molds used to shape lenses designed to focus a chemical blast onto the plutonium core of the "Gadget" Trinity Test bomb and the Nagasaki "Fat Man" bomb. These were of little, if any, use to the Soviets, given what Fuchs and Hall had already provided them, but they made great headlines. Meanwhile, the case and the trial were plagued with irregularities, including a biased "hanging" judge who was guilty of judicial misconduct, and, according to the recent release of previously secret grand jury questioning of David Greenglass, long-suspected perjured prosecution testimony— particularly his testimony implicating Ethel in the alleged spying.[10]

Julius and Ethel, who refused to confess or to testify against other spies or identify other Party members in return for clemency, were executed in the electric chair on June 19, 1953, leaving their two sons, ten-year-old Michael and six-year-old Robert, orphaned. Sobell was sentenced to thirty years in prison and was released after serving seventeen years and eight months. Ruth Greenglass, a known NKVD spy who had recruited her husband and testified falsely against her sister-in-law Ethel at the trial, was never charged as a spy.

With McCarthy's lurid, overblown claims that Communist subversion was everywhere, making him a staple in Congress and the news media, the conviction and death sentences meted out by Judge Irving R. Kaufman to Julius and Ethel Rosenberg were predictable. And the unprecedented severity of the punishment—no spy had ever been executed in peacetime in U.S. history—struck fear into the hearts of the many young Americans who had flirted with Communism and who were being asked to answer the question "Are you or have you ever been a Communist?" and sign employment application "loyalty forms" or to respond to such questions in Congress under oath.*

Among those who were seriously shaken and upset by the Rosenbergs' fate and worried about the U.S. political climate and how it might impact them personally were Ted and Joan Hall.

---

* So deep-rooted was the anti-Red paranoia in the United States that as late as 1978 when my keyboardist wife, formerly a member of Musician's Union local 802 in New York City, went to transfer to Los Angeles Local 47 when we moved there, she found a loyalty oath with the notorious question on the application form she was handed!

In a 2019 interview, Joan explained that she and Ted had joined the U.S. Communist Party in early 1948 not because of support for the Soviet Union, but for domestic reasons: "We saw an increasing fascist development in the US, and we also thought that the U.S. Communist Party was the only political organization in the country that was fighting against that and defending black people and opposing segregation in this county."[11]

After leaving the Party months later, they both participated actively in the allegedly Communist-supported presidential campaign of Henry Wallace. Wallace, who had been FDR's vice president during the New Deal and the wartime president's unprecedented third term, was the ailing but still popular president's preferred choice for a fourth-term running mate at the 1944 Democratic Convention. Instead, a coalition of conservative Southern Democrats and northern anti–New Deal powerbrokers successfully got one of their own—the conservative and comfortably racist Senator Harry Truman of Missouri—nominated instead. Truman went on to assume the presidency when Roosevelt died in 1945, just eighty-two days into his fourth term. In 1948, Wallace, who supported a friendly policy toward the postwar Soviet Union, ran a feisty but doomed third-party campaign against Truman as the candidate of the new Progressive Party, which he had helped establish in 1946. Truman won that close election by handily defeating Wallace and winning a surprise victory over Republican candidate Thomas Dewey.

Saville Sax was a Communist Party member at the same time and remained active in the Party longer, more comfortable with its twists and turns in policy as well as with the strict "democratic centralist" policy of requiring members to follow the decisions of Party leaders once made—a record both Ted and Joan found "disturbing."

Although they didn't know it at the time, the FBI, having learned very early in 1950 about Ted's spy work for the Soviets at Los Alamos, was initially dubious about his still spying in the late 1940s after learning that he had recently been active in the Communist Party. As FBI Chicago SAC Robert K. McQueen told Albright and Kunstel, U.S. spies typically were not allowed to be U.S. Communist Party members.[12] The rules of the NKVD, and later the KGB, directed its spies in the United States to steer clear of Party membership or political action in CP front organizations. Conversely, U.S. Party members should not engage in spying. However, at the same time, once Hoover decided to go after Ted Hall and Saville Sax, even a short history of flirtation with Marxism was enough to stoke the Communist-hating FBI director's interest in prosecution.

The Rosenberg case also weighed heavily on the minds of Ted and Joan, as they surely did on Saville and his wife, Susan, particularly after the Rosenbergs were convicted, sentenced to death, and locked up on the notorious death row of Sing Sing Prison, a New York State facility where 612 prisoners, including four high-profile federal prisoners, were executed. The Rosenbergs' execution in 1953 would increase that count to 614.

In a videotape made in 1998, a year before he died of kidney cancer and after he had been exposed publicly as a spy, Hall, asked what the risks were in that period of his having been an atomic spy, blew out a breath and said, "Whoo! Well, there was the Rosenbergs."[13]

It was obviously no coincidence that SAC McQueen, a veteran of the bureau's counterintelligence unit, decided to interrogate Hall and Sax just after the Rosenberg trial began. Naturally, Ted and Joan Hall and Saville and Susan Sax—both couples the parents of young children—were already horrified as they followed the arrest and trial of the Rosenbergs, particularly by how they were torn away from their two young sons. Even more horrifying was that the Rosenbergs were both charged with a capital crime and faced possible execution, which would leave their two young sons orphans. As Joan would recall seventy years later, still wincing at the memory at the age of ninety, "The idea of Ruthie being left to my mother was too horrible to contemplate."[14]

25

GOING AFTER ED HALL, THE AIR FORCE'S "ROCKET MAN"[1]

When brothers agree, no fortress is so strong as their common life.

—Antisthenes

In April 1950—three months before Julius and Ethel Rosenberg were arrested as suspected Soviet atomic spies—FBI director J. Edgar Hoover was well along in building his case against what the bureau was calling the "Rosenberg spy ring." But he and federal prosecutors on that case knew that claiming the ring had "stolen America's atomic secrets" would be hyperbole and that any Rosenberg role in spying on the U.S. atomic bomb project had at most been extremely minor. So part of their job in assembling witnesses to testify at the trial was to inflate the significance of what information machinist David Greenglass, the only spy recruited by Julius Rosenberg to have actually worked in the Manhattan Project, who was ready to admit to passing atomic bomb information to his Soviet handlers during his year working at Los Alamos, had to offer. But suddenly, with Ted Hall and Saville Sax, the publicity-seeking bureau director had some much bigger fish to catch (and perhaps fry).

By late October 1944, nineteen-year-old physicist Ted Hall had begun passing to the Soviet Union, via his friend and courier Saville Sax, major secrets about what was going on at the top-secret site in Los Alamos including the details of the plutonium bomb on which he was working. What

Hoover didn't know, even in 1951 when his agents in Chicago interrogated the two young men, was that by August 1945, just after the United States dropped the atomic bomb on Hiroshima, this young physicist/spy had provided the Soviet scientists with what Barnes Carr, author of a book on the capture of Morris and Lona Cohen, two of the NKVD's most important American spies, called "a complete diagram of the first A-Bomb" and a "schematic [that] contained all the parts of the puzzle."[2]

In early January 1950, Hall and Sax were the first Los Alamos spies to be identified, both by the actual names and their code names, MLAD and STAR, in the intercepted and decoded Venona Project cables sent between Soviet spies in the United States and Moscow NKVD headquarters. Hoover was immediately alerted to the breakthrough.

By 1950, of course, the Manhattan Project had long been shut down, replaced by the Atomic Energy Commission. President Harry Truman and the national security establishment, not satisfied with having stock-piled hundreds of fission weapons, each of which could destroy the heart of a city, had put this new agency to work developing the thermonuclear hydrogen fusion bomb, a weapon capable of destroying entire metropolitan regions or even whole countries. Ted had left Los Alamos in early 1946 after briefly doing some basic research related tangentially to that new nuclear project before losing his security clearance—but where had he gone from there?

Assigning a dragnet of FBI agents across the country to the case, Hoover soon learned that this teenage spy, by then in his early twenties, had been working since the war's end on a doctorate in biophysics at the University of Chicago and had married Joan Krakover, an eighteen-year-old fellow student, in 1947. He also learned the shocking and no doubt exciting fact that Ted's older brother, U.S. Air Force Major Edward Nathaniel Hall, was designing rocket engines for nuclear-capable missiles at a top-secret rocket facility located inside the heavily guarded security fence surrounding Wright-Patterson Air Force Base outside of Dayton, Ohio.

Even today, historians of atomic spying remain stunningly unaware of the incongruous careers of these two brothers: the teenage prodigy physicist/spy who helped both the United States and the USSR create the plutonium bomb, and his brother, eleven years older, a brilliant aeronautical engineer who created ICBMs that could deliver these devastating warheads to targets in the Soviet Union and other countries. Indeed, when Ed Hall died in 2006 at the age of ninety-one, obituaries published by the *New York Times* (in the city he was born and grew up), the *Los Angeles Times* (in the hometown he adopted later in life), and other national news media made much of his importance as a rocket scientist and inventor of the Minuteman and other missiles, yet all failed to even mention the easily discoverable enigma that he was the older sibling of known atomic spy Theodore Hall.[3]

This was true even though those same major news publications had written about Ted Hall's being exposed as an important atomic spy only a decade earlier, when his spying first became public knowledge, and again upon his death in 1999. These newspapers both had extensive and well-staffed "morgues"—in-house libraries where reporters could quickly order up all prior clips of articles published by their own publication—and since it was routine for obit writers at such publications to search for these clips, this is a rather astonishing omission. Amazingly, one week after publishing Ed Hall's obituary, the *New York Times* even published a correction—but it was about a misidentified aircraft company, not about the inexplicable failure to mention his fraternal relationship with a known, if never arrested or convicted, Soviet atomic spy.

Those historians and journalists who *were* aware of both men and their sibling bond puzzled over the question but couldn't convincingly explain why both Ted and Ed (and Saville Sax) managed to remain at large—or, in Ed's case, at work in his supersecret job—during the 1950s Red Scare. The 1950s were, after all, a time when merely having a relative or friend in the Communist Party, much less one who was a spy for the Soviet Union, was enough to end careers and even to lead to prosecution. Indeed, Robert Oppenheimer's brother was a member of the U.S. Communist Party, and his wife a former member. For this and other reasons, once the war was over and Russia had been reclassified from ally to enemy, the project's world-famous scientific director lost his security clearance and any chance to continue working in nuclear physics, spending the rest of his life battling false accusations that he was a spy (a charge only finally posthumously debunked in December 2022).[4]

Bombshell authors Joseph Albright and Marcia Kunstel came closest to tackling the connection, suggesting—as did Ted and Joan in his 1998 videotape—that perhaps Ed's importance to the U.S. ICBM program kept him and Sax from being arrested. That, however, was purely speculation. Now that story can be told, thanks to the 103 pages of FBI files on Ed Hall that I finally received through a FOIA appeal after an initial response from the bureau's FOIA office claiming incorrectly that there was no such file on him.

At the end of World War II, paranoia about Soviet espionage was rampant in the United States, spurred partly by propaganda and later by the

USSR's surprise successful detonation—years ahead of U.S. predictions—of its own atom bomb in August 1949. With Communism seemingly on the march first in Asia and Eastern Europe, and even in countries like France and Italy (where the new CIA had to resort to dirty tricks to prevent Communist election victories) as well as in Korea and Vietnam, it's easy to imagine how much Hoover, an obsessed anti-Communist, must have wanted to nail this case.

By the end of 1950 at least one atomic spy—Klaus Fuchs—had been caught and sentenced to fourteen years in prison.[5] As noted earlier, however, Fuchs was apprehended by Britain's MI5, not by Hoover's FBI. Ted Hall, however, was not just a Los Alamos physicist/spy, but an American one whose brother was a Cal Tech aerospace engineer and career U.S. Air Force officer—and a potential spy known to be working on the development of top-secret nuclear-tipped missiles, including the breakthrough large solid-fuel Minuteman ICBM. Hoover was closing in on a case that certainly offered the potential of being the biggest and most explosive of his career.

After having his agents intensively but surreptitiously investigate both Hall brothers and Sax for nearly nine months without their awareness—while keeping information about the case under tight wraps inside the bureau's counterintelligence unit—Hoover decided it was time to alert the Air Force. After all, the Pentagon would have jurisdiction over any prosecution of the still-in-uniform Major Hall, which would mean a court-martial and a military trial before a jury of U.S. Air Force officers.

As explained in chapter 22, Hoover accordingly sent a letter on January 6, 1951, to General Joseph F. Carroll, commander of the USAF Office of Special Investigation (OSI), alerting him to the spy and potential security risk in the air force's missile program. (See that letter in full at the end of the chapter.) Carroll was no stranger to the FBI director. A working-class Irish Catholic kid from Chicago who had financed his way through college and law school by working in Chicago's freight yards and as a department store bookkeeper before joining the FBI in 1940, Carroll had caught Hoover's attention after he helped nab notorious escaped Chicago mob boss Roger "Tough" Touhy. Before long, Carroll became a top Hoover aide. When Air Force Secretary Stuart Symington suggested picking Carroll as his OSI commander, Hoover immediately and enthusiastically endorsed him for the position.

The file provided by the FBI FOIA office on Ed Hall didn't include Carroll's response to what was surely shocking news coming from his former boss (or perhaps it is one of the pages in that file that was just a blank sheet of paper, allegedly withheld for reasons of privacy or national security, ludicrous as those would be at this late date). Efforts to find Carroll's communications regarding Major Hall in U.S. Air Force records have been unsuccessful.

My FOIA request to the Air Force OSI office and the Air Force Secretary's press office initially produced only word that neither office had a file on Ed Hall or any record of the collected correspondence of General Carroll, who, after spending a decade as the Air Force's first OSI director, left his post in 1961 to head the new Defense Intelligence Agency. He held that post until his retirement from the military in 1969. (Carroll died in 1991 after suffering from Alzheimer's.) Such files "may have existed," I was told by Roxanne M. Jensen, chief of the Air Force OSI's Information Release Branch, who added that they "could have been destroyed as part of a routine records purge."[6]

Fortunately, however, there is a second letter from Hoover to Carroll, dated March 27, 1951, contained in the FBI's Ed Hall file. In it, Hoover refers to written correspondence in both directions between himself and Carroll. That letter reads,

> Reference is made to my letter dated Jan. 6, 1951 . . . concerning Major Edward Nathaniel Hall . . . brother of Theodore Alvin Hall . . . the subject of a current espionage investigation by the Bureau. It is noted that *in your letter dated January 18, 1951, concerning captioned individuals* [author's emphasis], you advised that a limited inquiry would be conducted by your Department to determine whether Major Hall [is] engaged in activities inimical to the best interests of the United States.[7]

In this second letter to Carroll, Hoover reported that his agents had just interviewed Ted Hall, who "declared that he never furnished unauthorized information to anyone not entitled to receive it, and, furthermore, that he had never been approached by anyone, directly or indirectly, to furnish such information to unauthorized persons." He then noted that the Chicago FBI office leading the Ted Hall investigation "has requested that Major Hall, a regular Air Force officer on duty at Wright Patterson AFB, be interviewed re Theodore Hall, his younger brother."

Hoover added,

> This Bureau's investigation has now progressed to the point where interview of Major Hall concerning his brother, Theodore, is desirable. Accordingly, it will be appreciated if you would advise *at your earliest convenience* [author's

emphasis] whether you have any objection to an interview of Major Hall at this time by Bureau agents.[8]

Hoover's request to Carroll for the U.S. Air Force to allow federal agents to interview Ed Hall was eventually granted, although Carroll appears to have been in no rush to accommodate the "earliest convenience" part of it. Only on June 12—a full eleven weeks after Hoover's seemingly urgent request—were Cincinnati bureau agents finally permitted to conduct the interview (with an OSI officer observing, according to the postinterview report filed by the agents doing the interview). The report on that two-hour session, dated August 10, shows that Ed claimed ignorance of his brother's alleged Los Alamos espionage. It also shows that the questioning, as promised by Hoover to Carroll, was largely limited to asking what Ed knew of his brother's politics and actions.[9]

Evidence that the OSI's in-house investigation of Ed was underway at the time of Hoover's second memo comes from Ted's wife, Joan. Asked in an April 2022 phone interview about when Ed had first learned about Ted's spying, Joan suddenly recalled to me an incident she'd forgotten about in our previous in-person conversations. She told me that to the best of her recollection it happened on March 17, 1951, the Saturday morning directly after March 16, that unforgettable Friday when Ted and Sax had each been interrogated separately and aggressively for three and two hours, respectively, in the FBI's Chicago downtown office.

Joan remembered that on that cold, late winter weekend morning, a "jovial" man showed up uninvited in a lumberman's flannel jacket claiming to be a repairman sent by the phone company to "fix" their phone. The man tinkered with their black standard rotary phone and departed, declaring himself done. Shortly after he left, there was a second knock at the door of their Chicago home. It was Ted's brother, Ed, who, without calling ahead, had driven all night from Dayton, Ohio, a trip of some 275 miles that, before the advent of the Interstate Highway System, was a grueling stop-and-go journey of more than eight hours through a string of cities and small-town Main Streets. Checking the phone and indicating silently that it appeared to be bugged, he signaled Joan and Ted to join him outside. Once outside the house, he asked, "Okay, Ted, what kind of trouble did you get into this time?"[10] It was a question he had been compelled to drive those many miles and hours to get answered, because he clearly knew he couldn't risk calling his brother on the phone, based upon what he'd already learned from the line of questions OSI investigators had been plying him with.

Joan recalls that "Ted sort of smiled and said he'd been questioned about spying at Los Alamos, and Ed responded that he'd also been questioned about Ted's spying." She adds, "He didn't ask Ted if it was true he was a Soviet spy. He just told him he'd been questioned and that he had told the agents he knew nothing about any spying."

Following that brief exchange, the two brothers walked off, talking together and leaving Joan with their year-old daughter, Ruthie. The brothers returned almost an hour later, after which Ed returned to Dayton. While he may or may not have gotten a clear explanation from Ted about what he'd done, Ed didn't mention spying to Ted again in Joan's presence or to her knowledge until 1995, after his younger brother's spying had been exposed by the National Security Agency's declassification of the decrypted and translated Venona spy cables.[11]

Clearly, the questioning Ed mentioned during his surprise visit to their home had to have been by the OSI, not FBI agents, because Hoover's letter to Carroll requesting permission to have agents question Ed was dated March 27—ten days *after* Ed's quick surprise trip to his brother's house from Dayton. If the FBI had already questioned him, Hoover wouldn't have had to ask permission to question Ed again, as he finally was allowed to do only months later.

The FBI agents' report on that June 12 interview of Ed shows that he didn't mention his March 17 trip to Chicago, falsely informing them that his last visit with his younger brother had occurred a year earlier, in March 1950. This was a daring falsehood on Ed's part, since lying to the FBI is a felony, whether or not a person is under oath.[12]

According to his FBI file, Ed was interviewed four times by the OSI and once by the FBI, as well as once, over an entirely separate matter, in October 1945 by the Security Branch of the Atomic Energy Commission.[13] In his FBI interview, Ed claimed he hadn't seen his brother during the war years, as he'd been stationed in the United Kingdom, and that after the war he'd seen him only a few times. Admitting he'd been very close to Ted when they were young, he asserted that following his 1939 enlistment in the U.S. Army Air Corps, he'd been posted far from New York, in locations like Alaska, Indiana, and Ohio and then overseas, and that since then the two brothers had "not been particularly close."

That statement might have been true in terms of physical distance, but from a relationship perspective, Joan insists, it was simply "a lie." As she explained to me in our phone call, "They were always extremely close."

A big question is, if the FBI was investigating Ed Hall and monitoring his and Sax's actions and meetings with others, as it began doing at least by late

1950, why didn't they know he had visited the Ted and Joan on March 17, after they'd just interrogated Ted? This knowledge would have given them huge leverage over Ed because of his lie about not having seen his brother recently. They could have also used it in reinterviewing Ted to try to catch him denying that the visit had occurred. One reason none of this happened may be that the neighborhoods where Ted and Sax lived were not terribly safe—even for G-men.

As a somewhat hilarious pair of reports in the Sax/Hall FBI file illustrates, hanging around the two suspects' respective neighborhoods to surveil them proved to be unexpectedly risky. One report, dated March 16, 1951, the same day Hall and Sax were interrogated at the FBI office in downtown Chicago, is the account of an early morning surveillance effort on the very day of their interrogations gone embarrassingly south. It reads,

I was directed by Supervisor [BLANK] to take up a surveillance of Saville Sax on the morning of March 16, 1951. Agent [BLANK] and myself were together in radio car and Agent [BLANK] was in another radio car. We instituted this surveillance at the home of the subject, 1270 East 61st Street, at 7:15 a.m.

Subject SAX left his home at 8:15, proceeded to the Park Row Cafe at the corner of 55th and Lake Park Avenue. He thereafter took a bus to the Henry Horner Public School, 4113 S. Michigan Avenue, which he entered at 8:40 a.m.

Agent [BLANK] and myself parked our car on Michigan Avenue so as to observe the entrance to the school from Michigan Avenue, which he entered at 8:40 a.m.

Agent [BLANK] parked his car on 41st Street east of Michigan Avenue, so as to observe the north entrance to the school from 41st Street.

At approximately 9:44 a.m. I heard Agent [BLANK] on the 2-way radio advise the radio operator that 2 Negro men had attempted to hold him up, one of whom had taken a shot at him, and both fled after hearing the 2-way radio in the car.

Agent [BLANK] immediately entered his car with me and we cruised the area in an attempt to locate a policeman so that he could accompany us in an effort to locate the 2 colored men, since neither of us was armed at the time. Agent [BLANK] remained at the scene inasmuch as there were two possible witnesses to the incident and it was desired that he interview both as to their knowledge of the incident.

Agent [BLANK] then returned to the school and thereafter Agent [BLANK] left to go to the office and Agent [BLANK] and myself resumed the surveillance.[14]

The second report, by the agent who had been held up and was shot at, sounds harrowing. It reads,

> At approximately 9:40 a.m., a Negro man approached the right front of the Bureau car and asked me if I had a match. Immediately thereafter another Negro man opened the left front door, pushed a gun into my body and told me to move over. I immediately pushed the gun of the Negro man away from me and just then conversation emitted from the FM radio in the car. Both indivuduals, upon hearing the radio, immediately fled.
>
> I got out of the car, went around to the back, and the Negro man who asked me if I had a match fired one shot at me. He was about 15 feet away at the time. I was not injured nor was any property injured from this bullet to my knowledge. Both individuals fled.[15]

I submit that it's possible that after this close call, there may have been a delay the next day in getting monitoring agents in position at the two targeted homes while security issues were evaluated and agents took the time to arm up and perhaps don protective gear because of the evidence that the neighborhoods where they were going to be working made this case significantly more dangerous than they had anticipated. If so, and they were even just a little late in getting to their posts the next morning, Ed's surprise visit would have gone unnoticed. This could also explain why agents missed catching Ted and Joan loading up all their compromising material and dumping it into the Chicago Drainage Canal the evening after their simultaneous interrogation sessions—an action that could have constituted "obstruction of justice" by both of them. Significantly, there is no mention in either the Sax/Hall or the Edward Hall files of agents having seen Ed visit his brother on March 17 or at any other time between then and their interview of him on June 12.

Interestingly, Joan told Albright and Kunstel, who included it in their book, about the jovial "phone repairman" visiting them the day after Ted's March 16 FBI interrogation, and about them saying it was the first time they were certain their phone was being bugged and that they were under surveillance.[16] But Albright and Kunstel told me that Joan and Ted never mentioned anything to them about Ed's surprise visit right after the phone "repairman" had left.

The FBI report on the Cleveland bureau agents' questioning of Ted shows that while claiming to Ed that they were "not associating him with any responsibility for Theodore's actions," they did warn him bluntly that, given his plans for an Air Force career, his brother's refusal to cooperate with FBI investigators was "a matter in which he might have considerable concern." [17]

They suggested Ed visit his brother to urge him to cooperate with the Chicago agents. Ed promised to do this, and he did make another trip to see his brother on June 22, returning to Dayton on June 25. What he actually advised Ted to do on that visit is unknown, though urging him to cooperate doesn't seem like something Ed Hall would have done. Joan, for her part, told me in 2022 that "Ed never criticized Ted for his having provided important atomic bomb information to the Soviets and Ted never criticized Ed for helping to design nuclear missiles." Nor was Ed Hall unaware of how deadly serious U.S. security and law enforcement agencies could be, particularly in national security cases—especially in view of the just-concluded Rosenberg case that resulted in two death sentences. Nevertheless, the agents' report says that Ed later told them (after the June 22 visit he made at his inquisitors' request) that he had "failed to persuade his brother to cooperate." They said Ed told them Ted had complained that the agents who had interrogated him wanted him to give them the names of Progressive Party and leftist activists, something he told his brother he wouldn't do. [18]

The level of distrust the FBI had in Ed Hall shows in the report on their circumscribed and OSI-monitored interrogation of him. In that report, the agents note that following that interview,

> HALL was placed under discreet surveillance by Special Agents Stanley H. Hendelsohn and Terry R Anderson of the Cincinnati Office. HALL had stated that he planned to visit his brother, THEODORE ALVIN HALL, unannounced. The surveillance was conducted to determine whether or not he would make any attempt to telephone THEODORE immediately, following his, EDWARD'S, departure from the Dayton office.
>
> EDWARD proceeded directly home by auto, making no contacts en route. [19]

Looking at the long, close relationship between the two brothers, both Joan and I find it hard to believe that Ed Hall would have advised his younger brother to cooperate with the FBI.

There exists one more report of a brief questioning of Ed Hall by Cincinnati Bureau office SAC Carl A. Betsch. In a report dated October 17, 1951, Betsch wrote that he visited and interviewed (the by then) Lieutenant Colonel Edward Hall on October 11 at Hall's home following an August 18–24 family visit by Ted, Joan, and their infant daughter to Ed's home. Ted's family was apparently passing through on their way back to Chicago after a visit to Ted and Ed's father's home in New York City. Ed told Betsch that he had at that time asked Ted "what action he might have taken along the lines of furnishing further information" to the Chicago FBI. Betsch wrote that Lieutenant Colonel Hall told him that "Theodore had given the matter serious consideration," had consulted an attorney, who he did not identify to his brother, and that he had a "continuing view that further divulgence of information to the FBI would be a violation of his 'personal ethics.'" Ed Hall told the agent that "should he gain any information that Theodore had changed his position and would furnish further information in the future to the FBI in Chicago, Illinois, he would forthwith advise [Agent Betsch]."[20]

Ed never did that. The October 11 interview of Ed Hall ended bureau efforts to interrogate or further question not just Ed, but Ted too, at least using its own agents, though some investigation work continued in a minor way for much of the rest of the year (and for longer in the case of Sax). There are memos in the Saville/Hall part of their joint file indicating that agents asked Sax on a few later occasions over the years if he would talk with them and reporting that he had consistently refused.

If Hoover still harbored suspicions about Ed Hall, which he surely did, it is clear that Carroll and the Pentagon didn't share them. In what must have felt like a thumb in the eye to Hoover by his protégé Carroll, Major Hall was promptly promoted by the U.S. Air Force a few weeks after his interview by the FBI and was also made deputy chief of what became known as the Rockets & Ramjets Power Plant Lab—even *before* the OSI had formally concluded its investigation into Ed's loyalty. By August 10, the Cincinnati FBI agents' report on their questioning of Ed Hall refers to him as *Lieutenant Colonel* Hall—a significant promotion.

By October 25, the OSI had concluded its inquiry into Ted's loyalty. A letter dated November 20, 1951, from Charles W. Brown, special agent in charge of the Cincinnati FBI office, to the commandant officer of the Office of Special Investigations of the Air Force at Wright-Patterson Air Force Base reads,

Commanding Officer
Fifth District Office of Special Investigations
Wright-Patterson Air Force Base
Dayton, Ohio

Re: Edward Nathaniel Hall, Lt. Col., 0-434506
Philip Krakover, Private, AF 164342051

Dear Sir:

Reference is made to your letter of Oct. 25, 1951, enclosing copies of four OSI reports of investigation concerning the above individuals.

I have noted that your letter advises that OSI has closed its investigations of both Edward Nathaniel Hall and Philip Krakover.

Your request that your office be furnished any other information relative to Edward Nathaniel Hall or Philip Krakover in the event such information is developed in the future in the FBI investigation of Theodore Alvin Hall has been made known to the Chicago, Illinois Office of the FBI.

The Chicago, Illinois, Office of the FBI will furnish any further information directly to the OSI District Office #24, Chicago, Illinois, it being noted that the Chicago OSI Office is carrying this matter under their file number 27-7.

Very truly yours,

CHARLES W. BROWN

Special Agent in Charge

If any further evidence were needed linking that finding by the OSI regarding the importance of Ed Hall and its impact on Hoover's pursuit of Ted Hall and Saville Sax, it came later that same year when a frustrated SAC McQueen, head of the Chicago bureau office, was taken off the Hall/ Sax investigation and promoted to command of an internal security squad.[21] McQueen left the FBI in 1972 to become a state judge in Chicago. In an interview with the authors of *Bombshell*, who in 1997 visited him in Los Angeles, where he had retired, McQueen denied that the Hall/Sax case had been dropped at the time he was transferred out of the Chicago bureau office. In their book, they say he told them, "You certainly aren't going to close a case when you have information such as we had that these people had been involved in atomic espionage."[22]

And in a sense, he was right. For the rest of the Cold War 1950s, the FBI files suggest they put the case in cold storage—but they didn't close it out and just forget about it, either.

There was no sign of any FBI interest in the case when, in 1954—just as Senator Joseph McCarthy's controversial army hearings were trying to prove massive Communist infiltration in the armed forces began—Ed

Hall was named director of the entire USAF ballistic missile development program, a position he held until his retirement.[23] Nor was there any FBI concern shown when he was promoted to the rank of full colonel on February 20, 1957.[24]

In December 1959, Ed retired from the Air Force.[25] It wasn't an easy parting of ways. A frustrated Colonel Hall had decided to call it quits, but the Air Force and the Pentagon apparently didn't want him to go. Recognized as the lead developer of engines for the Atlas and Titan missiles in his official U.S. Air Force official biography, Ed Hall was, perhaps more significantly, *creator* of the entire Minuteman ICBM concept and designer of the revolutionary intercontinental solid-fuel missile itself.[26]

Indeed, Ed's daughter Sheila told me a humorous story. In 1959, she says, with the Minuteman I a success, her father announced his reluctant intention to call it quits, saying he was tired of having to work with the meddling and bureaucratic executives of the arms contractors on the project. The U.S. Air Force responded by saying if he would agree to stay on the program, developing more advanced versions of that missile, they'd promote him to the rank of general. "He told them he'd stay, but only if they'd replace the corporate executives he had to work with," she says with a laugh. "They told him they couldn't do that, so he retired." Sheila recalls that her mother was livid at her father for turning down the promotion offer because "it would have meant a substantial pay and pension increase for them."

But even out of the military, the Pentagon managed to keep Ed working on missiles for them after a fashion. Before he retired, at the urging of the Pentagon, Ed agreed to take on the job of leading the development of a fully French IRBM, the Diamant, giving France what President Charles de Gaulle wanted: an independent French nuclear force outside of NATO control. Hall completed that project in 1960.[27]

Ed clearly was considered vital to the U.S. (and NATO) ballistic missile program, at a time in the 1950s and early 1960s when the United States was perceived as lagging behind the Soviet Union in missile technology. And, as Peter Kuznick told me in an interview for this book, "If Ed was viewed as critical to the missile program, certainly the FBI couldn't have been allowed to arrest his brother as a Soviet spy because, especially in the 1950s, that would have made Ed radioactive no matter how confident the Air Force and the OSI's Gen. Carroll were [of Ed's] loyalty."

The question remains: Did the U.S. Air Force OSI effectively shut down Hoover's pursuit of Ed Hall and prevent the further investigation and any arrest and prosecution of Ted Hall and Saville Sax for more than a decade?

Carroll's son James, a self-described "Daniel Berrigan–style" Catholic priest and antiwar activist, now a staff columnist at the *Boston Globe*, thinks that's quite likely. "My dad revered Hoover," he told me in an interview for this book, "but he was someone who wouldn't have hesitated to stiff-arm him if he thought he was interfering with the prerogatives of the Air Force or OSI."

Whatever Hoover's reason for halting his pursuit of the two brothers, no word concerning Ted's spying—or Ed's relationship to a known Soviet spy—leaked or otherwise made it into the press until 1995, when the NSA finally began declassifying thousands of pages of decrypted Venona cables.

Interestingly, Ed never spoke publicly to anyone about his brother's Soviet spying, or even privately with his adult children. It's possible he didn't want to know about it so that he'd never have anything to hide, for example, on a polygraph test or in response to FBI questioning. But even after Ted's death in 1999, when Ed wrote a never-published memoir of his World War II work and his later work and bureaucratic struggles developing ICBMs for the USAF, he didn't mention a word about his brother's having been a Soviet atomic spy. He even left out the rather comical account, recounted earlier, about the letter from his wife to Ted, which the censors at Los Alamos had found and questioned the pair about.[28]

But both Joan and Sheila give a good illustration of the reality of his enduring affection and brotherly concern for his younger sibling. They told me separately the same story of how, in 1989, when Ted's cancer was diagnosed and he was told he had only a short time to live, Ed immediately flew with his wife and three children to Cambridge from their home in Los Angeles. A day or so later, as Ed was walking in Newnham with Joan, he collapsed on the sidewalk, and an ambulance had to be called. In the hospital he was diagnosed with a severe bleeding ulcer—something his daughter says he had dangerously kept to himself for some time. He was found by Cambridge's NHS hospital doctors to be so drained of blood that he had nearly died. Sheila says she asked him in the hospital why he hadn't told his family about the bleeding and how he could have taken the risk of such a long flight in that condition. "I wasn't going to lose that kid without coming to see him," she says her father told her.

As a significant late addition to this unusual tale of two brothers, Alexander Vassiliev, the former KGB operative who was given access to the KGB's atomic spying files, told me in 2022 that he agreed with the U.S. Air Force's assessment that Ed Hall was never a spy. "I never found his name mentioned in any document in the KGB archives," he said definitively.

The odds are, in fact, that the Soviet spy agency never even knew Ted Hall *had* a brother, much less one in the U.S. Air Force working on a top-secret ICBM development program.

In 1999, Ed Hall was inducted into the Air Force Space and Missile Hall of Fame.[29] He died in 2006 at age ninety-one.

26

TERROR, THEN A
STRANGE RESPITE
FROM FEAR

*It certainly brought home the fact that there were flames con-
suming people and that we were pretty close to being consumed.*

—Ted Hall, recalling the execution of
the Rosenbergs in June 1953

Nervously sweating through 1951 after their interrogation session at the
Chicago FBI building, Saville Sax and Ted Hall tried to alert the *Rezidentura* about the FBI interrogations and to say that they felt they were in
danger. They had no idea that the FBI was slowly, and perhaps reluctantly,
closing the drawer on their joint file.

The bureau certainly didn't politely notify the two spies that as of early
1952, its agents would no longer be watching and following them 24/7,
monitoring their mail, bugging their phones, and questioning associates, as
it had been doing aggressively for the prior two years since learning of their
spying from the Venona decrypts. Indeed, they had no way of even knowing
that officially—thanks to intervention by the U.S. Air Force to protect Ted's
brother, Ed, the rocket scientist running their ICBM development effort—J.
Edgar Hoover was having both Ted Hall and Saville Sax removed from the
Special Section of the FBI's Espionage-R Security Index list.[1]

That February, the FBI effectively dropped its active investigation of
Hall and Sax, moving them from the Special Section Security Index to the
Regular Section—a shift that meant these two known Soviet spies would no

longer be subject to overt or covert surveillance. A Chicago office memo in the file announcing the closure of the active case includes the letters UACB (Unless Advised to the Contrary by the Bureau) after the words Regular Section. The lack of significant additions to either Hall brother's file after that date makes it evident that the collection of physical surveillance, wiretaps, and mail covers (checking the target's written correspondence) halted at that point, for at least a decade in Ted's case and for good in Ed's. The Sax/Hall file, however, shows there *were* some periodic tabs kept on Sax (who died in 1980) well into the 1960s.[2] Hoover and the bureau seemed, judging by some of the entries in those reports, to think he might have had some link to the "Rosenberg ring," though memos in those files report that no such evidence ever materialized. That avenue of investigation wasted agents' time and led them into a blind alley, perhaps causing them to miss that Sax did maintain contact with the Soviet spy agency longer than Ted did.

As two memos added to their files put it:

Office Memorandum—United States Government

Date: January 22, 1952
To: Mr. A. H. Belmont
From: Mr. W. A. BRANIGAN. [then chief of the FBI's counterintelligence section in Washington, DC]
Subject: SAVILLE SAX, was,

ESPIONAGE-R

Purpose:

To recommend that subject's name be removed from the special section of the Security Index and placed in the regular section.

Observations:

It is felt that retention of Sax in the special section of the Security Index is no longer justified.

And:

Office Memorandum United States Government

To: Director, FBI DATE: FEB. 21, 1952

From: SAC [Special Agent in Charge], Chicago
Subject: Theodore Alvin Hall, was
Saville Sax. Was

ESPIONAGE-R

It is suggested that this case be closed after completion of possible dissemi-
nation of information relative to SAX as set out in relet. Sax and Hall would
thereafter be handled in accordance with current instructions pertaining
to Security Index subjects. This case will be so handled UACB. [Unless
Advised to the Contrary by the Bureau]

"I find it baffling that there was no continued surveillance by the FBI of
both Ted and Ed Hall through the 1950s," Peter Kuznick, a history professor and director of the Nuclear Studies Institute at American University told
me in an interview. "Certainly the FBI could have continued to keep an eye
on them." This was especially curious as Ted and Ed's families during the
latter part of that decade lived only an hour's drive apart in Connecticut and
saw each other frequently. And even if Ted had lost his security clearance,
Ed, working on top secret ICBM development, had certainly not.

The explanation of FBI officials and some Cold War historians for why
Hall escaped prosecution—that the FBI didn't want to reveal the United
States had cracked the Soviet spy code, and that absent such evidence or
a confession, they would have been unable to convict or even indict him—
simply doesn't hold up.

"Look how they handled that issue with Julius Rosenberg," said Kuznick.
He noted that like Hall, the real evidence in the Rosenberg case came from
the Venona decryptions, but that evidence was not presented at trial or in
questioning witnesses. It was information that remained secret for decades
after the couple's execution. "They just indicted Ethel too, to try and get
Julius to confess. It didn't work in that case but the FBI and Justice Department could certainly have indicted Joan as a co-conspirator to try and get a
confession from Ted." He adds that prosecutors also could have piled other
charges on Hall and Sax, like lying to the FBI, avoiding the need to mention
a decrypted NKVD cable.

For example, as noted in chapter 22, if they wanted to threaten him, the
FBI already had Sax in a lie involving his denial of an attempt to see Communist Party secretary general Earl Browder. That easy felony charge could
have given the bureau and the Justice Department tremendous leverage over
him.

Besides, the argument that the FBI was trying to keep the Soviets in the dark about the fact that their wartime coded messages had been recorded and their code cracked is pretty weak for another reason: The Soviets *knew* their code had been cracked, and had known this as early as 1945, thanks to a spy named William Weisband, who worked as a translator inside Arlington Hall, where the decryption process was taking place.[3] By 1950, Weisband, who failed to respond to a summons to appear before a grand jury investigating Communist activity, had been sentenced to a year in prison for contempt of court.[4] The FBI knew by that time that he was a spy from the cables, which they didn't want to disclose publicly, but they also clearly knew from them that he had by then alerted the Soviets to the breaking of their supposedly unbreakable code.

A vastly more compelling explanation for Ted Hall's and Saville Sax's escape from prosecution was the message sent by the U.S. Air Force, perhaps directly (if only missing Air Force files and unjustifiably redacted pages of Ed's FBI file could be obtained), but if not, certainly indirectly in a very obvious manner by the two rank and job promotions and Legion of Merit Awards and other honors bestowed upon Ed in short order beginning just weeks after his June 12 Cincinnati FBI office interview.

In Washington, DC, a city famous for leaks and packed with journalists looking for scoops—not to mention that in the 1950s, members of Congress and their staffs were looking for media attention by making accusations of Communists lurking all throughout the huge federal bureaucracy—it seems incredible that news about Ted's atomic spying and about Ed's relationship to a known Soviet spy never came out until 1995, when the NSA began declassifying and publishing hundreds of pages of decrypted Venona cables. Indeed, the first public awareness that Hoover even knew about Ed and Ted's relationship didn't come until an article I wrote in *The Nation* on January 4, 2022 (an article that formed the basis for chapter 25).

Nonetheless, even absent such news or any formal word that the Sax/Hall investigation had been shelved by the FBI, Joan Hall recalls that after that frightening year in 1951, when Ted and Sax were interrogated and Ed was questioned about his brother and agents were regularly spotted prowling around their homes and following them in cars, things changed. Even as the Rosenbergs were being tried, convicted, and left caged on death row at Sing Sing awaiting a rushed series of rejected appeals and petitions for clemency or for execution, all for doing vastly less in terms of atomic spying than what Ted Hall and Saville Sax had done, the Halls became aware by 1952 that any visible signs that they were being monitored seemed to have ceased.

In mid-1952, however, Ted was contacted at his home in Chicago by Savy Sax, who banged on his front door and told him to come with him "right away." Joan recalls that the two went off for three hours in Chicago to meet with a Soviet agent who suggested that if there were to come a time when it would be advisable to flee to the Soviet Union for safety, it would be "more convenient and easy if he and his family were located in the New York City vicinity, where there were more Soviet personnel available to help them escape the US safely."[5] So concerned were Ted and Joan about possible microphones inside their home at the time that after Ted returned, they repaired to the bathroom. There he conveyed to her the message on one of those "magic boards" popular with young kids in the 1950s, where one wrote with a wooden stylus on a bit of cellophane over a gray gel and letters appeared that vanished when the cellophane was lifted and put back down.

The message was that they needed to move.

Having earned a master's in physics and a doctorate in biophysics, and given his extraordinary work résumé, Ted already had several enticing job prospects, including an offer from his Chicago academic adviser Raymond Zirkle to help him find a good position in biophysics at the University of Chicago. But, taking the New York NKVD *Rezidentura* office's advice, he found a job opening at the Sloan Kettering Institute, conveniently located in Manhattan, as a research biophysicist. After he applied, he learned that the FBI had spoken to a senior administrator warning about him—a common harassment tactic of the bureau where unindicted suspected spies or even current or former Communists were involved. Ted was offered the position regardless—after all, the work had no connection with national security, much less nuclear bombs.

So the Halls moved to New York and a position offering a salary of $500 a month—adequate enough for them at that time, especially with the availability of a GI Bill mortgage, to buy a small frame house in Greenwich, Connecticut.

Before departing from Chicago, Joan recalls, they had gotten used to their home's being watched and to being tailed by easy-to-recognize black sedans, obviously from the FBI, when they drove anywhere. They'd also hear from time to time from friends and even family members that they had been questioned by the FBI agents who, following the March interrogations, evidently felt no need to work in the shadows (or perhaps *wanted* them to be on edge). It was an unsettling time, especially with the news about the Rosenbergs' appeal efforts to gain a new trial or to have their sentences commuted, which were going nowhere. The Halls could easily imagine the FBI coming back to them and to Savy and Susan Sax for more questioning—and finding themselves in the same situation as the doomed Rosenbergs.

In fact, Joan says that Ted, less concerned about himself and his family at that point, began feeling guilty about the grim fate the Rosenbergs increasingly appeared headed for. He told her, and his Russian contacts, that he was considering making an offer to the U.S. Justice Department: a deal where he would admit to his spying at Los Alamos if the government would release or at least drop the death penalty against the Rosenbergs. The NKVD was adamant in opposing the idea, saying it would lead to the destruction of their entire spying operation, including on U.S. bomb developments. Joan spoke out against it, too, for different reasons:

> Ted said he should be the one punished as whatever information the Rosenbergs had provided about the bomb was minor compared to what he had given them. I told him very forcefully that he could not do it because it would not work. The government would betray him and execute the Rosenbergs anyway, and him too, and perhaps me, and Ruthie would be left an orphan like the two Rosenberg boys. Thankfully he listened to me and gave up on his quixotic idea of sacrificing himself in a vain effort to save them.[6]

When informed of Ted's idea to trade himself for Ethel and Julius Rosenberg, their son Michael Meeropol, who was ten years old when his parents were executed, told me, "Joan was right. It wouldn't have saved my parents, and it could have ended up getting him killed."

Meanwhile, although the Rosenberg drama was painful for them to follow, life in Connecticut and Ted's job in New York with Sloan Kettering were going fairly smoothly. They were raising a young daughter, Ted was working in his field, and Joan, pregnant with their second daughter, found herself in the unwelcome role of suburban housewife: cooking meals, cleaning (badly, she confessed, as it was not something she wanted to do), and talking with women neighbors. "It was pretty boring," she says. "All talk about pregnancies, labor pains, nursing and so on. I mean it was interesting of course, but not all the time!"[7]

Then, lest they get too complacent about their situation, came June 19, 1953, the date of the Rosenbergs' execution. Ted, recalling the story in the tape he made before he died, explained: "I got an invitation to a dinner party at the home of my department head north of New York City. It was the day that the Rosenbergs were to be executed, and neither of us wanted to go, but it was not the kind of thing you could easily refuse."[8]

Joan, recalling the same story, picks up from Ted:

I got the best dress I could find, and we got in the car driving up into northern Westchester County. Ted was doing his usual competent driving. The sun was just setting as we passed a sign pointing to the turnoff for Sing Sing! We hadn't realized we were going to be passing the prison where the execution was to take place, but we knew that for some reason having to do with the Sabbath, it was being done after sunset. As we rode along, we couldn't talk. There was nothing to say! He turned on the radio, and the classical station was playing a piano concerto by Mahler (one of Ted's favorite composers). It was the last movement, called "The Departure."

It was painful! We didn't talk. What could we say?

We got to the party, and people were out in the back yard drinking and laughing, but we couldn't. We took the earliest opportunity to say good-bye and went back home.[9]

In the same interview, Joan recalls the horror she felt at the "lurid" newspaper accounts of the back-to-back executions, including Ethel's having to be given the jolt of current several times, and of the throngs mocking the funeral and the hearse procession to their burial the following day. "It was horrible!" she says, still wincing at the memory of it. "You think America is a bad place now? It was much worse then."

Ted, recalling that period after the Rosenberg executions, said in an unaired portion of a BBC interview from 1998, "It certainly brought home the fact that there were flames consuming people and that we were pretty close to being consumed. It could easily be imagined."[10]

That said, even as the Red Scare and the Cold War continued through the decade of the 1950s, the Halls did grow used to feeling more and more confident that the threat to them had for some reason subsided—or at least feeling less worried about the threat returning. They knew, of course, that it was always lurking there in the background and could come back to haunt them, but nothing seemed to be happening. FBI agents were nowhere to be seen, and none of their friends or family were reporting having been questioned anymore. But there was always the lingering concern that things could take a turn for the worse, and so, in early 1962, Ted reached out to Vernon Ellis Cossett, a famous biophysicist at Cambridge University who headed a program on electron microscopy, expressing interest in the renowned Cambridge Cavendish Physics Laboratory. This led to an invitation from Cossett to come to Cambridge for a year, which grew into decades at the Cav and later in Cambridge University's biology department.

Joan was ecstatic about the idea of leaving the United States, and so were their children—by that time, three girls: Ruth, who was twelve; Deborah, who was eight; and Sara, who was four at the time of the big move.

They moved into a row house in the little village of Newnham, which is just across the sleepy, meandering Cam River to the west of the university, within easy walking distance of the campus. Only a few streets lined with row houses at the time, mostly occupied by graduate students, young faculty, and university employees, Newnham was an almost rural setting, set as it was between the university campus and the Grantchester Meadows, a large land grant with open pastures to which Cambridge students would pole their dates in long wooden boats called punts for afternoon picnics, or where older folks would take leisurely walks. The younger two girls attended the local public elementary school, which was situated a block from their home.

The Halls settled in there easily, volunteering little about their past life in the United States. Britain was not paranoid about Communists or Reds in general and had even treated its captured atomic spies—like Fuchs and later, the Cohens—much more humanely than did the United States, even trading them to the Soviet Union so they ended up serving much less time behind bars than their sentences called for. This compared favorably to how such cases were handled in the United States, where the Justice Department executed two spies and punished others, like Harry Gold, with sentences so long they were effectively for life. Ted and Joan lived quietly, with Ted keeping his head down, making a name for himself in biophysics and the new field of electron microscopy and steering clear of politics. Unlike Savy Sax, who told all three of his children at a fairly young age—his daughter Sarah when she was just twelve—about his helping to give atomic bomb secrets to the Soviets, Ted and Joan kept their growing teenage girls in the dark about his past as long as possible. Ted didn't even tell them that he had worked on the Manhattan Project, fearing they would hate him for doing it. Joan, meanwhile, as her daughter Ruth explains, took up the study of both Italian and Russian at the Cambridgeshire Institute of Arts and Technology. She eventually became sufficiently proficient to be hired as a teacher of the two languages at the same school.

Ted's reticence about opening up to anyone about his wartime work at Los Alamos led to an understandable misperception that he was a loner. Many of his colleagues and friends in the Cambridge community were thus shocked when the news broke in 1995 that he had been a Manhattan Project spy for the Soviets. According to one colleague, physicist Mick Brown, most people in the university were accepting of his motives, believing they were understandable, and didn't hold his past against him. This vindicated the Halls' initial sense that Britain was a better place for them than the United States, where anti-Red and anti-Soviet mania reigned.

One indication of how quiet they kept about their past in their little adopted Newnham community* was that Michael Meeropol told me he had lived for a year in Newnham in the 1960s, less than a block from the Halls when he was doing graduate study at Cambridge, and though he likely passed them many times on the street, never met them. "I never knew them then," he said in a phone interview, "because nobody knew Ted had been an atomic spy in the U.S. I only learned about that in 1995, and then I quickly contacted them and flew to Cambridge to talk to them." He added that Joan and he count each other as close friends now.

---

* In another of those strange coincidences that popped up over and over when looking into this whole story, on my arrival in Newnham the first time my wife and I went to talk with Joan back in 2018, I was struck by how familiar the town looked. I had lived there, on Eltisly Avenue, a street running parallel to Owlstone Road, where the Hall's house is located, though I was nine and it was 1958, four years before the Halls moved there from Connecticut. But the houses looked the same—better maintained and prettified with new paint and in more colors—than when I was there; the school, in which I spent fourth grade while my father spent a sabbatical year working on an early analog computer in the Cambridge engineering school, was new too, but in the same location, and the old one had been attended by both Deborah and Sara Hall. The butcher shop across the street from the school was the same as I remembered it, with its delicious smell of preserved meats. The meadows, with their creative stiles for preventing cattle from leaving and wandering the town streets, were still the same, protected from any development or town expansion. One could easily see why the Halls were accepted, as my family and I had been, in that small cosmopolitan community, even after it was learned that Ted had been a Soviet atomic spy.

27

MI5 COMES CALLING

If I had to choose between betraying my country and betraying my friend, I hope I should have the guts to betray my country.

—E. M. Forster

Life in Cambridge had been a big change from the United States for the Halls. Arriving on July 17, 1962, in Southampton on the liner *Queen Mary*, they entered the country without a hitch, Ted having already obtained a one-year work visa for his research position at the Cavendish Lab. Leaving the bustle of the New York metro area and what Joan called the "boring conformity" of the Connecticut suburb they had lived in, after riding up to the northeast of London through the picturesque countryside of southern England, they found themselves in the cosmopolitan university town of Cambridge. There they moved into a brick row house in Newnham, a community filled with younger faculty, graduate students, and working people employed by Cambridge University. As their oldest daughter, Ruth—already a nonconformist in her thinking at the tender age of twelve—recalls, "It was wonderful. In Britain nobody cared if you were an atheist or even a Communist!"[1] For the younger daughters, Deborah and Sara, there was a local elementary school just a block away, and the meandering Cam River was less than a block away in the other direction. Most of the homes in Newnham were without central heating; people instead still using coal fires in fireplaces.* Few families had refrigerators at the time, so shopping in the little stores along the street was a daily chore and social occasion.

In such a bucolic setting, it was easy to forget the tense and sometimes frightening life Joan and Ted had been living for the past decade and a half in the United States. Ted began conducting his pioneering research into cellular structures and function using the lab's electron microscope equipment while Joan began working on a degree in Italian and Russian at Cambridge Tech, a public college located in Cambridge.

But the FBI had other ideas for them. It was a year later, in 1963, when Ted had to apply for his work visa renewal, that he was jolted with the realization that he had not left his past behind by leaving the United States. He heard nothing for weeks after dropping off his U.S. passport to have it stamped with a new work visa, and then, instead of being told to come pick it up, he was asked to come into the office for an interview.

As Joan recalls in an interview for the film *A Compassionate Spy*, a congenial and "persuasive" MI5 agent met Ted when he came into the passport office. "We know what you did," he said, adding, "Why don't you come in and tell us all about it? We're not the FBI. We won't arrest you or anything, and you'll be able to get it off your chest." *Bombshell* authors Joseph Albright and Marcia Kunstel write that they were told by Cleveland Cram, the CIA's former liaison in London, that his FBI counterpart in the United Kingdom had in fact been instructed by J. Edgar Hoover himself to have MI5 question Ted about his spying. The obvious reason the request came at that late date, eleven years after the case had been put on ice in Chicago, was that Ted's brother, Ed Hall, had retired from the U.S. Air Force and its ICBM development program at the end of 1959. By 1960, he had also successfully completed a project he had been assigned as a civilian at the urging of the Pentagon to help France, a NATO member with an independent streak, to develop a nuclear ballistic missile of its own. French president Charles de Gaulle wanted his country to possess an independent nuclear attack force (*Force de Frappe*) separate from and not dependent upon the rest of NATO and the United States, and Ed Hall helped them get their own intermediate-range ballistic missile (IRBM), the Diamant. With that project completed and Ed no longer in uniform or involved in any national security projects, and with Senator Joseph McCarthy long

---

* I vividly recall at age nine in the winter of 1958 rising ahead of the rest of the family in our Newnham row house and doing my assigned chore of turning on the electric heater by the living room fire to keep warm while getting the coal lit in the fire basket located in the living room's little fireplace.

dead and the Red Scare years fading away, there was no longer any reason for the Pentagon to worry about a public arrest and trial of Ed's brother as an atomic spy. The FBI's plan apparently was to use a block on Ted's work visa renewal to have MI5 bring him in and question him about his spying background. The hope was that he might be induced to confess, as they had done in the case of Klaus Fuchs.

Joan told me that Ted informed the MI5 officer that he would "think about it."

In an interview for the film *A Compassionate Spy*, Joan recalled that in the course of a long walk home from Cambridge down Grantchester Street in their neighborhood of Newnham after that meeting, Ted told her, "Maybe they're right. It would be good to be able to be honest about it all."

She added, "I stopped and turned to him and, speaking sternly in a voice I'd never used before with him, said, 'You'll do no such thing! You'll stick to your story! You did nothing!' He turned to me looking a bit shocked and said, 'You think?' And I said firmly, 'Yes!'"

She explained, "Ted was always a very honest person. He never lied. Even in matrimonial matters he didn't lie to me, and I didn't lie to him. It was really rather extraordinary. And he really didn't like having had to lie all this time about what he had done in the 1940s. I think he really *did* want to 'get it off his chest.' But fortunately for him, and for me and the girls, he did what I said, and MI5 left him alone after that."

Ted ignored the "invitation" to talk to the British security and counter-intelligence agency and heard nothing more from them. Eventually, in the middle of the fall, his passport was finally returned to him with the renewed work visa in it.

Hoover, who by that time was increasingly preoccupied with his shift in focus to a new enemy—the counterculture—was increasingly busy having his agents subvert and harass the civil rights and Black Power movements and the growing U.S. antiwar movement. The FBI director, it appears, gave up on the idea of pursuing Hall in the United Kingdom. Meanwhile, MI5 at that point showed little interest in pursuing on its own what was, after all, a U.S. domestic intelligence case, not a British one.

But Hoover still wasn't through with the Hall and Sax case. He clearly still wanted to nab them—especially Ted Hall—if he could. And so, on January 28, 1966, two agents from the Boston FBI office took another tack, contacting Ted's old Harvard schoolmate and friend, fellow young Manhattan Project physicist Roy Glauber, who had for a time occupied the dorm room adjacent to Hall's at Los Alamos, right at the time Hall first became a Soviet spy. After the war, Glauber had gone on to earn a doctorate at Harvard and had subsequently become a physics professor there. Another reason for the timing of that Bureau visit to Glauber was that by 1966, the NSA, successor to the old SIS, which had been continuing to decrypt the thousands of Soviet wartime spy cables in its Venona Project, had likely managed to translate the spy cable about the so-called "Grauber incident."

That was the NKVD's term for the time in January 1945 (described earlier, in chapter 13) when Ted, in a clumsy attempt at spy recruitment, had dropped to Glauber that he had just recently given information of an unspecified nature to Soviet authorities about the bomb project at Los Alamos. The FBI agent's report on their meeting with Glauber shows no indication that they told him anything about a translated spy cable, which is understandable. Before 1995, the NSA was still following the SIS's and FBI's earlier decision not to let on publicly—or even within most of the Washington national security establishment—that they had cracked the Soviet wartime spy code and were working through decrypting and translating as many of the captured cables from that time as possible, with progress accelerating as they proceeded.

The New Testament of the Bible recounts the story of how following the Last Supper, Jesus told his apostles that one of them would deny or disown him three times that night "before the cock crows." Peter, his favorite disciple, insisted he would never betray him, but when officials later that night were seeking Jesus to arrest him, Peter did, in fact—out of fear, the story goes—thrice deny knowing him.

Future Nobel Physics laureate Glauber, like St. Peter as a disciple of Jesus, had three occasions he could have reported on Ted's spying to protect himself. Instead, he not only kept that knowledge to himself but, when asked twice by the FBI, even denied being a close friend of his old college classmate and roommate (though, unlike St. Peter, Glauber's denials of his friendship with Ted were not a betrayal but rather were clearly courageous actions meant to protect him).

His first defense of his friend came after Ted disclosed to him in mid-January 1945 that he had given information about the atomic bomb to Soviet intelligence. Glauber was duty-bound at Los Alamos to report that act of spying, but instead, while cutting himself off from Ted and asking to be moved to a different dorm after Ted's admission, he kept the secret to himself, at considerable personal risk. The second occasion, as described in chapter 13, was in March 1951, when the FBI visited him at his family's home in New York City and he denied knowing anything about Ted or anyone else being a Soviet spy in the Manhattan Project. Admitting that he had known Hall and Sax as friends and roommates in the fall term of 1943 at Harvard, he falsely claimed that he wasn't close to Ted at Los Alamos.

When the FBI came to him again in 1966, to avoid endangering Ted Hall, he resorted to a number of evasions and lies, which he surely must have known was a risky action that put him potentially in serious legal jeopardy.

When contacted in early January by FBI special agents James T. Sullivan and Michael J. McDonegh of the Boston FBI field office, who asked him to come visit them at their building, Glauber, perhaps seeking a home-field advantage, asked them to instead meet with him in his lab at Harvard, explaining that he was "too busy with work" to go to their downtown Boston office. In their sixteen-page report, the agents describe Glauber at that session as having been "polite" and also characterize his responses to their questions as "cooperative, affable and forthright."

The report the two agents filed on the two-hour session conducted at Glauber's lab in Harvard's Lyman Laboratory on January 2, 1966, reads,

> In discussing his activities in conjunction with those of Theodore Alvin Hall, Glauber stated that the four young Harvard physicists no doubt were the youngest members of the theoretical work force at Los Alamos in 1944 and 1945. He stated that most of the other physicists were in their late twenties and thirties and that the four Harvard youngsters felt as though they had been left out of the main activities occurring at the base. He stated that the four of them were thrown together, that he and Kenneth Case worked in the same office and that Hall lived in the dormitory room next to his own. Hall usually attended the movies on the base with him, usually dined with the group comprised of the Harvard College classmates, and like the others, spent a good deal of time in his room reading. . . .
>
> Glauber stated he could not recall being introduced to any close friends or social acquaintances of Theodore Alvin Hall and Saville Sax by Hall and Sax. He recalled that Hall in particular was quite secretive about identifying various girl friends and that he, Glauber, was quite perturbed about this practice of Hall. He stated he recalled his feelings that any young man who had been a college roommate and who had been associated on a working project with another young man would have identified various female acquaintances and perhaps set up an opportunity for double dating. Hall, however, never did this. Glauber recalled that Hall used to write letters to various female acquaintances. The identity of those individuals, however, he never did learn. . . .
>
> Glauber stated he has no knowledge whether Saville Sax and Theodore Alvin Hall had any mutual acquaintances either during their college days at Harvard or during the period Hall was located at Los Alamos. He stated he

likewise had no knowledge that Saville Sax and Theodore Alvin Hall met at any time following Hall's departure from Harvard College in approximately December 1943 or January 1944. . . .

Glauber stated that while at Los Alamos, he never had any feeling or conviction that persons he knew as fellow workers at Los Alamos might have been recruited by the Soviets or that these individuals thereafter might have tried to recruit others for the Soviets. He stated he was not explicitly suspicious of any fellow worker at Los Alamos while there. He stated that he was only a youngster of eighteen years when he started his approximate two years employment at Los Alamos and that he had no knowledge of Communist Party activities or how espionage might be effected.

He stated that looking back on the widespread publicity [a year earlier] from the Klaus Fuchs case, he had been shocked. He stated he came to the conclusion that there were a lot of people working at Los Alamos who would never have passed current security regulations. He stated he had come to the conclusion that very little, if any, screening had been done and that the demand for capable scientists was so great that perhaps some persons who were admitted to Los Alamos should never have been admitted. It is his feeling that a number of people who were communists by conviction actually worked at Los Alamos. He stated he could not identify these individuals but recalled hearing various hearsay bits of information which upon retrospect seemed to indicate that Communist Party members or adherents to the philosophy of communism were employed there. . . .

Glauber stated that neither while at Los Alamos between 1944 and January 1946 nor in the years up to the present time, nor at any time, had he ever been approached by the Soviets to become an agent of theirs. He added also that he had never become aware either of such an agency by any of his scientific friends and associates. . . .

Glauber again referred to his amazement that an espionage ring had been uncovered which had operated at Los Alamos during World War II. He stated he had never known Julius Rosenberg and/or David Greenglass and had no information that any of his associates at Harvard and the Los Alamos Project knew these individuals while at Los Alamos.[2]

This FBI post-interview report shows that the two agents spent considerable time asking Glauber about what he knew about any spying at Los Alamos by his fellow scientists during the war, and especially about his friend and Harvard classmate Ted Hall. His answers show that in response to those questions he lied and said he had never heard of anyone spying at Los Alamos, and certainly not Ted Hall. He made no mention to the agents about Hall's having admitted to him, after returning from his visit to New York in October 1944, that he had told the Soviets about the bomb project.

Another prevarication involved his living situation at Los Alamos. Glauber explained that after he had traveled to the Los Alamos job on the same train with Hall from New York's Pennsylvania Station, he found himself assigned to a dorm room inside the Manhattan Project compound located directly next to Hall's room. He claimed to the agents, however, that when Hall was drafted several months later, he had been required to move away to the military barracks located elsewhere on the Los Alamos compound, presumably leaving Glauber in his same room. This differs from the account by John Earl Haynes, Harvey Klehr, and Alexander Vassiliev in *Spies*, which quotes an NKVD cable sent by Leonid Kvasnikov (ANTON) from the *Rezidentura* to Moscow telling headquarters what Saville Sax had related to him after a trip to meet with Ted in New Mexico. In that version, Kvasnikov said that Glauber, upon hearing Hall's admission that he had shared information about the bomb with the Soviets "got scared, started taking back everything that he had said, and two weeks later he even moved out of MLAD's room and has since stopped being his friend."[3]

Stressing that he had worked, as part of the Theoretical Division, in an entirely different building from Hall, who was in the Experimental Division, Glauber also failed to mention the interesting though likely innocent fact that he and Hall had swapped assignments shortly after arriving at Los Alamos—information the agents might have viewed with suspicion if they'd known about it. While this was not technically a lie, it was extremely misleading about the circumstances of his having ended up in the T-Division and not the P-Division during his tenure at Los Alamos.

There were also factual issues with his account. Glauber twice told the agents "how amazed he was when he learned that an espionage ring had been uncovered that had operated at Los Alamos during World War II." Glauber also specifically told Hoover's gumshoes that he had "no knowledge of Hall's meeting Sax while at Los Alamos" and added that "while at Los Alamos he never had any feeling or conviction that persons he knew as fellow workers at Los Alamos might have been recruited by the Soviets or that those individuals thereafter might have tried to recruit others for the Soviets."[4]

The agents' report on Glauber's responses to their questions shows the physicist risked his reputation and possibly even prosecution by lying to the FBI to save his old pal while "betraying his country"—though his decision to protect Ted Hall, not once but three times, surely would have earned him novelist E. M. Forster's praise for putting friendship above patriotism. By 1993, Vassiliev's discoveries in the opened KGB archives (of which U.S. intelligence was acutely aware) were available in Russian. Even so, although Glauber was still in his late sixties—and Hall, while terminally ill, was still alive—no efforts were made by the FBI to question him to see if they could trip him up, or to prosecute him for having lied to FBI agents earlier about his knowledge in 1945 that his friend Ted Hall was a spy in the Manhattan Project or for his failure to immediately report Ted as a spy to Los Alamos security officials.

If Ted Hall's account to Sax of the "Grauber Incident," as relayed with the name misspelled by his handler to the New York *Rezidentura* and transmitted in code from the NKVD office in Manhattan to Moscow, is accurate—and there is no reason to suspect it is not—Glauber was lying brazenly at several points in his 1966 FBI interview. By the questions the agents asked during their interview in Glauber's Harvard lab, it seems clear the FBI had by then received from the NSA a transcript of the cable from Kvasnikov to Moscow explaining belatedly how Ted Hall had put himself in jeopardy by offering his friend Glauber a way to contact the Soviets. Glauber was thus in serious legal jeopardy both for lying to the FBI at that time and also for failing to report what he knew immediately to Los Alamos security officials after it happened. That he told these lies means that even in 1966, two decades after he had last seen his old friend at a dinner during a short train stop in Chicago, he did not wish to betray his college classmate and Manhattan Project colleague.

Glauber, who went on to receive a Nobel Prize in Physics in 2005 (joining a long list of Manhattan Project veterans who went on to win one), died in 2018 at the age of ninety-three, three months before I began researching this story and before I knew of his close connection to it. Multiple efforts to interview his adult son and daughter concerning his relationship with Hall and Sax, made by both phone and email, were met with no response.

Albright and Kunstel write in *Bombshell* that they interviewed Glauber during the mid-1990s and learned from him about two of his interviews by the FBI, including "in the '60s." He told them he "hadn't a clue as to what the 'Grauber incident' might entail." He went on to tell them: "It's very bizarre. Because I cannot associate anything at all with that period of time. That doesn't ring true."[5]

The authors do not speculate about Glauber's truthfulness regarding Hall and their post-Harvard and postwar relationship, but when I asked them about that they pointed out that they did not, when they were researching and writing their book, have access to the FBI's files on Hall and Sax, nor did they have access to the Boston FBI agents' report on their two-hour interview of Glauber in 1966.

—⌒⌒

One clear conclusion that can be drawn from these two attempts by the FBI in the mid-1960s to reactivate its pursuit of Ted Hall is that speculation among some atomic historians that he might have "come in from the cold" and turned on his former Soviet spy handlers to avoid prosecution is simply wrong. If, twelve to fifteen years *after* they hauled him and Savy Sax into their Chicago office and grilled the two young spies—and then suddenly dropped their investigation—they reopened it, then there's absolutely no basis for suspicion that he had become a double agent. In fact, if the FBI still wanted to nail Hall as a spy for what he had done at Los Alamos, as the evidence in their files shows they did as late as 1966, he certainly had not already cut a deal with them to avoid prosecution.

After the agents departed Glauber's lab, the FBI's effort to catch and prosecute Ted Hall as a Soviet spy finally died a quiet death. At that point, Hoover, with the U.S. war in Vietnam growing in terms of cost and blood and with popular opposition to it mounting dramatically and with the Black Power and civil rights movements increasingly allying with that opposition appears to have moved on from hunting Communists and Soviet spies to a new obsession: hounding unkempt leftist hippies and Black, beret-wearing, gun-toting Panthers—and perhaps assassinating Black leaders.[6] Indeed, Ted, who assured his anxious NKVD handlers in early 1945 that he trusted Glauber not to rat him out to Los Alamos security—though he never learned of his old friend's heroic stand when questioned by the FBI more than two decades later—had been right in his faith in that bond of friendship.

Ted subsequently visited the United States several times, both to visit family and to attend a scientific conference at which he was honored. He was never challenged or stopped at passport control on those trips back to his native land.

28

TELLING THE KIDS

What did you do in the war, Daddy?

—Common question from children born in
the years following World War II

Living with secrets as a parent is sure to be hard, both practically and emotionally. Ted and Joan Hall were in the position of keeping Ted's history as an atomic scientist and spy secret from their daughters, born in 1950, 1954, and 1958. They worried that telling their older daughters, Ruth and Debby, when they were old enough to keep a secret even from friends, could still lead to their youngest daughter's hearing about it, inadvertently putting them in legal jeopardy. Even his work on the Manhattan Project was kept secret from them as long as possible, and it was not until Sara confronted her father as a twenty-year-old college student that they all learned about his history.

Sara, the youngest Hall daughter, speaking on camera for the film *A Compassionate Spy* in 2020, confided that not knowing their secret, she wondered why her parents didn't seem to act on their professed concern about war and nuclear weapons, saying, "The way I looked at Joanie and Teddy growing up, I had known them to be utterly, through and through, desiring a better world and believing that everybody seemed necessary, but not acting, not action, being activists. And so growing up as a teenager, I was a bit scornful."

Her mother Joan, who was listening to the interview from across the kitchen table, looked serious and even a bit pained as Sara said that. "Scornful?" she asked.

Sara replied, "A little bit, yes, because while they always talked about wanting a better world, they never seemed to *do* anything about it." Then one day when she was "about 20" and a student at college living away from home, she said she found herself listening to a BBC program about the Manhattan Project. As she recalled in that same filmed interview,

> I listened to it and then I phoned up and asked Teddy and said I just heard this radio program, "Were you there?" And then he said, "Yes," [she laughed, adding] of course he said yes! And then he explained to me that "we had . . . the motivation was to develop the bomb before the Germans." That was how [he] justified doing it. And then he told me about how he felt when they tested it, how he wasn't celebrating as everybody else and had gone back to his room. I just thought, "Shit! It's him! He's been involved in designing and making the most horrendous thing on earth and not something to be proud of."
>
> I didn't know that he'd mitigated it by making sure it was shared information. And it never occurred to me. And then when they told me, the penny dropped. [Here her two hands made the motions of a penny falling down a set of double ladders, clicking her tongue as it dropped: Tchik, tchik, tchik . . .] Everything. It made sense of us, and our lives.[1]

She broke down at that point in the interview and couldn't keep talking, saying to stop the camera as she couldn't continue. Only later, at director Steve James's gentle urging, did she agree reluctantly to allow the segment to be included in the film (though she later came to appreciate its importance and impact as she saw how close friends reacted to it).

Ruth, the oldest sister and a committed progressive activist, including against war and the nuclear bomb, says she first had an inkling that her father may have done something like give the bomb secret away one day when she was a teenager relaxing with her father out in their backyard. Already a peace and antinuke activist, she was complaining about the limited approach to nuclear weapons being taken by the British and American disarmament movements during the Nuclear Freeze campaign, saying it was premised on the concept of mutual assured destruction: that as long as two rival nations have even a relatively few nuclear weapons, but enough to wreak havoc on a nuclear rival, there will be no war and no need to add more weapons. "It would never work," she told her father resolutely. As she recounts, "He looked at me with a funny smile and said, 'Are you sure it wouldn't work?' And I remember having this feeling of 'He must have done something to help create that kind of situation that we're in.' And it's true. He did."

There were other clues too, Ruth said, some that she recognized only looking back later. She recalls,

> I remember the Cuban missile crisis [in October 1962, when Ruth was about twelve], and there was a demonstration going past, of loads of people like, "Don't bomb!" And I was there tugging at Ted's arm saying, "Come on, come on! You know. What are we waiting for? You know, come!" And I remember him standing there, just standing, and he said, "What the hell!" and he took me by the arm and we went and we joined the demonstration. And I couldn't understand.

Back in 1966, when she was sixteen, Ruth says her mother took her to the Cambridge railway station so they could talk, explaining cryptically, "because it's a noisy place." She says her mother then told her, "There are some things you can't be told. There are some things that can't be told until one of us has died, and it will depend on who dies first." She continues, "They said whatever it was it didn't stop me from going to demonstrations. I think that it worried them, but they decided to let me go. So I guess I'd have to say I'd been scratching at the issue."

Later, when Ruth was living in Chicago with a boyfriend who had "political smarts," she says, "We were in a park and he was saying, 'You know, Ted was at the Manhattan Project and it could be he was a spy.' I thought about it, and realized it could be true. There was a book in the house about the Rosenbergs—probably Joan's—and it stuck in my mind. There was this hesitancy to talk about that case and then suddenly the book had disappeared."

Deborah, the middle Hall daughter, was thirty-seven years old in 1992 when she was hit by a truck as she was riding her bike on a London street. The activist law school student, violinist, and mother of two was killed on her way to class. The tragedy struck the family a scant three years after Ted had learned he had terminal kidney cancer, no doubt contracted as a result of the work with dangerous radioactive materials he routinely dealt with in the P-Division at Los Alamos. Two years later, in a fiftieth anniversary Harvard class note, Ted wrote, "I'm afflicted with Parkinson's disease and an inoperable cancer, and I recently experienced the death of a dearly loved daughter. Some of the horrors in the world scene are incomprehensible. But life still seems amazing and beautiful."[2]

Ruth says that before her sister Debbie was killed, the two of them had talked about their suspicions that their father had been a spy for good reason. "She guessed it," Ruth says confidently.

29

DENOUEMENT

*What Americans totally fail to understand is that their weap-
ons of mass destruction are just as much a problem as are those
of Iran.*

—Richard Rhodes[1]

The release of the Venona cable decrypts in 1995 outed Ted publicly
as an important Soviet spy in the Manhattan Project bomb development operation at Los Alamos. A world press scrum suddenly seemed to be
everywhere around the Hall home, part of an attached row of brick houses
on Owlstone Road in Newnham, even including photographers popping
out from behind streetside shrubs as Ted and Joan walked past. Meanwhile,
British tabloids and some U.S. publications were running blaring headlines
about the "teenage atomic spy." But as the Halls stayed largely quiet, the
excitement died down after a few weeks.

Instead of facing the electric chair, as the minor atomic spy Julius Rosenberg and his wife, Ethel (who refused to save herself and let her husband
take the heat alone), had done, sitting on death row for two years waiting to
be killed by the state, Ted Hall died peacefully in his sleep in a hospital bed.
Joan, his wife of fifty-one years, got the news of his passing shortly after she
arrived home from a visit to him at the hospice where he had been slowly
fading from the ravages of an incurable kidney cancer and Parkinson's
disease.

"I rushed back to the hospital and went into his room telling him that I loved him. I kissed him and mumbled a lot of sweet things to him, but he was gone," she recalls in a poignant interview in the film *A Compassionate Spy*.

Joan organized a secular memorial service for Ted on the Cambridge campus shortly after his death. The service was attended by friends of Ted and the family, as well as by work colleagues, mostly from Cambridge, and included a eulogy delivered by friend and fellow physicist Mick Brown. He went over Ted's many pioneering discoveries as a biophysicist, and then, toward the end of his speech, said,

It came as a bolt from the blue that Ted was an "atomic spy." We knew vaguely that he had worked on the Manhattan Project which built the first atomic weapons used decisively at Hiroshima and Nagasaki to end the war against Japan. He was one of several scientists active in Cambridge in the 1960s who had been involved in it and were reluctant to talk about their experiences to our antinuclear groups. But the news that Ted had been a brilliant, youthful recruit to Los Alamos, where he had at the age of eighteen headed a team designing the implosion trigger used to detonate the Nagasaki bomb came literally as a "bombshell" to me. *Bombshell* is the title of a book by Joseph Albright and Marcia Kunstel, published by Times Books/Random House, and still not available in the UK. As they describe, he conveyed information about the new technology to the Soviet spy network. There is no doubt in my mind that he did this for the highest of motives: to help break a U.S. monopoly of the deadly weapons. It is important for younger readers to understand the situation; in 1945 the American military held unchallenged control of nuclear power, which could with impunity threaten the destruction of large cities, such as Moscow, which could be—and might have been—used for decades to impose American conditions upon the shattered world emerging from World War II. It is probable the military establishment underestimated the scientific skills and accomplishments of the Russians, and therefore the likely duration of their monopoly. The Americans appeared surprised by the short time interval—four years—between the American bombs and the first Russian explosions. Perhaps the secrets revealed to the Russians shortened somewhat the time interval. In the feverish atmosphere of the day, other alleged spies—the Rosenbergs—were executed in the USA, the physicists Klaus Fuchs and Alan Nunn May imprisoned in Britain, and other famous agents, [Donald] Maclean, [Kim] Philby, and [Guy] Burgess, exiled to Russia. . . . Ted was allowed to live modestly in Cambridge and the role he played was not publicly known. Certainly we, his friends and colleagues, knew nothing of it.

The most eloquent defense of Ted's behavior against the charge of treason is his own: "Maybe the course of history, if unchanged [by my action], could have led to atomic war in the past fifty years; for example, the bomb might have been dropped on China in 1949 or the early 1950s. Well, if I helped to prevent that, I accept the charge." In his early phase of his life, yes, he was using his mastery of physics for the good of the world. He was certainly not a blind follower of Russian propaganda, but an independent thinker as well as a man who could take practical action.

Ted in Cambridge must have suffered acutely because of the enforced concealment of his youthful career in the Manhattan Project. It was always painful every year to apply for renewal of his resident's visa, and a great relief to be given leave to reside indefinitely. It was too risky ever to apply for [British] citizenship. It is tragic that his life was cut too short by cancer for him to have become what he deserved to be: a living example of selfless courage, and a hero to the present younger generation of science students. They should learn from him, and we his survivors should remember the proper pursuit of science is in the service of man.[2]

Physicist Frank Close, in his book on Klaus Fuchs, speculated about what that brilliant physicist/spy might have done had he not been exposed by the Venona cables (which were basically all the government had on him) and instead had managed to continue as head of the Oxford atomic research program at Harwell:

> But for Venona, Fuchs's espionage would probably have remained undetected for the rest of his life. His close friend Rudolf Peierls was knighted, his junior colleague Brian Flowers and the leader of the British Atomic Bomb project, William Penny, were both enobled. Would Fuchs, the brains behind the British weapon project, guru at Harwell, have achieved anything less?[3]

As for Ted Hall, his wife told me he had hoped, after nothing came of the MI5 call in the mid-1960s, that by 1985, when he reached sixty, he could retire, leave his biophysics work behind, and "return to the theoretical physics and the quantum questions that he loved." Had he been able to do that, with his brilliant mind intact, who knows what he might have discovered? But some combination of nature, the genetic roll of the dice, and the high-energy radiation and alpha-emitting nucleotides he was exposed to at Los Alamos conspired against that life plan as the diagnosis of an inoperable malignancy and advancing Parkinson's took their toll on his energy, his time, and his life, so we'll never know.

Joan and their two surviving daughters, Ruthie and Sara, scattered his ashes as he wished, under a magnificently branching hornbeam tree he loved on a green just off the Cambridge campus and a stone's throw from the Cam River. It is a huge, stately tree past which he for years had walked twice a day on his way to and from the Cambridge campus. Joan, an accomplished poet, wrote after Ted's death:

What If

What if I had died instead
and left you here behind
alone in your eighties?

How would you have lived
Would you have solved the riddle
of quantum mechanics?

Of course you'd have kept the audio
system in working order, go on
listening to your music.

Always a better housekeeper than I, you'd
have kept things much tidier. Though
come to think of it when I recall

the state of your study I sometimes wonder.
And would you have learnt to cook?
Frozen ready meals, I suppose.

But no doubt you'd have been invited
to dinner every day by one or another
of your women friends, who once

were my women friends. How would you
have remembered me? Anyway, soon
you'd surely have married again, one

of those women who loved you and envied me.
And for long years of Indian summer you
would drive along together and talk

in the car and in bed, my grey ashes melted
silently into the earth under that tall tree
in the park. Ah, now I'm jealous.

I want to be your second wife.

—Joan Krakover Hall

EPILOGUE

What Ted's Spying Accomplished and Didn't, and Where He Left Us

Seven decades later . . . the survival of life on Earth in the atomic age may be due to the mutually assured destruction that . . . Fuchs and Ted Hall helped to mature.

—Frank Close[1]

In early 2022, as Russian troops and vast amounts of heavy military equipment—tanks, huge artillery, bombers and attack aircraft, long-range missiles, and cruise missile–armed ships in the Azov and Black seas—were assembled for what would become a brutal all-out Russian invasion of Ukraine, the United States and the nations of NATO—and NATO itself—declared clearly that they would not be sending troops or air forces to defend the erstwhile second-largest state in the former Soviet Union, nor would they use NATO planes to establish any kind of no-fly zone over the threatened country established in 1991 after the break-up of the Soviet Union.

There was only one reason for such an advance declaration on the part of the United States and NATO member nations: recognition of the reality that Russia has in its arsenal the largest number of deliverable nuclear weapons in the world, many of them able to hit every part of the United States, not to mention every NATO member country.

The sense of crisis has worsened as the war has ground on for more than a year, with Ukrainian forces proving tougher than Russia expected, in no small measure thanks to the more than $70 billion in arms the United

States and many NATO countries have provided to the Ukrainian military, including advanced U.S. weapons and training for Ukrainian troops to be able to use them. This aid, including targeting assistance provided by U.S. spy satellites and drones, has allowed Ukrainian forces to hit Russian troop positions while remaining themselves out of range of less capable Russian artillery. As well, sophisticated U.S. antiaircraft weapons have kept Russian aerial attacks and troop support to a minimum. As Ukrainian forces started pushing Russian troops out of occupied territory, some reportedly even abandoning their still-functioning heavy vehicles and tanks, Russian president Vladimir Putin and his backers began hinting that any threat to Russia itself—and here he pointedly included Crimea and occupied portions of the eastern oblasts Donetsk and Luhansk—by NATO forces could lead to Russia's using "all available means to protect Russia and our people."[2]

That language was understandably taken by the United States and other NATO countries—and by most NATO country media—to mean nuclear weapons.[3] (It's important to note that while there has been a lot of speculation in U.S. media and government circles, aided by statements by Russian commentators, about Russian forces in Ukraine proactively turning to "tactical" nukes in that conflict, Putin himself has to date not overtly said such a thing, perhaps fearing causing a panic among Russians.)

Many people, both in Russia and in the NATO nations, quite reasonably wonder whether this Ukrainian war is going to be how the world ends. But I think that fear is overblown. The United States, remember, threatened to use its nuclear weapons multiple times—in Korea, twice in Vietnam, in the Cuban and Suez Crises, in the Berlin Crisis, and during the crisis over the Soviet shoot-down of a Korean 747 flying over Soviet-owned Sakhalin Peninsula—but it never acted on those threats, despite sometimes coming perilously close.

It has been clear even to the biggest anti-Russian politicians and militarists in Washington and the capitals of Europe that going to Ukraine's defense *directly* against Russia with NATO or U.S. military forces would almost inevitably lead to a nuclear war that would likely destroy the world.

The reason most rational humans outside Ukraine have had a reluctance to go to war there against an invading Russia, even when its ground forces have proven to be less formidable than U.S. and NATO strategists expected or predicted, is the same reason that none of those many crises have led to world- or European-wide wars (as much smaller conflicts did twice in the last century). Since August 29, 1949, when Russia exploded its first atom bomb and joined the United States as a nuclear power, it has been too dangerous for U.S., Soviet (or Russian), or any other nuclear nation's military to get involved in head-to-head nuclear conflict because of the near certainty that whichever combatant begins to lose would turn (or at least threaten to turn) to nuclear weapons.

War game after war game, whether played out in Washington, Moscow, Beijing, or elsewhere, has shown this to be true: Within days or hours of any modern war between nuclear powers, the conflict goes nuclear and everyone is destroyed. As Christopher Chivvas, a senior fellow at the Carnegie Endowment for Peace and a political scientist at the Defense Department–linked RAND Corporation, writes,

> Scores of war games carried out by the United States and its allies in the wake of Russia's 2014 invasion of Ukraine make it clear that Putin would probably use a nuclear weapon if he concludes that his regime is threatened. . . . Based on war games I ran in the wake of Putin's 2014 invasion, a more likely option would be a sudden nuclear test or a high-altitude nuclear detonation that damages the electrical grid over a major Ukrainian or even NATO city. Think of an explosion that makes the lights go out over Oslo. . . .
>
> Those war games indicated that the best U.S. response to this kind of attack would be first to demonstrate U.S. resolve with a response in kind, aimed at a target of similar value, followed by restraint and diplomatic efforts to de-escalate. In most games, Russia still responds with a second nuclear attack, but in the games that go "well," the United States and Russia manage to de-escalate after that, although only in circumstances where both sides have clear political off-ramps and lines of communication between Moscow and Washington have remained open. *In all the other games, the world is basically destroyed.*[4]

But that fear of nuclear catastrophe works on both sides of the Ukrainian border. Putin, just like a string of U.S. presidents going back to Truman, has been bluffing. Whether this is because he doesn't really want to have Russia destroyed by a U.S. nuclear attack or because he is afraid if he orders the use of tactical nukes, his generals will ignore such a suicidal order—or, worse for him, will turn on him and remove or kill him—the result is the same. Knowing the disaster turning to "tactical nukes" would be for themselves and all Russia, nuclear threats, whether veiled or overt, from the Kremlin have remained just that.

The constraint of mutual assured destruction is the reason that in the seventy-eight years since the United States dropped the only two nuclear bombs ever used in war, leveling Hiroshima and Nagasaki, no other nuclear weapon has been used in battle and no two nuclear nations have risked engaging in direct combat between their conventional forces. MAD is also the reason the war in Ukraine has stayed in Ukraine, why U.S. and NATO troops have not joined the battle, and why nuclear weapons—even "small" ones—have not been used. I'm also confident in predicting that because of MAD, those weapons will continue not to be used. Humanity has come frighteningly close to nuclear catastrophe several times, but saner heads or courageous junior officers on both sides, forced to make their own decision, have made the right one (often at great personal and career risk) and refused to launch a nuclear attack or to resort to using even a single nuclear weapon.

As atomic bomb historian Richard Rhodes writes in the foreword to the twenty-fifth anniversary edition of his highly praised book on the making of the atomic bomb,

> When the Soviet Union exploded a copy of the "Fat Man" plutonium bomb built from plans supplied by Klaus Fuchs and Ted Hall and went on to develop a comprehensive arsenal of its own, matching the American arsenal; when the hydrogen bomb increased the already devastating destructiveness of nuclear weapons by several orders of magnitude; when the British, the French, the Chinese, the Israelis and other nations acquired nuclear weapons, the strange new nuclear world matured. . . .
>
> So cheap, so portable, so holocaustal did nuclear weapons eventually become that even nation-states as belligerent as the Soviet Union and the United States preferred to sacrifice a portion of their national sovereignty— preferred to forgo the power to make total war—rather than be destroyed in their fury. Lesser wars continue, and will continue . . . but world war at least has been revealed to be historical, not universal, a manifestation of destructive technologies of limited scale. In the long history of human slaughter that is no small achievement.[5]

It's a lousy situation, to be sure, one that has led to the unconscionable deaths of millions (mostly civilians) in proxy wars. As Ted Hall, speaking in a clip from a tape made in 1998, a year before his death, concluded at the end of the film *A Compassionate Spy*, the people of the world must "compel governments to ensure that the world never again comes close to catastrophe."[6]

It's way past time for the nuclear-armed nations of the world to recognize the futility of their nuclear weapons and the terrible risk their existence poses of some mistake leading to disaster, and just get rid of them. Not just most but all of them.

When nineteen-year-old Ted Hall provided his Soviet spy handlers with the detailed plan for making the implosion system for the plutonium bomb and the method for controlling that unstable element plutonium to produce a massive blast instead of a weak "fizzle," he had no way of knowing what the result would be. Instead of recognizing they were in a stalemate and banning the weapon they by mid-1949 both possessed, as he had hoped would happen, Washington and Moscow embarked on a decades-long and incomprehensibly expensive and wasteful competition to try to achieve supremacy over each other such that one of them could launch a first strike on the other with impunity. Thankfully, that atomic strategists' dream and humanitarian nightmare has never been realized, and now nuclear weapons are so numerous and so powerful that even a "successful" strike by one country that takes out all of an adversary's retaliatory capability, would by itself destroy all complex life forms on earth, making "victory" pyrrhic and thus utterly pointless.

We have Ted Hall and Saville Sax (along with Klaus Fuchs) to "thank" for that, if such a word can be used.

In 1954, just months before his death, Albert Einstein confided to a visiting Linus Pauling, a Nobel laureate chemist, Nobel Peace Prize laureate, and antinuclear activist: "I made one great mistake in my life when I signed the letter to President Roosevelt recommending that atom bombs be made."[7]

Ted Hall, who later in his life had grave misgivings about his spying because of the enormous cost of the arms race that ensued and because of the undeniable truth about the horrors inflicted on the Soviet people by Joseph Stalin's decades-long rule of terror, at least didn't go to his death regretting what he had done. His wife Joan told me that he only regretted that he had to be the one who shared the bomb instead of someone else at Los Alamos.

Maybe the information shared by Ted Hall and Klaus Fuchs about the plutonium bomb's design and construction, taken together, gave the Soviets their own atom bomb four or five years ahead of when they would have gotten it on their own, or perhaps what they provided only advanced Soviet development of their own bomb by a year. Either way, it's likely that Ted Hall's spying effort did prevent the nightmare of a U.S. monopoly on nuclear weapons and a genocidal nuclear attack against the Soviet people in the early 1950s.

Certainly one elderly Russian nuclear scientist thought so.

Hugh Gusterson, a professor of anthropology and public policy at the University of British Columbia, writing in the *Bulletin of the Atomic Scientists*, recalls how in the mid-1990s, he met with a nuclear weapons designer who had witnessed the first test in August 1949 of the Soviet atomic bomb he (and Ted Hall) helped to create. He writes:

> In what was admittedly an inartfully phrased question, I asked, "How did you feel when you realized you had given Stalin the bomb?" He looked at me steadily from under craggy eyebrows as the question was translated, then said evenly, "I felt at last I could sleep again after four years. Finally we were safe from the Americans."[8]

Imperfect as is the mutual assured destruction that Ted's spying helped to create, until the nine nuclear nations of the world join the 120 nations that in early 2022 voted to declare nuclear weapons illegal under the UN Charter, it's pretty much the best, or only, system we have to rely on to deter such weapons from being used. Since it is a flawed system, we all—especially those of us in those nine nations—need to work, as Hall said in the last year of his life, to ban such weapons entirely as was done after World War I with germ and chemical weapons.

APPENDIX

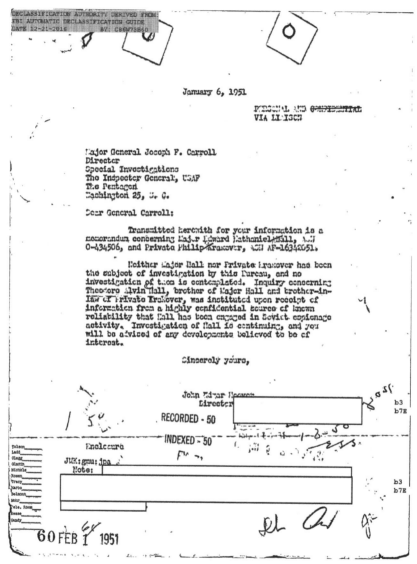

January 6, 1951

PERSONAL AND CONFIDENTIAL
VIA LIAISON

Major General Joseph F. Carroll
Director
Special Investigations
The Inspector General, USAF
The Pentagon
Washington 25, D. C.

Dear General Carroll:

Transmitted herewith for your information is a
memorandum concerning Major Edward Nathaniel Hall, ASN
0-434506, and Private Philip Krakover, ASN AF-16342051.

Neither Major Hall nor Private Krakover has been
the subject of investigation by this Bureau, and no
investigation of them is contemplated. Inquiry concerning
Theodore Alvin Hall, brother of Major Hall and brother-in-
law of Private Krakover, was instituted upon receipt of
information from a highly confidential source of known
reliability that Hall has been engaged in Soviet espionage
activity. Investigation of Hall is continuing, and you
will be advised of any developments believed to be of
interest.

Sincerely yours,

John Edgar Hoover
Director

RECORDED - 50

INDEXED - 50

Enclosure

JMK:gmu:jpa
Note:

b3
b7E

b3
b7E

Tolson
Ladd
Clegg
Glavin
Nichols
Rosen
Tracy
Harbo
Belmont
Mohr
Tele. Room
Nease
Gandy

60 FEB 1 1951

January 6, 1951

RE: MAJOR EDWARD NATHANIEL HALL,
ASN O-434506;
PRIVATE PHILIP KRAKOVER,
ASN AF-16342051

During the course of an investigation of Theodore Alvin Hall, who resides at 6002 University Avenue, Chicago, Illinois, it has been ascertained that both he and _____ have been extremely active in the affairs of the Progressive Party of Illinois. A reliable confidential source has advised that the Progressive Party of Illinois is actually under the control of the Communist Party. Hall was graduated from Harvard University in 1944 with a B.S. degree in Physics, and is presently employed by the Institute of Radio Biology and Biophysics of the University of Chicago. Hall and his wife have been extremely active in soliciting signatures to the "Stockholm Peace Pledge" and signatures to place the Progressive Party on the Illinois ballot for the November, 1950 election. On May 3, 1950, _____ was elected corresponding secretary of the Fifth Ward (Chicago) Progressive Party, and membership meetings of that club have been held at the Hall residence.

On July 9, 1950, Hall and four associates were taken into custody by the Chicago Police Department for soliciting signatures to petitions to place the Progressive Party on the Illinois ballot and to outlaw the Atom Bomb, but were released without charges being lodged against them. Hall also has been active in the affairs of the Chicago Tenants Action Council, which organization has been described by informants of known reliability as a "Communist front organization" which is receiving active support from the Communist Party. Most of Hall's associates in Chicago have a background of past or present membership in the Communist Party or other Communist organizations.

b6
b7C

Tolson
Ladd
Clegg
Glavin
Nichols
Rosen
Tracy
Harbo
Belmont
Mohr
Tele. Room
Nease
Gandy

J.M. Kelly:gmu

b3
b7E

Figure D.1   (continued)

Investigation has disclosed that Theodore Alvin
Hall is a brother of Major Edward Nathaniel Hall, ASN O-434506.
Major Hall, as of September 27, 1950, was assigned to the
Power Plant Laboratory, Engineering Division, Wright-Patterson
Air Force Base, Dayton, Ohio, and was reportedly working on a
highly secret and confidential project.

It has also been determined that Philip Krakover,
_____ is a Private in the United States
Air Force, ASN AF-16342051, and as of October 28, 1950, was
assigned to the 3726th Training Squadron, Lackland, Texas, Air
Force Base.

b6
b7C

b3
b7E

- 2 -

Figure D.1   (continued)

Operation Dropshot
Strategic Air Offensive
Program

Soviet Industry:

Degree of Collapse of Industry	Several Years	1–1½ Years	1 Year
Target Systems to Be Attacked	Petroleum, Electric Power, and Steel	Electric Power and Steel	Petroleum and Electric Power
Atomic Bombs on Target (in 30 days)	180	141	109
Tons of Conventional Bombs on Target (by D + 4 mos.)	12,620 tons	10,420 tons	10,420 tons
Percentages of Industry Destroyed or Eliminated from Production.			
Electric Power	66–70	66	66
Petroleum	95	70	95
Steel	85	85	76
Alumina	100	100	100
Aluminum	100	100	100
Magnesium	100	100	100
Autos and Trucks	100	100	100
Hvy. Elec. Eq.	97	97	97
Syn. Ammonia	98	98	98
A/C Assembly	92	92	92
A/C Engines	89	89	89
Elec. Tubes	91	97	91
Lt. Elec. Eq.	82	82	82
Coke	100	100	100
Hv. and Med. Bomb Gps. Reqd. for Atomic Effort	7	5	4
Hv. and Med. Bomb Gps. Reqd. for Conv. Effort	6	5	5

Figure D.2   Early Dropshot bombing program for hitting the Soviet Union and other Communist nations with 180 Nagasaki-sized nuclear bombs to destroy the USSR as an industrial society. *Document created by author based on information from the National Archives*

NOTES

PREFACE

1. Shannon Duffy, "Loyalists," Center for Digital History, Washington Library at George Washington's Mt. Vernon, https://www.mountvernon.org/library/digitalhistory/digital-encyclopedia/article/loyalists/.

2. "Dunmore's Proclamation," History.com, October 26, 2021, https://www.history.com/topics/american-revolution/dunmores-proclamation.

3. Ed Crews, "Voting in Early America," *Colonial Williamsburg Journal*, Spring 2007, https://research.colonialwilliamsburg.org/Foundation/journal/Spring07/elections.cfm.

PROLOGUE

1. Saville Sax/Theodore Hall FBI file #65-3348 Memorandum from Albuquerque FBI office to multiple FBI offices, May 4, 1959. (Also appears in 1964 document in FBI file on Edward Hall.)

2. Herbert Romerstein and Eric Breindel, *The Venona Secrets: Exposing Soviet Espionage and America's Traitors* (New York: Regency Publishing, 2000), 205.

3. Romerstein and Breindel, *The Venona Secrets*, 203.

4. "Secrets, Lies and Atomic Spies," a documentary on PBS's program *Nova*, aired February 5, 2002. Transcript at https://www.pbs.org/wgbh/nova/transcripts/2904_venona.html.

5. Daniel Fienberg, "'A Compassionate Spy' Review: Steve James Doc Is a Nuanced Portrait of Love and Espionage," *Hollywood Reporter*, September 2, 2022, https://www.hollywoodreporter.com/movies/movie-reviews/a-compassionate-spy-steve-james-ted-hall-1235210819/; Alex Billington, "Alex's 8 Favorite Films at the Invigorating 2022 Venice Film Festival," *First Showing*, September 22, 2022, https://www.firstshowing.net/2022/alexs-8-favorite-films-at-the-invigorating-2022-venice-film-festival/; Robert Abele, "'A Compassionate Spy' Film Review: Steve James Doc Examines a WWII Scientist's Moral Espionage," *The Wrap*, September 22, 2022, https://www.thewrap.com/a-compassionate-spy-documentary-review-steve-james-ted-hall-ussr-atomic/.

CHAPTER 1: THE NUTURING OF A YOUNG GENIUS

1. Joan Hall, "A Memoir of Ted Hall," History Happens, 2003, https://web.archive.org/web/20070607215311/http://www.historyhappens.net/archival/manproject/joanhalldoc/joanhall.htm.
2. Maurice Isserman, "When New York City Was the Capital of American Communism," *New York Times*, October 20, 2017, http://www.nytimes.com/2017/10/20/opinion/new-york-american-communism.html.
3. Joseph Albright and Marcia Kunstel, *Bombshell: The Secret Story of America's Unknown Atomic Spy Conspiracy* (New York: Times Books, 1997), 35.
4. Hall, "A Memoir of Ted Hall."

CHAPTER 2: EDWARD HALL JOINS THE ARMY AIR CORPS AND SHIPS OFF TO ENGLAND

1. Edward N. Hall, *A Nation at Risk* (unpublished manuscript, 2000–2003), 2.
2. Hall, *A Nation at Risk*, 3.
3. Hall, *A Nation at Risk*, 19.
4. Hall, *A Nation at Risk*, 16.
5. Hall, *A Nation at Risk*, 18.
6. Hall, *A Nation at Risk*, 21.

CHAPTER 3: EINSTEIN WARNS FDR ABOUT A POSSIBLE GERMAN A-BOMB

1. Albert Einstein and Leo Szilard, "Einstein's Letter to Roosevelt," The Manhattan Project, An Interactive History, https://www.osti.gov/opennet/manhattan-project-history/Events/1939-1942/einstein_letter.htm.

2. Einstein and Szilard, "Einstein's Letter to Roosevelt."

CHAPTER 4: TED HALL

1. "Mass Media Specialist at U of H," *Hartford Courant*, September 22, 1974.
2. Nicholas Cox, "John Reed Clubs," Society for US Intellectual History, December 1, 2017, https://s-usih.org/2017/12/john-reed-clubs/.
3. Ellen W. Schrecker, *No Ivory Tower: McCarthyism and the Universities* (New York: Oxford University Press, 1986), 3.
4. Chandler Davis, "An Extremum Problem for Plane Convex Curves," in *Convexity: Proceedings of Symposia in Pure Mathematics*, vol. VII, ed. Victor L. Klee, pp. 181–85 (Providence, RI: American Mathematical Society, 1963).
5. Original handwritten letter in the possession of Joan Hall.
6. Original handwritten letter in the possession of Joan Hall.
7. Joseph Albright and Marcia Kunstel, *Bombshell: The Secret Story of America's Unknown Atomic Spy Conspiracy* (New York: Times Books, 1997), 57.
8. Joan Hall, "A Memoir of Ted Hall," History Happens, 2003, https://web.archive.org/web/20070607215311/http://www.historyhappens.net/archival/manproject/joanhalldoc/joanhall.htm.

CHAPTER 5: ENTER SAVILLE SAX

1. Boria Sax, *Stealing Fire: Memoir of a Boyhood in the Shadow of the Atomic Espionage* (Mount Vernon, NY: Decalogue Books, 2014), 15.
2. Sax, *Stealing Fire*, 16.
3. Sax, *Stealing Fire*, 27.
4. Joan Hall, interview in Steve James, dir., *A Compassionate Spy* (Participant Films, 2022).
5. Boria Sax, interview in *A Compassionate Spy*.
6. Joseph Albright and Marcia Kunstel, *Bombshell: The Secret Story of America's Unknown Atomic Spy Conspiracy* (New York: Times Books, 1997), 57.
7. Saville Sax/Theodore Hall FBI file #65-3348, May 2, 1950.

CHAPTER 6 : HIRED ONTO THE MANHATTAN PROJECT AT LOS ALAMOS

1. Joseph Albright and Marcia Kunstel, *Bombshell: The Secret Story of America's Unknown Atomic Spy Conspiracy* (New York: Times Books, 1997), 60–61.

2. Albright and Kunstel, *Bombshell*, 60.

3. Herbert Romerstein and Eric Breindel, *The Venona Secrets: Exposing Soviet Espionage and America's Traitors* (New York: Regency Publishing, 2000), 200.

4. Romerstein and Briendel, *The Venona Secrets*, 200.

5. Albright and Kunstel, *Bombshell*, 60–61.

CHAPTER 7: THE SOVIET BOMB PROJECT

1. Venona cable #1699, New York to Moscow, December 2, 1944.

2. William Burr, "The British Bomb and the United States," National Security Archive, March 13, 2021.

3. Atomic Heritage Foundation, "The British Nuclear Program," https://ahf.nuclear museum.org/ahf/history/british-nuclear-program/.

4. Frank Close, *Trinity: The Treachery and Pursuit of the Most Dangerous Spy in History* (New York: Penguin, 2020), 162–65.

5. Close, *Trinity*, 285–86. A Venona cable from October 4, 1944, identified a spy code-named REST, while a second, on October 5, named a spy CHARLES or Charle-Z, who had "moved to Camp No. 2 [Los Alamos], and would be visiting his sister in December." Sleuthing work by FBI and MI5 did the rest, identifying the sister as Fuchs's younger sister, Kristel Fuchs Heineman, and GOOSE and ARNO as Fuchs's courier, Harry Gold.

6. Close, *Trinity*, 295.

7. U.S. Department of Energy, Office of Legacy Management, "Manhatttan Project Background Information and Preservation Work," https://www.energy.gov/lm/manhat tan-project-background-information-and-preservation-work#.

CHAPTER 8: TED HALL AT LOS ALAMOS

1. Joseph Albright and Marcia Kunstel, *Bombshell: The Secret Story of America's Unknown Atomic Spy Conspiracy* (New York: Times Books, 1997), 67.

2. Albright and Kunstel, *Bombshell*, 69.

3. Kai Bird and Martin J. Sherwin, *American Prometheus: The Triumph and Tragedy of J. Robert Oppenheimer* (New York: Vintage Books, 2006), 582.

4. David Hawkins, Edith C. Truslow, Ralph Carlisle Smith, and Los Alamos Scientific Laboratory, *Project Y: The Los Alamos Story* (Los Angeles: Tomash Publishers, 1983), 203.

5. "Los Alamos. Wayside; Now We Have Our Bomb," Manhattan Project National Historical Park plaque, Los Alamos.

6. Ted Hall, speaking in Steve James, dir., *A Compassionate Spy* (Participant Films, 2022).

CHAPTER 9: 1944 AND THE WAR'S END IS IN SIGHT

1. Kai Bird and Martin J. Sherwin, *American Prometheus: The Triumph and Tragedy of J. Robert Oppenheimer* (New York: Vintage Books, 2006), 288.

2. Niels Bohr, "Niels Bohr's Memorandum to President Roosevelt," Atomic Archives, https://www.atomicarchive.com/resources/documents/manhattan-project/bohr-memo.html.

3. Joseph Albright and Marcia Kunstel, *Bombshell: The Secret Story of America's Unknown Atomic Spy Conspiracy* (New York: Times Books, 1997), 100.

4. Pugwash Conference on World Affairs, https://pugwash.org/.

5. Albright and Kunstel, *Bombshell*, 86.

6. Bird and Sherwin, *American Prometheus*, 286.

7. Albright and Kunstel, *Bombshell*, 89–90.

8. Theodore Hall, unpublished essay explaining his reason for becoming a Los Alamos spy, circa 1995–1997, in the possession of Joan Hall.

9. Jonathan M. Katz, "The Plot against American Democracy That Isn't Taught in Schools," *Rolling Stone*, January 21, 2022, https://www.rollingstone.com/politics/politics-features/coup-jan6-fdr-new-deal-business-plot-1276709/.

10. Rachel Maddow, "Ultra," six-part documentary podcast, October 10, 2022, https://www.msnbc.com/rachel-maddow-presents-ultra.

11. Transcript of a taped conversation by Ruth Hall London made on her cell phone with her mother, Joan Hall, on October 12, 2022.

CHAPTER 10: FINDING A SOVIET SPY TO SIGN UP WITH

1. Joseph Albright and Marcia Kunstel, *Bombshell: The Secret Story of America's Unknown Atomic Spy Conspiracy* (New York: Times Books, 1997), 206.

2. Venona Decrypt, Soviet Cable NY-Moscow, November 12, 1944.

3. Alexander Vassiliev, Yellow Notebook #1, Wilson Center Digital Archive, https://digitalarchive.wilsoncenter.org/document/vassiliev-yellow-notebook-1, 19–22.

4. Albright and Kunstel, *Bombshell*, 97.

CHAPTER 11: EDWARD HALL AT WAR IN GREAT BRITAIN

1. Edward N. Hall, *A Nation at Risk* (unpublished manuscript, 2000–2003), 27.

2. Hall, *A Nation at Risk*, 29.

3. Hall, *A Nation at Risk*, 29.

4. Hall, *A Nation at Risk*, 32.

5. Hall, *A Nation at Risk*, 33.

6. Hall, *A Nation at Risk*, 34.

7. U.S. Air Force, "Col. Edward N. Hall, Inducted 1999," https://www.afspc.af.mil/Portals/3/documents/Pioneers/AFD-100405-065.pdf.

8. Hall, *A Nation at Risk*, 36.

CHAPTER 12: THE VENONA DECRYPTION PROJECT

1. Peter Wright, *Spycatcher: The Candid Autobiography of a Senior Intelligence Officer* (Richmond, Victoria: Heinemann, 1987), 185.

2. "Julius Rosenberg: Soviet Spy," Atomic Heritage Foundation, https://ahf.nuclearmuseum.org/ahf/profile/julius-rosenberg/.

3. Harold Jackson, "Obituary: Theodore Hall, US Scientist Spy Who Escaped Prosecution and Spent 30 Years in Biological Research at Cambridge," *Guardian*, November 15, 1999, https://www.theguardian.com/news/1999/nov/16/guardianobituaries.haroldjackson.

4. Venona cable #1585 from New York to Moscow, November 12, 1944.

5. Herbert Romerstein and Eric Breindel, *The Venona Secrets: Exposing Soviet Espionage and America's Traitors* (New York: Regency Publishing, 2000), 27.

6. Romerstein and Breindel, *The Venona Secrets*, 207.

CHAPTER 13: THE "GRAUBER INCIDENT"

1. Ted Hall, in a clip from a video made shortly before his death, which appears at the beginning of Steve James, dir., *A Compassionate Spy* (Participant Films, 2022).

2. Alexander Vassiliev, Yellow Notebook #1, Digital Archive, Wilson Center, 227, https://digitalarchive.wilsoncenter.org/document/vassiliev-yellow-notebook-1.

3. Vassiliev, Yellow Notebook #1, 342.

4. Vassiliev, Yellow Notebook #1, 343.

5. New York Report, FBI, 4-28-51 Re: "Theodore Alvin Hall, Saville Sax," Espionage-R #65-59122-263 (18).

6. Joseph Albright and Marcia Kunstel, *Bombshell: The Secret Story of America's Unknown Atomic Spy Conspiracy* (New York: Times Books, 1997), 211.

CHAPTER 14: KLAUS FUCHS

1. Otto Frisch and Rudolf Peierls, "Memorandum, March 1940," https://ahf.nuclearmuseum.org/ahf/key-documents/frisch-peierls-memorandum/.

2. Frisch and Peierls, "Memorandum, March 1940."

3. Robert Chadwell Williams, *Klaus Fuchs: Atom Spy* (Cambridge, MA: Harvard University Press, 1987), 17.

4. Williams, *Klaus Fuchs*, 22.

5. Williams, *Klaus Fuchs*, 23.

6. Williams, *Klaus Fuchs*, 33.

7. Richard M. Langworth, "Churchill, Refugees and Aliens," The Churchill Project, Hillsworth College, April 27, 2017, https://winstonchurchill.hillsdale.edu/churchill-refugees-aliens/.

8. Williams, *Klaus Fuchs*, 34.

9. Atomic Heritage Foundation, "Klaus Fuchs, Atomic Spy, Los Alamos," https://www.atomicheritage.org/profile/klaus-fuchs.

10. Maud Committee, "MAUD Committee Report," March 1941, https://ahf.nuclearmuseum.org/ahf/key-documents/maud-committee-report/.

11. Atomic Heritage Foundation, "Klaus Fuchs, Atomic Spy, Los Alamos."

12. John Earl Haynes, Harvey Klehr, and Alexander Vassiliev, *Spies: The Rise and Fall of the KGB in America* (New Haven, CT: Yale University Press, 2009), 93.

13. Haynes, Klehr, and Vassiliev, *Spies*, 93.

CHAPTER 15: TED'S SPYING BEGINS IN EARNEST

1. Joan Hall, "A Memoir of Ted Hall," History Happens, 2003, https://web.archive.org/web/20070607215311/http://www.historyhappens.net/archival/manproject/joanhalldoc/joanhall.htm.

2. Joseph Albright and Marcia Kunstel, *Bombshell: The Secret Story of America's Unknown Atomic Spy Conspiracy* (New York: Times Books, 1997), 100.

3. Ted Hall, interview taped in 1998, shown in Steve James, dir., *A Compassionate Spy* (Participant Films, 2022).

4. Hall, "A Memoir of Ted Hall."

5. Sarah Pruitt, "8 Spies Who Leaked Atomic Bomb Intelligence to the Soviets," History.com, August 18, 2021, https://www.history.com/news/atomic-bomb-soviet-spies; William Broad, "Fourth Spy Unearthed in US Atomic Bomb Project," *New York Times*, November 23, 2019, https://www.nytimes.com/2019/11/23/science/manhattan-project-atomic-spy.html; Michael Walsh, "George Koval: Atomic Spy Unmasked," *Smithsonian*, May 2009, https://www.smithsonianmag.com/history/george-koval-atomic-spy-unmasked-125046223/.

6. Sam Roberts, "The Nation: The Rosenbergs, 50 Years Later; Yes, They Were Guilty. But of What Exactly?" *New York Times*, June 15, 2003, https://www.nytimes.com/2003/06/15/weekinreview/nation-rosenbergs-50-years-later-yes-they-were-guilty-but-what-exactly.html.

7. From Joan Hall's files; also quoted in her "Memoir of Ted Hall."

8. Joan Hall, telephone interview with the author, December 2022.

9. John Earl Haynes, Harvey Klehr, and Alexander Vassiliev, *Spies: The Rise and Fall of the KGB in America* (New Haven, CT: Yale University Press, 2009), 98.

10. Haynes, Klehr, and Vassiliev, *Spies*, 98.

11. Haynes, Klehr, and Vassiliev, *Spies*, 99.

12. Albright and Kunstel, *Bombshell*, 165.

13. Haynes, Klehr, and Vassiliev, *Spies*, 214.

CHAPTER 16: THE SUCCESSFUL TRINITY TEST OF THE "GADGET"

1. From the video recording Hall made shortly before his death at the urging of his attorney Benedict Birnberg. This clip appears in Steve James, dir., *A Compassionate Spy* (Participant Films, 2022).

2. Hugh Selby, et al., "A New Yield Assessment for the Trinity Nuclear Test, 75 Years Later," *Nuclear Technology* 207, sup. 1 (October 11, 2021): 321–25.

3. William Leonard Laurence, *Dawn Over Zero: The Story of the Atomic Bomb* (New York: Knopf, 1946), 14.

4. James Temperton, "'Now I Am Become Death, the Destroyer of Worlds': The Story of Oppenheimer's Infamous Quote," *Wired*, August 8, 2017, https://www.wired.co.uk/article/manhattan-project-robert-oppenheimer.

5. Kenneth T. Bainbridge, "All in Our Time—A Foul and Awesome Display," *Bulletin of the Atomic Scientists* (May 1975): 40.

6. Hall and Birnberg, in *A Compassionate Spy*.

7. Leo Szilard, Petition to President Truman, U.S. National Archives, Record Group 77, Records of the Chief of Engineers, Manhattan Engineer District, Harrison-Bundy File, folder #76, July 17, 1945, http://www.dannen.com/decision/45-07-17.html.

8. "Unexpected Opposition," Atomic Archive, 6, https://www.atomicarchive.com/history/atomic-bombing/hiroshima/page-6.html#.

CHAPTER 17: LONA COHEN REPLACES SAVILLE SAX AS COURIER

1. Venona Project Soviet spy cable from New York consulate to Moscow NKVD headquarters, May 26, 1945.

2. Joseph Albright and Marcia Kunstel, *Bombshell: The Secret Story of America's Unknown Atomic Spy Conspiracy* (New York: Times Books, 1997), 150–51.

3. Pavel and Anatolil Sudoplatov, with Jerrold L. and Leona P. Schechter, *Special Tasks: The Memoirs of an Unwanted Witness—A Soviet Spymaster* (Boston: Back Bay Books, 1995), 191.

4. Albright and Kunstel, *Bombshell*, 152.

5. Sudoplatov and Sudoplatov, *Special Tasks*, 201.

6. Barnes Carr, *Operation Whisper: The Capture of Soviet Spies Morris and Lona Cohen* (Lebanon, NH: University Press of New England, 2016), 268.

CHAPTER 18: THE CONTROVERSIAL ATOMIC BOMBING OF JAPAN

1. Reuters Staff, "Quote of the Day," Reuters, August 6, 2008.

2. Susan Montoya Bryan, "Reports on Trinity Test Fallout, Cancer Cases to Be Released," *Las Vegas Sun*, August 31, 2020, https://lasvegassun.com/news/2020/aug/31/reports-on-trinity-test-fallout-cancer-cases-to-be/.

3. Paul Ham, "As Hiroshima Smoldered, Our Atom Bomb Scientists Suffered Remorse," *Newsweek*, August 5, 2015, https://www.newsweek.com/hiroshima-smouldered-our-atom-bomb-scientists-suffered-remorse-360125.

4. Ham, "As Hiroshima Smoldered."

5. Peter Kuznick, "Nuking of Japan was 'Totally Unnecessary' and Didn't End World War II, US Historian Explains," *Interregnum*, August 7, 2020, https://theinterregnum.net/nuking-of-japan-was-totally-unnecessary-and-didnt-end-world-war-ii-us-historian-explains/.

6. "'The World Will Note': President Truman Announces the Atom Bomb," delivered on August 6, 1945 (transcript and sound recording), from the Truman Library, *Hawaii Free Press* archives, August 6, 2022, http://www.hawaiifreepress.com/Articles-Main/ID/2612/This-Day-in-History-Truman-Announces-Hiroshima-Bombing.

7. Terry Gross and Dave Davies, "Looking Back at the Decision to Drop Atomic Bombs on Hiroshima and Nagasaki," NPR "Fresh Air" program, August 11, 2023. https://www.npr.org/2023/08/11/1193189051/looking-back-at-the-decision-to-drop-atomic-bombs-on-hiroshima-and-nagasaki.

8. Gar Alperovitz, "The War Was Won before Hiroshima—And the Generals Who Dropped the Bomb Knew It," *Nation*, August 6, 2015, https://www.thenation.com/article/world/why-the-us-really-bombed-hiroshima/.

9. Dwight D. Eisenhower, *Mandate for Change: 1953–56: The White House Years, a Personal Account* (New York: Doubleday, 1963), 312–13.

10. "'The World Will Note.'"

11. Barton J. Bernstein, "Reconsidering Truman's Claim of 'Half a Million American Lives' Saved by the Atomic Bomb: The Construction and Deconstruction of a Myth," *Journal of Strategic Studies* 22, no. 1 (1999): 54–95, https://doi.org/10.1080/01402399908437744.

12. Amy Briggs, "Twists of Fate Made Nagasaki a Target 75 Years Ago," *National Geographic*, August 5, 2020, https://www.nationalgeographic.com/history/article/twists-fate-made-nagasaki-target-atomic-bomb.

13. Geoff Brufield, "Why Did the U.S. Choose Hiroshima?" Morning Edition, National Public Radio, August 6, 2015, https://www.npr.org/2015/08/06/429433621/why-did-the-u-s-choose-hiroshima.

14. Atomic Heritage Foundation, "Bombings of Hiroshima and Nagasaki—1945," June 5, 2014, https://www.atomicheritage.org/history/bombings-hiroshima-and-nagasaki-1945.

15. Atomic Heritage Foundation, "Bombings of Hiroshima and Nagasaki."

16. Michio Kaku and Daniel Axelrod, *To Win a Nuclear War: The Pentagon's Secret War Plans* (Boston: South End Press, 1986), 44.

17. Gar Alperovitz, *The Decision to Use the Atomic Bomb* (New York: Vintage Books, 1995), 34.

18. Matt Juul, "Remembering the American POWs Who Died at Hiroshima," *Boston*, May 27, 2016, https://www.bostonmagazine.com/arts-entertainment/2016/05/27/remembering-american-soldiers-hiroshima/.

19. United States Adjutant General's Office, *Army Battle Casualties and Nonbattle Deaths in World War II, Final Report, 7 December 1941–31 December 1946* (Washington, DC: Department of the Army, 1953), 42, https://archive.org/details/ArmyBattleCasualtiesAndNonbattleDeathsInWorldWarIiPt1Of4.

20. Robert F. Dorr, "The Last American to Die in World War II," Defense Media Network, August 14, 2015, https://www.defensemedianetwork.com/stories/the-last-american-to-die-in-world-war-ii/.

21. History.com, "Firebombing of Tokyo," November 16, 2009, https://www.history.com/this-day-in-history/firebombing-of-tokyo.

22. Alperovitz, *The Decision to Use the Atomic Bomb*, 413.

23. Pad Kumlertsakul, "Soviet-Japan and the Termination of the Second World War," *National Archives Blog*, September 2, 2020, https://blog.nationalarchives.gov.uk/soviet-japan-and-the-termination-of-the-second-world-war/.

24. Kumlertsakul, "Soviet-Japan and the Termination of the Second World War."

25. Joan Hall, interview with the author, September 2022.

CHAPTER 19: TED LEAVES LOS ALAMOS FOR CHICAGO AND MEETS JOAN KRAKOVER

1. Joseph Albright and Marcia Kunstel, *Bombshell: The Secret Story of America's Unknown Atomic Spy Conspiracy* (New York: Times Books, 1997), 163.

2. Albright and Kunstel, *Bombshell*, 164.

3. Albright and Kunstel, *Bombshell*, 162.

4. Letter in possession of Joan Hall, also published in Albright and Kunstel, *Bombshell*, 162–63.

5. Albright and Kunstel, *Bombshell*, 165.

6. Gregg Herken, *Brotherhood of the Bomb: The Tangled Lives and Loyalties of Robert Oppenheimer, Ernest Lawrence, and Edward Teller* (New York: Henry Holt, 2002), 63–67.

7. Albright and Kunstel, *Bombshell*, 167.

8. Albright and Kunstel, *Bombshell*, 166.

9. Albright and Kunstel, *Bombshell*, 167.

10. Saville Sax/Theodore Hall FBI file, Espionage-R, File # 65-3348 The first censored words of the first sentence in the memo almost certainly were "The NSA."

11. Joan's recollections in this section are taken from interview with her in Steve James, dir., *A Compassionate Spy* (Participant Films, 2022).

CHAPTER 20: THE SOVETS' FIRST ATOMIC BOMB

1. Joan Hall, in Steve James, dir., *A Compassionate Spy* (Participant Films, 2022).

2. Colum Lynch, "How the US Found Out about Russia's First Nuclear Test 70 Years Ago," *Foreign Policy*, October 4, 2019, https://foreignpolicy.com/2019/10/04/how-us-detected-russia-first-nuclear-test-document/.

3. Michio Kaku and Daniel Axelrod, *To Win a Nuclear War: The Pentagon's Secret War Plans* (Boston: South End Press, 1986), 53–54.

4. Kaku and Axelrod, *To Win a Nuclear War*, 30.

5. Goodreads, "Einstein Quotable Quote," https://www.goodreads.com/quotes/14977-i-know-not-with-what-weapons-world-war-iii-will.

6. Federation of Atomic Scientists, "About FAS," https://fas.org/about-fas/.

7. Albert Einstein and Bertrand Russell, "The Russell-Einstein Manifesto," July 9, 1955, https://pugwash.org/1955/07/09/statement-manifesto/.

8. "Joseph Rotblat: The Nobel Peace Prize, 1995," Nobel Prize website, https://www.nobelprize.org/prizes/peace/1995/rotblat/facts/.

9. Joseph Albright and Marcia Kunstel, *Bombshell: The Secret Story of America's Unknown Atomic Spy Conspiracy* (New York: Times Books, 1997),192.

10. Albright and Kunstel, *Bombshell*, 194.

11. Albright and Kunstel, *Bombshell*, 195.

12. Albright and Kunstel, in a November 17, 2002 email response to my request for those sources, hint that the "close confidante" of Ted's was someone they had "good reason to believe" I had interviewed already. My guess would be that it is Joan Hall.

13. Albright and Kunstel, *Bombshell*, 221–22.

14. Ann Hagedorn, *Sleeper Agent: The Atomic Spy in America Who Got Away* (New York: Simon & Schuster, 2021), 203–5.

15. Harvey Klehr, interview with the author, December 2022.

16. John Earl Haynes and Harvey Klehr, "The Atomic Spy Who Never Was: 'Perseus' and KGB/SVR Atomic Espionage Disinformation," *International Journal of*

Intelligence and Counterintelligence 35, no. 3 (2022): 397–428, https://doi.org/10.108
0/08850607.2021.1894835.

17. Hagedorn, *Sleeper Agent*, 183–84.

18. Hagedorn, *Sleeper Agent*, 123–26.

19. Amy Hagedorn, email to the author, February 19, 2023.

CHAPTER 21: THE HIDDEN DANGER YEARS OF THE NUCLEAR ERA

1. Michael Peck, "America's Cold-War Master Plan to Nuke Russia," The National Interest, December 23, 2015, https://nationalinterest.org/feature/americas-cold-war -master-plan-nuke-russia-14714.

2. Peter Kuznick, "A Tragic Life: Oppenheimer and the Bomb," *Arms Control Today* 35 (July/August 2005), https://www.armscontrol.org/act/2005_07-08/Kuznick.

3. Kuznick, "A Tragic Life."

4. Michio Kaku and Daniel Axelrod, *To Win a Nuclear War: The Pentagon's Secret War Plans* (Boston: South End Press, 1986), 44.

5. Kaku and Axelrod, *To Win a Nuclear War.*

6. Atomic Heritage Foundation, "Soviet Atomic Program—1946," June 5, 2014, https://ahf.nuclearmuseum.org/ahf/history/soviet-atomic-program-1946/.

7. Kaku and Axelrod, *To Win a Nuclear War*, 32.

8. Kaku and Axelrod, *To Win a Nuclear War*, 54.

9. National Museum of the United States Air Force, "Mark-17 Thermonuclear Bomb," https://www.nationalmuseum.af.mil/Visit/Museum-Exhibits/Fact-Sheets/Dis play/Article/197628/mark-17-thermonuclear-bomb/.

10. Daniel Axelrod, email to the author, February 15, 2023.

11. Corydon Ireland, "How'd the Soviets Get the H-bomb?" *Harvard Gazette*, May 21, 2009, https://news.harvard.edu/gazette/story/2009/05/howd-the-russians-get-the -h-bomb/.

12. Atomic Heritage Foundation, "Soviet Hydrogen Bomb Program," August 8, 2014, https://ahf.nuclearmuseum.org/ahf/history/soviet-hydrogen-bomb-program/.

13. Robert Chadwell Williams, interview with the author.

14. Kaku and Axelrod, *To Win a Nuclear War*, 29.

15. Kaku and Axelrod, *To Win a Nuclear War*, 29–30.

16. Project for a New American Century, *Rebuilding America's Defenses: Strategy, Forces, and Resources for a New Century* (September 2000), ii, https://idoc.pub/docu ments/rebuilding-americas-defenses-pnac-6vylykjd4mwr.

17. Anthony Leviero, "H-Bomb Air Drop Missed by Four Miles," *New York Times*, June 16, 1956, https://timesmachine.nytimes.com/timesmachine/1956/06/16/86615 366.pdf.

18. Kaku and Axelrod, *To Win a Nuclear War*, 60.

19. Kaku and Axelrod, *To Win a Nuclear War*, 61; emphasis mine.

20. Kaku and Axelrod, *To Win a Nuclear War*, 63.

21. Kaku and Axelrod, *To Win a Nuclear War*, 63; emphasis mine.

22. Kaku and Axelrod, *To Win a Nuclear War*, 61.

23. Dwight D. Eisenhower, "The Chance for Peace" (transcript), 1953, https://alphahistory.com/coldwar/eisenhowers-chance-for-peace-speech-1953/.

CHAPTER 22: STILL SEEKING A REAL LOS ALAMOS SPY

1. Frank Close, *Trinity: The Treachery and Pursuit of the Most Dangerous Spy in History* (New York: Penguin, 2020), 212.

2. John Earl Haynes, Harvey Klehr, and Alexander Vassiliev, *Spies: The Rise and Fall of the KGB in America* (New Haven, CT: Yale University Press, 2009), 287.

3. John Simkin, "Judith Coplon," Spartacus Educational, September 1997 (updated 2021), https://spartacus-educational.com/Judith_Coplon.htm.

4. Saville Sax/Theodore Hall FBI file, #65-3348, August 25, 1951.

5. Sax/Hall FBI file, #65-3348, August 25, 1951.

6. Sax/Hall FBI file, #65-3348, May 2, 1950.

7. Sax/Hall FBI file, #65-3348, May 2, 1950.

8. President Harry Truman signed United States Executive Order 9835, sometimes known as the "Loyalty Order," on March 21, 1947. The order established the first general loyalty program in the United States, designed to root out communist influence in the U.S. federal government.

9. Sax/Hall FBI file, #65-3348, August 25, 1951.

10. Edward Nathaniel Hall FBI file, January 6, 1951.

CHAPTER 23: BUSTED!

1. Ed Hall FBI file, January 6, 1951, correspondence marked "Personal and Confidential" from FBI director J. Edgar Hoover to U.S. Air Force OSI director Joseph F. Carroll, informing him that USAF rocket engineer and designer Edward Hall was the brother of a known Soviet atomic spy.

2. Both reports appear, first the Ted Hall one and then the Saville Sax one, in their combined FBI Chicago File #65-3403, dated 3/31/51 for period 3/16/51. The Hall report is listed as having been written by Robert K. McQueen. Oddly, though, McQueen was not present at Sax's interrogation, which was handled by agents W. Rulon Paxton and L. Hoyt McGuire, the report is described as being compiled by SAC McQueen, which could have rendered its contents hearsay and unusable as impeaching evidence had there been any trial.

3. Theodore Alvin Hall et al. FBI file, # 65-3403, covering March 16–19, 1951, FBI FOI Archive, March 31, 1951.

4. Theodore Alvin Hall et al. FBI file, # 65-3403, covering March 16–19, 1951.

5. Theodore Alvin Hall et al. FBI file, # 65-3403, covering March 16–19, 1951.

6. Theodore Alvin Hall et al. FBI file, # 65-3403, covering March 16–19, 1951.

7. Harry Bridges, fiery leader of the International Longshore and Warehouse Union, was one of the most progressive labor leaders in the U.S. labor movement during the 1930s–1970s. Because of his militancy and popularity with the union membership, the U.S. government and FBI hounded the Australian-born Bridges with accusations of being a Communist and attempted multiple times in court to use that claim to have him deported, finally winning a conviction on a charge of lying about his alleged Communist Party membership, a case that was eventually tossed out by the U.S. Supreme Court, but his union was thrown out of the Confederation of Industrial Organizations (CIO) because of an unproven claim that it was a Communist front organization. See University of Washington Civil Rights and Labor History Consortium, "Harry Bridges: Life and Legacy," https://depts.washington.edu/dock/Harry_Bridges_intro.shtml.

8. Theodore Alvin Hall et al. FBI file, # 65-3403, covering March 16–19, 1951.

9. Theodore Alvin Hall et al. FBI file, # 65-3403, covering March 16–19, 1951.

10. Archived FBI files identifying FBI informants in the U.S. Communist Party, Internet Archive, https://archive.org/details/ernie1241_fbiinformants.

11. Saville Sax/Theodore Hall FBI file, #65-3348, May 10, 1950, New York bureau report on Saville Sax.

12. Joseph Albright and Marcia Kunstel, *Bombshell: The Secret Story of America's Unknown Atomic Spy Conspiracy* (New York: Times Books, 1997), 229–30.

13. Joan Hall, interview with the author, 2022.

CHAPTER 24: THE RED SCARE YEARS

1. From a clip of the historical film *Mission to Moscow*, directed by Michael Curtiz (Warner Bros., 1943), quoted in Steve James, dir., *A Compassionate Spy* (Participant Films, 2022).

2. Alex Lo, "Why the U.S. Kept Making Enemies Who Wanted to Be Friends: Castro, Ho Chi Minh and Putin," *South China Morning Post*, October 20, 2022, https://www.scmp.com/comment/opinion/article/3196657/why-us-kept-making-enemies-who-wanted-be-friends-castro-ho-chi-minh-and-putin.

3. Frank Close, *Trinity: The Treachery and Pursuit of the Most Dangerous Spy in History* (New York: Penguin, 2020), 211–12.

4. Peter Reid, "This Day in History: Joseph McCarthy Said Communists Have Infiltrated the State Department," *American Military News*, February 9, 2019, https://www.history.com/this-day-in-history/mccarthy-army-hearings-begin.

5. Allen M. Hornblum, *The Invisible Harry Gold: The Man Who Gave the Soviets the Atom Bomb* (New Haven, CT: Yale University Press, 2010), 206–7.

6. Close, *Trinity*, 254.

7. Close, *Trinity*, 254.

8. Close, *Trinity*, 266, 423, 425.

9. Encyclopedia.com, "Rosenbergs Trial," https://www.encyclopedia.com/law/encyclopedias-almanacs-transcripts-and-maps/rosenbergs-trial.

10. "Irving R. Kaufman: Judge in Rosenbergs' Spy Trial," *Los Angeles Times*, February 4, 1992, https://www.latimes.com/archives/la-xpm-1992-02-04-mn-1246-story.html; "Transcripts Suggest Ethel Rosenberg May Have Been Convicted, Executed on Perjured Testimony," Fox News, January 13, 2015, https://nsarchive2.gwu.edu/news/20150714-Rosenberg-spy-case-Greenglass-testimony/.

11. Joan Hall, interview with the author in *A Compassionate Spy*.

12. Joseph Albright and Marcia Kunstel, *Bombshell: The Secret Story of America's Unknown Atomic Spy Conspiracy* (New York: Times Books, 1997), 217.

13. Ted Hall, unaired BBC interview, 1998, outtake from *A Compassionate Spy*.

14. Joan Hall, interview in *A Compassionate Spy*.

CHAPTER 25: GOING AFTER ED HALL, THE AIR FORCE'S ROCKET MAN

1. A shorter version of this chapter was originally published in *The Nation* on January 4, 2022, https://www.thenation.com/article/world/ted-hall-espionage-fbi/.

2. Barnes Carr, *Operation Whisper: The Capture of Soviet Spies Morris and Lona Cohen* (Lebanon, NH: University Press of New England, 2016), 165.

3. Douglas Martin, "Edward Hall, 91, Developer of Missile Programs, Dies," *New York Times*, January 18, 2006, https://www.latimes.com/archives/la-xpm-2006-jan-18-me-hall18-story.html; Thomas H. Maugh, "Edward N. Hall, 91; Rocket Pioneer Seen as the Father of the Minuteman ICBM," *Los Angeles Times*, January 18, 2006, https://www.latimes.com/archives/la-xpm-2006-jan-18-me-hall18-story.html.

4. William J. Broad, "J. Robert Oppenheimer Cleared of 'Black Mark' After 68 Years," *New York Times*, December 16, 2022, https://www.nytimes.com/2022/12/16/science/j-robert-oppenheimer-energy-department.html.

5. Atonic Heritage Foundation, "Klaus Fuchs: Early Years," https://ahf.nuclearmuseum.org/ahf/profile/klaus-fuchs/.

6. Roxanne M. Jensen, letter from Air Force Office of Special Investigations, Information Release Branch, July 8, 2021.

7. J. Edgar Hoover, letter to USAF OSI Director Joseph F. Carroll, March 27, 1951; emphasis mine.

8. Edward Nathaniel Hall FBI file, March 27, 1951; emphasis mine.

9. Edward Nathaniel Hall FBI file, August 10, 1951.

10. This was a reference to the incident during Ted's first year at Los Alamos when censors questioned Ed and his wife about the contents of a letter.

11. Joan Hall, telephone interview with the author, April 2022.

12. FBI file of Edward Hall's FBI interview at Wright Patterson AFB on June 12, 1951, File 3.

13. An FBI memo in Ed Hall's file dated March 13, 1945, notes that Major Hall had been questioned in the United Kingdom by the Atomic Energy's Los Alamos Security Branch in October 1945 in connection with his wife's intercepted letter to Ted concerning Guy Fawkes Day. It reports that Ed had not known about the atomic bomb until the United States announced its existence publicly on August 6, 1945. But he explained that "when the announcement was made he recognized the mention of Santa Fe, New Mexico as being near the site at which the trial of the Atomic Bomb had been staged and, knowing that his brother, TED HALL, had worked in that region as a civilian and then as a soldier on secret work, he guessed the latter's connection to the bomb."

14. FBI File # Bufile 65-59122, Chicago bureau Hall and Sax file, March 16, 1951.

15. FBI File # Bufile 65-59122, Chicago bureau Hall and Sax file, March 16, 1951.

16. Joseph Albright and Marcia Kunstel, *Bombshell: The Secret Story of America's Unknown Atomic Spy Conspiracy* (New York: Times Books, 1997), 231.

17. Edward Hall FBI file (no FBI file number given). Report on Cincinnati Bureau agents' June 12, 1951 interview of Edward Hall written by Cincinnati SAC Carl A. Betsch on August 10, 1951.

18. Edward Hall file (no number shown), op. cit. report on Edward's June 22 visit to Ted Hall's home.

19. Edward Hall FBI file (no number provided in documents received through FOIA), Cincinnati Bureau field office, August 10, 1951, op. cit.

20. Edward Hall FBI File (number censored), written by Cincinnati FBI SAC Carl A. Betsch, October 17, 1951.

21. Albright and Kunstel, *Bombshell*, 233.

22. Albright and Kunstel, *Bombshell*, 233.

23. Martin, "Edward Hall, Developer of Missile Programs, Dies."

24. Department of the Air Force Special Order 35, signed by Air Force Chief of Staff N. F. Twining and Colonel Charles F. McDermott, Acting Air Adjutant General, original in possession of Sheila Hall.

25. Edward N. Hall, *A Nation at Risk* (unpublished manuscript, 2000–2003), 79.

26. Air Force Missile and Space Museum, "Colonel Edward N. Hall," https://web.archive.org/web/20120614172528/http://www.afspc.af.mil/shared/media/document/AFD-100405-065.pdf; GlobalSecurity.org, "LGM-30A/B Minuteman I," Maugh, "Edward N. Hall, 91; Rocket Pioneer Seen as the Father of Minuteman ICBM."

27. Martin, "Edward Hall, 91, Developer of Missile Programs, Dies."

28. Albright and Kunstel, *Bombshell*, 166.

29. Maugh, "Edward N. Hall, 91; Rocket Pioneer Seen as the Father of Minuteman ICBM."

CHAPTER 26: TERROR, THEN A STRANGE RESPITE FROM FEAR

1. See FOIA FBI file 65-3403, Saville Sax, January 22, 1951, and Theodore Hall, February 21.

2. A series of brief entries regarding Sax's current address and employment running from 1954 through October 2, 1969, show that the FBI didn't give up easily on him, often noting that he is "disheveled" and "lives in a dream world." But there are repeated memos from the Chicago bureau office saying they would maintain a six-month check on Sax's whereabouts, suggesting that the FBI's interest in the Hall/Sax spy case, while inactive, was not shut down.

3. John Simkin, "William Weisband," Spartacus Educational, September 1997 (updated 2020), https://spartacus-educational.com/William_Weisband.htm.

4. David C. Martin, *Wilderness of Mirrors: Intrigue, Deception and the Secrets that Destroyed Two of the Cold War's Most Important Agents* (New York: Skyhorse Publishing, 2003), 44.

5. Joseph Albright and Marcia Kunstel, *Bombshell: The Secret Story of America's Unknown Atomic Spy Conspiracy* (New York: Times Books, 1997), 235.

6. Joan Hall, interview in Steve James, dir., *A Compassionate Spy* (Participant Films, 2022).

7. Joan Hall, interview in *A Compassionate Spy.*

8. Ted Hall, video recording made in late 1998, as shown in *A Compassionate Spy.*

9. Ted Hall, video recording.

10. Ted Hall, unaired BBC interview, 1998, as shown in *A Compassionate Spy.*

CHAPTER 27: MI5 COMES CALLING

1. Joan Hall, interview in Steve James, dir., *A Compassionate Spy* (Participant Films, 2022).

2. Saville Sax/Theodore Hall FBI file #65-58236, February 10, 1966, Boston agents' report on Glauber interview.

3. John Earl Haynes, Harvey Klehr, and Alexander Vassiliev, *Spies: The Rise and Fall of the KGB in America* (New Haven, CT: Yale University Press, 2009), 116.

4. Sax/Hall FBI file #65-58236, February 10, 1966, Boston agents' report on Glauber interview.

5. Joseph Albright and Marcia Kunstel, *Bombshell: The Secret Story of America's Unknown Atomic Spy Conspiracy* (New York: Times Books, 1997), 143.

6. Kevin Sack and Emily Yellin, "Dr. King's Slaying Finally Draws a Jury Verdict, but to Little Effect," *New York Times*, December 19, 1999; David Alm, "'The Murder of Fred Hampton' Still Has Much to Teach," *Forbes*, January 3, 2020, https://www.forbes

.com/sites/davidalm/2020/06/03/the-murder-of-fred-hampton-still-has-much-to-teach
-watch-it-here/?sh=a6ec84312f4b; Jonathan Allen and Brendan O'Brien, "Malcolm X's
Daughter to Sue CIA, FBI, New York Police over Assassination," Reuters, February 21,
2023, https://www.reuters.com/legal/malcolm-xs-daughter-sue-cia-fbi-new-york-police
-over-assassination-2023-02-21/.

CHAPTER 28: TELLING THE KIDS

1. All recollections in this chapter from Joan, Ruth, and Sara Hall are taken from
interviews shown in Steve James, dir., *A Compassionate Spy* (Participant Films, 2022).

2. Harvard Class of 1944 50th Reunion Yearbook, "Class Notes." The reunion book
for the class of 1944's fiftieth reunion is in Joan Hall's possession, which is where I saw
it. But copies of such volumes are usually available in the university's library.

CHAPTER 29: DENOUEMENT

1. Richard Rhodes, *The Making of the Atomic Bomb: The 25th Anniversary Edition*
(New York: Simon & Schuster, 2012), 8.

2. This passage is an excerpt of the eulogy Professor Brown delivered at Ted Hall's
memorial, which he shared with me.

3. Frank Close, *Trinity: The Treachery and Pursuit of the Most Dangerous Spy in
History* (New York: Penguin, 2020), 425.

EPILOGUE

1. Frank Close, *Trinity: The Treachery and Pursuit of the Most Dangerous Spy in
History* (New York: Penguin, 2020), 417.

2. Guy Faulconbridge, "Factbox: Has Putin Threatened to Use Nuclear Weapons?" Reuters, October 27, 2022, https://www.reuters.com/world/europe/has-putin
-threatened-use-nuclear-weapons-2022-10-27/.

3. Faulconbridge, "Factbox."

4. Christopher S. Chivvas, "How Does This End?" Carnegie Endowment for Peace,
March 3, 2022, https://carnegieendowment.org/2022/03/03/how-does-this-end-pub
-86570.

5. Richard Rhodes, *The Making of the Atomic Bomb: The 25th Anniversary Edition*
(New York: Simon & Schuster, 2012), 5.

6. From a never-used video interview of Ted Hall made by historian Martin Sherwin
in 1998.

7. *The Ultimate Quotable Einstein* (Princeton, NJ: Princeton University Press, 2010), https://libquotes.com/albert-einstein/quote/lby3i1m.

8. Hugh Gusterson, "A Tale of Two Suspects: 'Oppenheimer' versus 'A Compassionate Spy,'" *Bulletin of the Atomic Scientists*, August 16, 2023, https://thebulletin .org/2023/08/a-tale-of-two-suspects-oppenheimer-versus-a-compassionate-spy/.

ACKNOWLEDGMENTS

1. Dave Lindorff, "Two Soviet Spies Who Deserve a Posthumous Nobel Peace Prize," ThisCantBeHappening.net, https://thiscantbehappening.net/page/4/?s=hiroshima; Dave Lindorff, "Two Soviet Spies Who Deserve a Posthumous Nobel Peace Prize," *Counterpunch*, October 20, 2017, https://www.counterpunch.org/2017/10/20/two -soviet-spies-who-deserve-a-posthumous-nobel-peace-prize/.

2. Dave Lindorff, "One Brother Gave the Soviets the A-Bomb. The Other Got a Medal," *The Nation*, January 4, 2022, https://www.thenation.com/article/world/ted -hall-espionage-fbi/.

ACKNOWLEDGMENTS

The origins of this book date to October 17, 2017, when I wrote a short article[1] proposing that two Manhattan Project physicists, Theodore Alvin Hall and Klaus Fuchs, both of whom worked as part of the massive Manhattan Project during World II, should be awarded posthumous Nobel Peace Prizes, not because they helped build the bomb, but because they provided crucial information about its design construction to the USSR, a key U.S. ally in the war against Nazi Germany that was being kept in the dark about the atomic bomb project by the United States. I had focused particularly in that article on Ted Hall, a teenage Harvard physics major who I was astonished to learn was still only 18 years old when he made his fateful decision to volunteer as a Soviet atomic spy.

There are many people, too numerous to mention, who helped me pursue this story, but one stands out—the then 87-year-old woman who, a few weeks after my article ran, sent me an email from her home in Newnham, England, reading, "Dear Dave, I'm reading your article about Ted Hall with tears in my eyes. I'm Ted's widow, and you are the first person who 'got' him."

Joan Krakover Hall, an energetic and articulate American woman of 88 when I got to know her in person, was a fount of knowledge about her husband and what he had done, and the half-century they kept his secret until he was publicly identified as an atomic spy in decrypted Soviet wartime coded spy cables released by the U.S. National Security Agency in 1995.

Joan, who died in her sleep on June 14, 2023, at the age of 94, was generous and open in sharing her encyclopedic knowledge of that entire period, both for the book and for *A Compassionate Spy*, the film I was a producer on along with director Steve James and his colleague and regular producer, Mark Mitten. Without Joan's insights and memory, which she continued to share with me right through 2023 when she was much frailer and in and out of hospital, neither the book nor the film would have been possible. Joan and Ted's two surviving daughters, Sara Hall and Ruth London, were also important contributors to my learning Ted's story and who he was as a person, as were Sarah and Boria Sax, children of Ted's friend and spy courier, Saville Sax, who died in 1986. Without their help, it would have been much harder to tease out what kind of people these two men were.

Also important to my writing this book were Steve James and Mark Mitten, who I approached about Ted's story to see if they would be interested in taking it on as a documentary film. Both were enthusiastic when I explained the basics of what Ted had done. They rightly recognized that the idea of a documentary about Ted would hinge on how compelling Joan would be on film. Steve sprang for travel costs for himself, Mark, and his director of photography, Tom Bergman, to fly to the United Kingdom for a three-day filming of Joan in Newnham. I joined them, along with my videographer son Jed, on our dime. After viewing what we'd taped, Steve, who found Joan to be as compelling a figure as I did, said on his return to Chicago that he definitely wanted to make a film about Ted and Joan's story with me, the length depending on what funding we could obtain. Steve and Mark were fantastic collaborators on the film project for the next three years, and even when we disagreed about something, our conversations helped make the film better and also helped me immeasurably as I worked on this book.

Kartemquin Films immediately offered $50,000 in seed funding, and Participant Films followed with a commitment to fully fund a feature-length documentary, including the making of short reenactments using young actors to play out narrations by Joan and Ted (the latter possible thanks to a videotape Ted had made in 1998, a year before his death from cancer, at the suggestion of his attorney—a never-before-seen tape that brings Ted to life and which Joan generously made available for use in the film).

I am forever indebted to Kartemquin and Participant Films as well, because the producer's fee and expenses they paid me, much of which was for my work finding the story and doing the research for and lining up interview subjects for the film, did double duty funding my research and

writing of this vastly more in-depth book about Ted's spying and its historical impact.

Special thanks go to Jake Bonar, acquisitions editor at Prometheus
Books, who also recognized the importance of this book, sold it to the Prometheus editorial board, and was so enthusiastic himself that he asked if I
would agree to his being my editor on it, too.

I owe a huge debt of gratitude to journalists Joseph Alsop and Marcia
Kunstel, who wrote *Bombshell* (1997), the only book before this one to focus
on Ted Hall. They were generous in offering information they had found in
their pioneering investigation, were wonderful interviews in the film, and
had information I could never have gotten on my own because they were
able to interview Ted himself while he was still alive.

I meanwhile had something to work with that they did not have, and
that was the FBI files on Ted Hall, Saville Sax, Roy Glauber, and, most
interestingly and revealingly, Ted's older brother, rocket scientist Edward
Nathaniel Hall, none of which were available through FOIA when they were
writing their book.

Thank you to Don Guttenplan, editor at *The Nation* magazine, who
helped me hone a crucial and fascinating part of the story: how Ed Hall's
role to the U.S. Air Force as a genius rocket scientist ended up protecting his
brother Ted and Ted's spy courier and friend Saville Sax from FBI pursuit
and prosecution. Don gave me the opportunity to publish that part of the
story in the magazine early on,[2] which contributed to garnering interest from
Jake and Prometheus in my book proposal, in addition to helping boost my
funding for work on researching and writing the story.

Numerous other people also need to be thanked, including Ed Hall's
daughter Sheila, who scoured old albums to locate photos of her late father
and Ted's families and, most importantly, provided me with the unpublished manuscript of a memoir her father wrote about his years in World
War II in the United Kingdom repairing bombers and designing and building U.S. intercontinental ballistic missiles in the Cold War during the 1950s
and 1960s.

Thanks to Academy Award–winning documentarian and friend David
Goodman, who, upon hearing that I was planning to present my Ted Hall
film idea to Steve James and Mark Mitten, advised me to first develop a
gripping "elevator pitch" to ensure their interest. It worked (although the
elevator pitch I produced was more suited to a high-rise office tower, they
read the entire thing and liked it!).

My agent, Ron Goldfarb, deserves special praise for recognizing the importance of this book and going the distance to get it done. It was a hard sell, especially with the U.S. government and media in full propaganda mode with the war in Ukraine, to make the case that a U.S. spy who gave the Soviet Union crucial information to help Soviet scientists develop a nuclear bomb did a noble and heroic thing, preventing the United States from again using nuclear weapons as in Hiroshima and Nagasaki. Despite every major publisher he approached rejecting my book proposal with excuses ranging from "people are tired of spy stories" to "I'm not going to buy a book that lionizes a U.S. traitor," Ron kept at it with small presses, caring more about seeing the book in print than getting an agent's fee. Thank you, Ron, for your dedication and persistance.

I especially want to thank Joyce, my wife of 52 years and still my best editor. She put up with my preoccupation with and obsessive pursuit of this story, and the writing and editing of the book, and has never tired of pointing out my run-on sentences and the times I missed the real lead of a particular part of the story. Her patience, love, and support even when the project sometimes was all-consuming, were unflagging.

Finally, I want to thank FDR and the Social Security program he founded for the generous monthly federal stipend—my personal "Federal Writer's Project" grant—which has been supporting my writing habit now for more than four years.

INDEX

ABOUT THE AUTHOR

Dave Lindorff, a journalist since 1972, when he began covering three small towns near the mouth of the Connecticut River for the feisty daily *Middletown Press*, has made a name for himself as a tenacious investigative reporter. During a varied career in daily newspapers, he cofounded in Los Angeles the independent alternative weekly *Los Angeles Vanguard*. He was also bureau chief for the *Los Angeles Daily News*, covering Los Angeles County government; an investigative reporter/producer for KCET-TV PBS affiliate's Peabody-winning *28 Tonight* news program; a correspondent for *Business Week* based in Hong Kong, where he covered Hong Kong and China in the 1990s; and a freelance magazine writer and book author. For his work as a contributor to *The Nation* magazine, Lindorff was honored with an "Izzy" Award in 2019 for "outstanding independent journalism" from the Park Center for Independent Media based at Ithaca College. Most recently, he was coproducer of the documentary film *A Compassionate Spy*, directed by Steven James and released this year, about the same teenage Manhattan Project spy Theodore "Ted" Hall who is the subject of this book.

Lindorff is a magna cum laude graduate of Wesleyan University, where he majored in Chinese, and earned an MS in journalism from the Columbia Grad School of Journalism. His work has included exposés of unarmed people killed by police in Los Angeles, the ongoing disaster of for-profit medicine in the United States, the Pentagon's decades of trillion-dollar accounting fraud, the impeachable crimes of President George W. Bush and Vice President Dick Cheney, a half-century and more of horrific U.S. war crimes, the metastasizing national security state and normalization of militarized policing, and the looming threat sea level rise poses to the fifty thousand "sanitary" landfills located on land less than ten feet above sea level along all three U.S. coastlines.

Earlier critically acclaimed books have included *Marketplace Medicine: The Rise of the For-Profit Hospital Chains* (1992), *Killing Time: An Investigation into the Death Penalty Case of Mumia Abu-Jamal* (2003), and *The Case for Impeachment* (2006, coauthored with Barbara Olshansky).